ULTIMATE
Skillet
COOKBOOK

Taste
of Home
BOOKS

RDA ENTHUSIAST BRANDS, LLC
MILWAUKEE, WI

Taste of Home

EDITORIAL

Editor-in-Chief: Catherine Cassidy
Vice President, Content Operations: Kerri Balliet
Creative Director: Howard Greenberg

Managing Editor, Print & Digital Books: Mark Hagen
Associate Creative Director: Edwin Robles Jr.

Editor: Amy Glander
Layout Designers: Catherine Fletcher, Courtney Lovetere
Editorial Production Manager: Dena Ahlers
Editorial Production Coordinator: Jill Banks
Copy Chief: Deb Warlaumont Mulvey
Copy Editors: Chris McLaughlin, Mary-Liz Shaw
Contributing Copy Editor: Kristin Sutter
Business Analyst, Content Tools: Amanda Harmatys
Content Operations Assistant: Shannon Stroud
Editorial Services Administrator: Marie Brannon

Food Editors: Gina Nistico; James Schend;
 Peggy Woodward, RDN
Recipe Editors: Sue Ryon (lead); Mary King; Irene Yeh

Test Kitchen & Food Styling Manager: Sarah Thompson
Test Cooks: Nicholas Iverson (lead), Matthew Hass,
 Lauren Knoelke
Food Stylists: Kathryn Conrad (lead), Leah Rekau,
 Shannon Roum
Prep Cooks: Bethany Van Jacobson (lead), Megumi Garcia,
 Melissa Hansen
Culinary Team Assistant: Megan Behr

Photography Director: Stephanie Marchese
Photographers: Dan Roberts, Jim Wieland
Photographer/Set Stylist: Grace Natoli Sheldon
Set Stylists: Melissa Franco, Stacey Genaw, Dee Dee Jacq
Set Stylist Assistant: Stephanie Chojnacki

Editorial Business Manager: Kristy Martin
Editorial Business Associate: Samantha Lea Stoeger
Contributing Editorial Business Assistant: Andrea Polzin

BUSINESS

Vice President, Group Publisher: Kirsten Marchioli
Publisher: Donna Lindskog
General Manager, Taste of Home Cooking School: Erin Puariea

For other Taste of Home books and products,
visit us at tasteofhome.com.

International Standard Book Number: 978-1-61765-551-7
Library of Congress Control Number: 2016930444
Component Number: 250022197S

Cover Photographer: Jim Wieland
Set Stylist: Dee Dee Jacq
Food Stylist: Shannon Roum

Pictured on front cover: Deep-Dish Sausage Pizza Frittata,
page 60

Pictured on back cover: Stovetop Hamburger Casserole,
page 49; Skillet Blueberry Slump, page 217; Deep-Dish Sausage
Pizza, page 14; Campfire Cheese Hash Brown Packets, page 245

Pictured on spine: Queso Fundido, page 229

Printed in USA.
3 5 7 9 10 8 6 4 2

CONTENTS

74

89

228

114

163

Create skillet sensations!

Looking to sizzle up something fast, delicious and smokin' hot? It's never been easier!

There's always time for a savory homemade meal when you have a skillet and this brand-new cookbook in hand.

Featuring everyday ingredients and easy-to-follow instructions, the 301 recipes inside *Taste of Home Ultimate Skillet Cookbook* guarantee you will find the ideal stovetop dish for every day and every occasion.

Cooking up a hearty, fast meal perfect for breakfast, lunch or dinner (even dessert!) has never been easier. From classic family favorites to skillet novelties, let these can-do recipes make dinnertime a sizzling success!

CHEESY ONION CHICKEN SKILLET, PAGE 115

HANDY ICONS IN THIS BOOK

⑤ INGREDIENTS 52 dishes use 5 or fewer ingredients. Recipes may also call for water, salt, pepper, and canola or olive oil.

FAST FIX 198 recipes are table-ready in 30 minutes or less.

46

193

SKILLET COOKWARE

The right cookware can simplify meal preparation when cooking on the stovetop. The basic skillets every kitchen needs include a 10- or 12-in. skillet with lid and an 8- or 9-in. saute/omelet pan.

SELECTING COOKWARE

Good quality cookware conducts heat quickly and cooks food evenly. The type of metal and thickness of the pan affect its performance. There are pros and cons to each of the most common cookware metals:

Copper conducts heat the best. However, it is expensive, it tarnishes (and usually requires periodic polishing) and it reacts with acidic ingredients, which is why the interior of a copper pan is usually lined with tin or stainless steel.

8-IN. SAUTE/OMELET PAN

Aluminum is a good conductor of heat and it is less expensive than copper. Aluminum reacts, however, with acidic ingredients.

Anodized Aluminum has the same good qualities as aluminum, but the surface is electrochemically treated so it will not react to acidic ingredients. The surface is resistant to scratches and is nonstick.

12-IN. SKILLET WITH LID

Cast Iron conducts heat very well. It is usually heavy. Cast iron also needs regular seasoning to prevent sticking and rust.

10-IN. SKILLET

Stainless Steel is durable and retains its new look for years. It isn't a good conductor of heat, which is why it often has an aluminum or copper core or bottom.

Other factors to consider when choosing cookware: Thicker-gauge cookware heats and cooks more evenly than thinner-gauge cookware of the same material, and is heavier. Nonstick surfaces make for easy cleanup and are great for skillets and saute pans, but are not necessary for saucepans and Dutch ovens. All lids should be tight-fitting. Handles should stay cool during cooking and ideally be oven-safe at high temperatures.

COMMON STOVETOP COOKING TECHNIQUES

FRYING

Pour about ½ in. oil into a skillet. Heat over medium-high heat until hot. The oil is ready when it shimmers (gives off visible waves of heat). Never leave the pan unattended, and don't overheat the oil or it will smoke. Pat food dry before frying and, if desired, dip in batter or coat it with crumbs. Don't overcrowd the pan, as the food will steam rather than fry. Fry, uncovered, until food is golden brown and cooked through.

SAUTEING

Pour a small amount of oil into a skillet. Heat over medium-high heat until hot. For best results, the food should be cut into uniformly sized pieces and patted dry. Don't overcrowd the pan. Stir frequently while cooking.

SEARING

Heat oil in a large cast-iron or other ovenproof skillet over medium-high heat until it begins to smoke. Cook the meat, poultry or fish until a deeply colored crust has formed. Reduce the heat if the food browns too quickly. Pat the food dry and don't overcrowd the pan.

TOP TIPS
FOR CAST-IRON SKILLETS

- Season your cast-iron skillet before first use and re-season it regularly. To season your pan, heat it up on the stovetop until it gets very hot, then rub a little oil into it and let it cool. You can easily maintain the seasoning by using your pan regularly. The more you cook, sear or fry in it, the better it gets!

- Always make sure your skillet is dry when not in use. Water can lead to rust spots.

- Hand wash the skillet after each use. Wash with mild, soapy water. Dry immediately and rub with a light coat of oil. Do not use harsh detergent or metal scouring pads. Do not put in the dishwasher or microwave.

- Match pan size to burner size.

- If cooking on a gas stove, don't let the flames extend up the side of the pan.

28

BONUS
Campfire Classics

Let's go camping! You just can't beat the fun of sitting around a crackling campfire. But if cooking a delicious meal over a fire seems a little daunting, fear not. Eating in the great wide open can be an enjoyable and nostalgic experience that will leave you savoring every bite.

All you need is a packed cooler (or two), an open flame and a few good recipes. Don't forget aluminum foil, skewers and a reliable, heavy-duty pan. Turn to page 238 for recipes that will fire up your appetite for the great outdoors. Then, head outside and cook up a fiery favorite!

242

240

**ALICE BEARDSELL'S
HOMEY MAC & CHEESE** *PAGE 25*

Top 10 Cast-Iron Skillet Recipes

Cast-iron skillets are back! No longer your grandma's griddle, this workhorse sizzles up all of your favorites, whether they're prepared over a campfire, on the stovetop or in the oven. Here you'll find 10 classics!

CARAMEL-APPLE SKILLET BUCKLE

My grandma used to make a version of this for me when I was a little girl. She would make it using fresh apples from her tree in the back yard. I've adapted her recipe because I love the combination of apple, pecans and caramel.

—EMILY HOBBS SPRINGFIELD, MO

PREP: 35 MIN.
BAKE: 1 HOUR + STANDING
MAKES: 12 SERVINGS

- ½ cup butter, softened
- ¾ cup sugar
- 2 large eggs
- 1 teaspoon vanilla extract
- 2 cups all-purpose flour
- 2½ teaspoons baking powder
- 1¾ teaspoons ground cinnamon
- ½ teaspoon ground ginger
- ¼ teaspoon salt
- 1½ cups buttermilk

TOPPING
- ⅔ cup packed brown sugar
- ½ cup all-purpose flour
- ¼ cup cold butter
- ¾ cup finely chopped pecans
- ½ cup old-fashioned oats
- 6 cups thinly sliced peeled Gala or other sweet apples (about 6 medium)
- 18 caramels, unwrapped
- 1 tablespoon buttermilk
  Vanilla ice cream, optional

1. Preheat oven to 350°. In a large bowl, cream butter and sugar until light and fluffy. Add eggs, one at a time, beating well after each addition. Beat in vanilla. In another bowl, whisk flour, baking powder, cinnamon, ginger and salt; add to creamed mixture alternately with buttermilk, beating well after each addition. Pour into a greased 12-in. cast-iron or ovenproof skillet.

2. For topping, in a small bowl, mix brown sugar and flour; cut in butter until crumbly. Stir in pecans and oats; sprinkle over batter. Top with apples. Bake 60-70 minutes or until apples are golden brown. Cool in pan on a wire rack.

3. In a microwave, melt caramels with buttermilk; stir until smooth. Drizzle over cake. Let stand until set. If desired, serve with ice cream.

CARAMEL–APPLE SKILLET BUCKLE

ANYTIME FRITTATA

ANYTIME FRITTATA

We enjoy frittatas often at our house. They're a great way to use up vegetables, cheese and meat. Enjoy this hearty recipe with fruit and biscuits for a light dinner.

—LYNNE VAN WAGENEN SALT LAKE CITY, UT

START TO FINISH: 30 MIN.
MAKES: 4 SERVINGS

1¼ cups egg substitute
2 large eggs
½ teaspoon dried oregano
⅛ teaspoon pepper
1 small onion, chopped
1 garlic clove, minced
1 teaspoon butter
3 plum tomatoes, chopped
½ cup crumbled feta cheese
2 tablespoons capers, drained

1. In a small bowl, whisk the egg substitute, eggs, oregano and pepper; set aside. In a 10-in. cast-iron or ovenproof skillet, saute chopped onion and garlic in butter for 2 minutes. Stir in plum tomatoes; heat through.
2. Pour reserved egg mixture into skillet. Reduce the heat; cover and cook eggs for 4-6 minutes or until nearly set.
3. Sprinkle with cheese and capers. Broil 3-4 in. from the heat for 2-3 minutes or until eggs are completely set. Let stand for 5 minutes. Cut the frittata into wedges.

TOP TIP

Cast-iron pans should be seasoned before use to protect the surface and prevent food from sticking. One way to season a cast-iron skillet is to brush the inside with vegetable oil or coat it with shortening. Bake at 300° for 1 hour. Another method is to heat it up on the stovetop until it gets very hot, then rub a little oil into it and let it cool. Once cool, wipe it dry with paper towels. Repeat one or two times.

DEEP-DISH SAUSAGE PIZZA

My grandma made the best meals when we stayed with her on her farm. Her deep-dish sausage pizza, hot from the oven, was covered with cheese and boasted fragrant herbs in the crust. Now I'm proud to serve this to my own family.

—MICHELE MADDEN
WASHINGTON COURT HOUSE, OH

PREP: 30 MIN. + RISING
BAKE: 30 MIN. + STANDING
MAKES: 8 SLICES

- 1 package (¼ ounce) active dry yeast
- ⅔ cup warm water (110° to 115°)
- 1¾ to 2 cups all-purpose flour
- ¼ cup vegetable oil
- 1 teaspoon each dried oregano, basil and marjoram
- ½ teaspoon garlic salt
- ½ teaspoon onion salt

TOPPINGS

- 4 cups (16 ounces) shredded part-skim mozzarella cheese, divided
- 2 medium green peppers, chopped
- 1 large onion, chopped
- ½ teaspoon each dried oregano, basil and marjoram
- 1 tablespoon olive oil
- 1 cup grated Parmesan cheese
- 1 pound bulk pork sausage, cooked and drained
- 1 can (28 ounces) diced tomatoes, well drained
- 2 ounces sliced pepperoni

1. In a large bowl, dissolve yeast in warm water. Add 1 cup flour, oil and seasonings; beat until smooth. Add enough remaining flour to form a soft dough.

2. Turn onto a floured surface; knead until smooth and elastic, about 6-8 minutes. Place in a greased bowl; turn once to grease top. Cover and let rise in a warm place until doubled, about 1 hour.

3. Punch dough down; roll out into a 15-in. circle. Transfer to a well-greased 12-in. cast-iron or heavy ovenproof skillet, letting dough drape over edges. Sprinkle with 1 cup mozzarella.

4. In a skillet, saute the green peppers, onion and seasonings in oil until tender; drain. Layer half of the mixture over crust. Layer with half of the Parmesan, sausage and tomatoes. Sprinkle with 2 cups mozzarella. Repeat layers. Fold the crust over to form an edge.

5. Bake at 400° for 20 minutes. Sprinkle with pepperoni and remaining mozzarella. Bake 10-15 minutes longer or until crust is browned. Let stand for 10 minutes before slicing.

DEEP-DISH SAUSAGE PIZZA

FIESTA BEEF & CHEESE SKILLET COBBLER

I tweaked my beefy skillet cobbler until it achieved the wow factor. I must have gotten it right, because it's now a family tradition. Top it off with lettuce, avocado, cherry tomatoes and a tangy dollop of sour cream.

—GLORIA BRADLEY NAPERVILLE, IL

PREP: 40 MIN. • **BAKE:** 15 MIN. + STANDING
MAKES: 8 SERVINGS

- 1 **pound ground beef**
- 1 **can (15 ounces) black beans, rinsed and drained**
- 1 **can (14½ ounces) diced tomatoes with mild green chilies**
- 1 **can (10 ounces) enchilada sauce**
- 1 **teaspoon ground cumin**
- 4 **tablespoons chopped fresh cilantro or parsley, divided**
- 1½ **cups biscuit/baking mix**
- 1½ **cups (6 ounces) shredded Colby-Monterey Jack cheese, divided**
- 4 **bacon strips, cooked and crumbled**
- ⅔ **cup 2% milk**
- 1 **large egg, lightly beaten**
  Sour cream, optional

1. Preheat oven to 400°. In a 10-in. cast-iron or ovenproof skillet, cook beef over medium heat 5-7 minutes or until no longer pink, breaking into crumbles; drain. Stir in beans, tomatoes, enchilada sauce and cumin; bring to a boil. Reduce heat; simmer, uncovered, for 20 minutes to allow flavors to blend, stirring occasionally. Stir in 2 tablespoons cilantro.

2. In a bowl, combine baking mix, ½ cup cheese, bacon and remaining cilantro. Add milk and beaten egg; stir just until a soft dough is formed. Spoon over the beef mixture.

3. Bake, uncovered, for 13-15 minutes or until golden brown. Sprinkle with remaining cheese; bake 2-3 minutes longer or until cheese is melted. Let stand for 10 minutes before serving. If desired, serve with sour cream.

FIESTA BEEF & CHEESE SKILLET COBBLER

**BASIL-BUTTER STEAKS
WITH ROASTED POTATOES**

BASIL-BUTTER STEAKS WITH ROASTED POTATOES

A few ingredients and 30 minutes are all you'll need for this incredibly satisfying meal. A simple basil butter gives these steaks a very special taste.

—TASTE OF HOME TEST KITCHEN

START TO FINISH: 30 MIN.
MAKES: 4 SERVINGS

- 1 package (15 ounces) frozen Parmesan and roasted garlic red potato wedges
- 4 beef tenderloin steaks (1¼ inches thick and 6 ounces each)
- ½ teaspoon salt
- ½ teaspoon pepper
- 5 tablespoons butter, divided
- 2 cups grape tomatoes
- 1 tablespoon minced fresh basil

1. Bake the frozen potato wedges according to the package directions.

2. Meanwhile, sprinkle the tenderloin steaks with salt and pepper. In a 10-in. cast-iron skillet, brown steaks in 2 tablespoons butter. Add tomatoes to skillet. Bake, uncovered, at 425° for 15-20 minutes or until the meat reaches desired doneness (for medium-rare, a thermometer should read 145°; medium, 160°; well-done, 170°).

3. In a small bowl, combine basil and remaining butter. Spoon over steaks and serve with potatoes.

CORNED BEEF HASH AND EGGS

CORNED BEEF HASH AND EGGS

Sunday breakfasts have always been special in our house. It's fun to get in the kitchen and cook with the kids. No matter how many new recipes we try, the kids always rate this "No. 1"!

—RICK SKILDUM MAPLE GROVE, MN

PREP: 15 MIN. • **BAKE:** 20 MIN.
MAKES: 8 SERVINGS

- 1 **package (32 ounces) frozen cubed hash browns**
- 1½ **cups chopped onion**
- ½ **cup canola oil**
- 4 **to 5 cups chopped cooked corned beef**
- ½ **teaspoon salt**
- 8 **large eggs**
  Salt and pepper to taste
- 2 **tablespoons minced fresh parsley**

1. In a large cast-iron or ovenproof skillet, cook hash browns and onion in oil until potatoes are browned and onion is tender. Remove from the heat; stir in corned beef and salt.

2. Make eight wells in the hash browns. Break one egg into each well. Sprinkle with salt and pepper. Cover and bake at 325° for 20-25 minutes or until eggs reach desired doneness. Garnish with parsley.

DID YOU KNOW?

Consider breakfast an investment in your health. Not only does a nutrient-dense meal boost your vitamin and mineral intake, it can help you stay focused and energized all morning long. By fueling your body right, you may stop yourself from overindulging at the next meal.

GRAM'S FRIED CHICKEN

As a boy, I would wolf down my grandmother's fried chicken. I never knew how she made it, but I think my recipe using potato flakes comes pretty close.

—**DAVID NELSON** LINCOLNTON, NC

PREP: 20 MIN. + CHILLING
COOK: 10 MIN.
MAKES: 4 SERVINGS

- 1 **large egg**
- 1 **cup 2% milk**
- 2 **cups mashed potato flakes**
- 1 **tablespoon garlic powder**
- 1 **tablespoon each dried oregano, parsley flakes and minced onion**
- ½ **teaspoon salt**
- ¼ **teaspoon coarsely ground pepper**
- 4 **boneless skinless chicken breast halves (6 ounces each)**
  Oil for frying

1. In a shallow bowl, whisk egg and milk. In another shallow bowl, toss potato flakes with seasonings. Remove half of the mixture and reserve (for a second coat of breading).

2. Pound chicken with a meat mallet to ½-in. thickness. Dip chicken in egg mixture, then in potato mixture, patting to help coating adhere. Arrange chicken in an even layer on a large plate. Cover and refrigerate chicken and remaining egg mixture for 1 hour. Discard remaining used potato mixture.

3. In a 12-in. cast-iron or other deep skillet, heat ½ in. of oil over medium heat to 350°. For the second coat of breading, dip chicken in remaining egg mixture, then in unused potato mixture; pat to coat. Fry the chicken for 4-5 minutes on each side or until golden brown and chicken is no longer pink. Drain on paper towels.

HOW TO

FLATTEN CHICKEN BREASTS

1 Place boneless chicken breasts between two pieces of waxed paper or plastic wrap or in a resealable plastic bag.

2 Starting in center and working out to edges, pound lightly with the flat side of a meat mallet or tenderizer until chicken is even in thickness. Use a lighter touch than you would for tenderizing a beef round steak; if pounded too hard, the chicken will fall apart and be mushy.

3 Discard the plastic bag and sanitize all surfaces.

GRAM'S FRIED CHICKEN

HOMEY MAC & CHEESE

HOMEY MAC & CHEESE

I also call this "My Grandson's Mac & Cheese." Zachary has been to Iraq and Afghanistan with both the Marines and the Navy, and I've been privileged to make his favorite casserole for him for over 20 years.
—**ALICE BEARDSELL** OSPREY, FL

PREP: 20 MIN. • **BAKE:** 25 MIN.
MAKES: 8 SERVINGS

- 2½ **cups uncooked elbow macaroni**
- ¼ **cup butter, cubed**
- ¼ **cup all-purpose flour**
- ½ **teaspoon salt**
- ¼ **teaspoon pepper**
- 3 **cups 2% milk**
- 5 **cups (20 ounces) shredded sharp cheddar cheese, divided**
- 2 **tablespoons Worcestershire sauce**
- ½ **teaspoon paprika**

1. Preheat oven to 350°. Cook macaroni according to package directions for al dente.

2. Meanwhile, in a large saucepan, heat butter over medium heat. Stir in flour, salt and pepper until smooth; gradually whisk in milk. Bring to a boil, stirring constantly; cook and stir 2-3 minutes or until thickened.

3. Reduce heat. Stir in 3 cups cheese and Worcestershire sauce until cheese is melted.

4. Drain macaroni; stir into sauce. Transfer to a greased 10-in. cast-iron or ovenproof skillet. Bake, uncovered, 20 minutes. Top with remaining cheese; sprinkle with paprika. Bake 5-10 minutes longer or until bubbly and cheese is melted.

TURKEY BISCUIT STEW

This chunky stew makes a hearty supper and is especially comforting in the fall and winter. It's also a great way to use up extra turkey around the holidays.

—**LORI SCHLECHT** WIMBLEDON, ND

PREP: 15 MIN. • **BAKE:** 20 MIN.
MAKES: 6-8 SERVINGS

- ⅓ cup chopped onion
- ¼ cup butter, cubed
- ⅓ cup all-purpose flour
- ½ teaspoon salt
- ⅛ teaspoon pepper
- 1 can (10½ ounces) condensed chicken broth, undiluted
- ¾ cup milk
- 2 cups cubed cooked turkey
- 1 cup cooked peas
- 1 cup cooked whole baby carrots
- 1 tube (10 ounces) refrigerated buttermilk biscuits

1. In a 10-in. cast-iron or ovenproof skillet, saute onion in butter until tender. Stir in the flour, salt and pepper until blended. Gradually add broth and milk. Bring to a boil. Cook and stir for 2 minutes or until thickened and bubbly. Add the turkey, peas and carrots; heat through. Separate biscuits and arrange over the stew.
2. Bake at 375° for 20-25 minutes or until biscuits are golden brown.

TURKEY BISCUIT STEW

CORN BREAD WITH A KICK

To me, nothing says good old-fashioned Southern cooking like crisp corn bread made in a cast-iron skillet. I'm lucky to have a vintage skillet that once belonged to my great-aunt.

—**GEORDYTH SULLIVAN** CUTLER BAY, FL

PREP: 20 MIN. • **BAKE:** 20 MIN.
MAKES: 8 SERVINGS

- ⅔ **cup all-purpose flour**
- ⅔ **cup cornmeal**
- 1 **tablespoon sugar**
- ½ **teaspoon baking powder**
- ½ **teaspoon salt**
- ¼ **teaspoon baking soda**
- 1 **large egg**
- 1 **cup buttermilk**
- 3 **tablespoons butter**
- 3 **chipotle peppers in adobo sauce, drained and chopped**
- 6 **bacon strips, cooked and crumbled**

1. In a large bowl, combine the first six ingredients. In another bowl, whisk egg and buttermilk.

2. Place butter in an 8-in. cast-iron or ovenproof skillet; heat skillet in a 425° oven for 3-5 minutes or until butter is melted. Meanwhile, stir egg mixture into dry ingredients just until moistened. Fold in peppers and bacon.

3. Carefully swirl the butter in the skillet to coat the sides and bottom of pan; add batter. Bake at 425° for 18-22 minutes or until a toothpick inserted near the center comes out clean. Cut corn bread into wedges; serve warm.

CORN BREAD WITH A KICK

**JENNY DUBINSKY'S
BEEF & SWEET PEPPER SKILLET**
PAGE 37

30 Entrees In 30

Time-crunched cooks, rejoice! Beat the clock on busy nights with surprisingly easy, fast-to-fix skillet entrees, all ready in just 30 minutes or less.

PORK QUESADILLAS WITH FRESH SALSA

PORK QUESADILLAS WITH FRESH SALSA

I threw these together one night when I was in the mood for quesadillas but didn't feel like going out. The homemade salsa is so tasty and versatile, you might want to double the recipe.

—ADAM GAYLORD NATICK, MA

START TO FINISH: 30 MIN.
MAKES: 4 SERVINGS (¾ CUP SALSA)

- 1 tablespoon olive oil
- 1 each small green, sweet red and orange peppers, sliced
- 1 medium red onion, sliced
- ¾ pound thinly sliced cooked pork (about 3 cups)
- ¼ teaspoon salt
- ⅛ teaspoon pepper

SALSA
- 2 medium tomatoes, seeded and chopped
- 1 tablespoon chopped red onion
- 1 tablespoon minced fresh cilantro
- 2 teaspoons olive oil
- 1 to 2 teaspoons chopped seeded jalapeno pepper
- 1 teaspoon cider vinegar
- ⅛ teaspoon salt
    Dash pepper

QUESADILLAS
- 4 flour tortillas (10 inches)
- 1½ cups (6 ounces) shredded part-skim mozzarella cheese

1. In a large skillet, heat the oil over medium-high heat. Add peppers and onion; cook 4-5 minutes or until tender, stirring occasionally. Stir in pork, salt and pepper; heat through. Meanwhile, in a small bowl, combine salsa ingredients.

2. Place tortillas on a griddle. Layer one-half of each tortilla with ¼ cup cheese, 1 cup pork mixture and 2 tablespoons cheese; fold other half over filling.

3. Cook over medium heat 1-2 minutes on each side or until golden brown and cheese is melted. Cut into wedges. Serve with salsa.

NOTE *Wear disposable gloves when cutting hot peppers; the oils can burn skin. Avoid touching your face.*

CHICKEN TORTELLINI SKILLET

Dinner's on the table in no time with this tasty chicken and pasta recipe. I'm a graduate student and live alone, so the recipes I favor are budget-friendly and make just a few servings.

—CHANDRA BENJAMIN EDEN PRAIRIE, MN

START TO FINISH: 25 MIN. • **MAKES:** 2 SERVINGS

- 2 **cups frozen cheese tortellini**
- ½ **pound boneless skinless chicken breast, cubed**
- 1 **tablespoon canola oil**
- 1 **cup meatless spaghetti sauce**
- ½ **cup shredded part-skim mozzarella cheese**

1. Cook tortellini according to package directions. Meanwhile, in a large skillet, cook chicken in oil over medium heat until juices run clear.

2. Drain tortellini; add to skillet. Stir in spaghetti sauce. Sprinkle with cheese. Reduce heat to low. Cover and cook for 3-5 minutes or until the cheese is melted.

PRESTO PASTA

PRESTO PASTA

When the temperature and humidity rise—or when you just want something light—this pasta is the ticket.
—DEBBIE VERDINI YARDLEY, PA

START TO FINISH: 20 MIN. • **MAKES:** 9 SERVINGS

- 8 **ounces linguine**
- 4 **cups fresh baby spinach**
- 1½ **cups julienned roasted sweet red peppers**
- 4 **garlic cloves, minced**
- 3 **tablespoons olive oil**
- 1 **can (6 ounces) pitted ripe olives, drained**
- ¼ **teaspoon salt**
- ⅛ **teaspoon pepper**

1. Cook linguine according to the package directions. Meanwhile, in a large skillet over medium heat, cook the spinach, peppers and garlic in oil until spinach is wilted.

2. Drain linguine; toss with spinach mixture, olives, salt and pepper. Serve pasta warm or at room temperature.

CHICKEN TORTELLINI SKILLET

FAST FIX

VEGGIE TACOS

These yummy vegetarian tacos are stuffed with a blend of sauteed cabbage, peppers and black beans that is so flavorful and filling no one will miss the meat. Let guests top their own with avocado, cheese or a dollop of sour cream.

—*TASTE OF HOME* TEST KITCHEN

START TO FINISH: 20 MIN.
MAKES: 4 SERVINGS

- 8 taco shells
- 3 cups shredded cabbage
- 1 cup sliced onion
- 1 cup julienned sweet red pepper
- 2 tablespoons canola oil
- 2 teaspoons sugar
- 1 can (15 ounces) black beans, rinsed and drained
- 1 cup salsa
- 1 can (4 ounces) chopped green chilies
- 1 teaspoon chili powder
- 1 teaspoon minced garlic
- ¼ teaspoon ground cumin
- ½ cup shredded cheddar cheese
- 1 medium ripe avocado, peeled and sliced

1. Heat taco shells according to package directions. Meanwhile, in a large skillet, saute cabbage, onion and red pepper in oil for 5 minutes or until crisp-tender. Sprinkle with sugar.

2. Stir in the beans, salsa, chilies, chili powder, garlic and cumin. Bring to a boil. Reduce the heat; cover and simmer for 5 minutes or until heated through. Spoon into the taco shells. Garnish with cheese and avocado.

FAST FIX

CREAMY SHELLS AND CHICKEN

This is a great weeknight dinner dish. While it simmers, I can throw together a salad or steam some broccoli, and I have a tasty meal ready in a flash.

—TRISHA KRUSE EAGLE, ID

START TO FINISH: 30 MIN.
MAKES: 3 SERVINGS

- ½ pound boneless skinless chicken breasts, cut into 1-inch strips
- ¼ teaspoon salt
- ¼ teaspoon pepper
- 2 tablespoons canola oil, divided
- 2 tablespoons butter, divided
- ½ cup chopped onion
- ½ cup chopped green pepper
- ½ cup chopped sweet red pepper
- 1⅓ cups water
- ½ cup milk
- 1 package (4.9 ounces) creamy garlic shells
- Shredded Parmesan cheese

1. Sprinkle chicken with salt and pepper. In a large skillet, cook the chicken over medium heat in 1 tablespoon oil and 1 tablespoon butter for 4-5 minutes or until no longer pink. Remove strips and keep warm.

2. In the same skillet, saute the onion and peppers in remaining oil and butter until crisp-tender. Stir in the water, milk and shells. Bring to a boil. Reduce the heat; simmer, uncovered, for 10-12 minutes or until pasta is tender, stirring occasionally. Add the chicken; cook 2-3 minutes longer or until heated through. Sprinkle with cheese.

NOTE *This recipe was prepared with Lipton Italian Sides creamy garlic shells.*

CREAMY SHELLS AND CHICKEN

OASTED
ED PEPPER
AUSAGE SKILLET

two busy teenagers make sure ey're home on nights I serve a mforting pasta dish. Eat it on its wn, or pair it with breadsticks, green salad and apple slices.

JANET TEAS ZANESVILLE, OH

ART TO FINISH: 30 MIN.
AKES: 5 SERVINGS

4 **cups uncooked egg noodles**
½ **pound bulk Italian sausage**
1 **small onion, chopped**
1 **small green pepper, chopped**
½ **cup chopped fresh mushrooms**
2 **jars (7½ ounces each) roasted sweet red peppers, drained and coarsely chopped**
1 **can (10¾ ounces) condensed golden mushroom soup, undiluted**
3 **ounces cream cheese, cubed**
⅓ **cup 2% milk**
½ **cup shredded smoked provolone cheese**

Cook noodles according to e package directions; drain. Meanwhile, in a large skillet, cook sausage, onion, green epper and mushrooms over medium heat until sausage is o longer pink and vegetables re tender, breaking up sausage into crumbles; drain.

Stir in the red peppers, soup, cream cheese and milk; heat through. Stir the noodles into sausage mixture; sprinkle with provolone cheese. Let mixture and, covered, for 5 minutes or until cheese is melted.

ROASTED RED PEPPER SAUSAGE SKILLET

**BEEF & SWEET
PEPPER SKILLET**

BEEF & SWEET PEPPER SKILLET

I love Mexican-inspired food. I also enjoy experimenting with recipes to make them healthy, satisfying and down-home good!

—**JENNY DUBINSKY** INWOOD, WV

START TO FINISH: 30 MIN. • **MAKES:** 6 SERVINGS

- **1 pound lean ground beef (90% lean)**
- **2 cups water**
- **1 can (14½ ounces) diced tomatoes with mild green chilies, undrained**
- **1 tablespoon chili powder**
- **2 teaspoons beef stock concentrate**
- **¼ teaspoon salt**
- **⅛ teaspoon garlic powder**
- **2 cups instant brown rice**
- **1 medium sweet red pepper, sliced**
- **1 medium green pepper, sliced**
- **1 cup (4 ounces) shredded Colby-Monterey Jack cheese**

In a large skillet, cook beef over medium heat 6-8 minutes or until no longer pink, breaking into crumbles; drain.

Add water, tomatoes, chili powder, beef stock concentrate, salt and garlic powder; bring to a boil. Stir in the rice and peppers. Reduce heat; simmer, covered, 8-10 minutes or until liquid is absorbed. Remove from the heat; sprinkle with cheese. Let stand, covered, until cheese is melted.

TOP TIP

Make easy work of slicing a sweet bell pepper. Holding the pepper by the stem, slice from the top of the pepper down, using a chef's knife. Scrape out any seeds and discard. Use this technique to slice around the seeds when a recipe calls for julienned, sliced or chopped peppers.

GROUND TURKEY AND HOMINY

Hominy is a favorite of mine, so when I saw this fast-to-fix recipe, I had to try it. With its flavorful combination of spices, it makes a warming meal on a cool night.

—**ESTHER HOFF-SHERROW** DENVER, CO

START TO FINISH: 20 MIN. • **MAKES:** 8 SERVINGS

- **1½ pounds ground turkey**
- **1 large onion, chopped**
- **2 tablespoons olive oil**
- **1 teaspoon minced garlic**
- **2 cans (14½ ounces each) diced tomatoes, undrained**
- **1 tablespoon chili powder**
- **1½ teaspoons ground cumin**
- **1 teaspoon salt**
- **½ teaspoon ground mustard**
- **½ teaspoon dried thyme**
- **¼ teaspoon ground cinnamon**
- **¼ teaspoon ground allspice**
- **¼ teaspoon pepper**
- **2 cans (15½ ounces each) hominy, rinsed and drained**

In a large skillet, cook turkey and onion in oil over medium heat until meat is no longer pink. Add garlic; cook 1 minute longer. Drain. Stir in tomatoes and seasonings; heat through. Add hominy and heat through.

⑤ INGREDIENTS | FAST FIX

BLUE CHEESE-CRUSTED SIRLOIN STEAKS

My wife loves when I fix this steak for her. It's the ideal dish for Friday night after a long week.
—**MICHAEL ROUSE** MINOT, ND

START TO FINISH: 30 MIN.
MAKES: 4 SERVINGS

- 2 **tablespoons butter, divided**
- 1 **medium onion, chopped**
- 1 **beef top sirloin steak (1 inch thick and 1½ pounds)**
- ¾ **teaspoon salt**
- ½ **teaspoon pepper**
- ⅓ **cup crumbled blue cheese**
- 2 **tablespoons soft bread crumbs**

1. In a large ovenproof skillet, heat 1 tablespoon butter over medium heat. Add onion; cook and stir until tender. Transfer to a small bowl.

2. Cut the steak into four equal portions; season with salt and pepper. In the same skillet, heat remaining butter over medium heat. Brown steaks for about 5 minutes on each side. Meanwhile, add blue cheese and bread crumbs to onion; mix well. Spread over steaks.

3. Broil the steaks 4-6 in. from the heat for 3-5 minutes or until the steaks reach the desired doneness (for medium-rare, a thermometer should read 145°; medium, 160°; well-done, 170°).

FAST FIX

SHRIMP FRIED RICE

This delectable shrimp dish is filled with color and flavor that makes it quickly vanish from the dinner table. The best part is that it all cooks in one pan, so prep and cleanup is a breeze. Consider it when you're looking for a new entree or even a brunch item.
—**SANDRA THOMPSON**
WHITE HALL, AR

START TO FINISH: 20 MIN.
MAKES: 8 SERVINGS

- 4 **tablespoons butter, divided**
- 4 **large eggs, lightly beaten**
- 3 **cups cold cooked rice**
- 1 **package (16 ounces) frozen mixed vegetables**
- 1 **pound uncooked medium shrimp, peeled and deveined**
- ½ **teaspoon salt**
- ¼ **teaspoon pepper**
- 8 **bacon strips, cooked and crumbled, optional**

1. In a large skillet, melt 1 tablespoon of butter over medium-high heat. Pour eggs into skillet. As eggs set, lift edges, letting the uncooked portion flow underneath. Remove eggs and keep warm.

2. Melt remaining butter in the skillet. Add the rice, vegetables and shrimp; cook and stir for 5 minutes or until shrimp turn pink. Meanwhile, chop eggs into small pieces. Return eggs to the pan; sprinkle with the salt and pepper. Cook until heated through, stirring occasionally. Sprinkle with bacon if desired.

SHRIMP FRIED RICE

ROSEMARY CHICKEN WITH SPINACH & BEANS

ROSEMARY CHICKEN WITH SPINACH & BEANS

I have kids who are constantly on the go, so simplifying meals is key. Since this recipe uses just one skillet, it's a cinch to prepare when I only have a half hour to make dinner.

—SARA RICHARDSON LITTLETON, CO

START TO FINISH: 30 MIN.
MAKES: 4 SERVINGS

- 1 **can (14½ ounces) stewed tomatoes**
- 4 **boneless skinless chicken breast halves (6 ounces each)**
- 2 **teaspoons dried rosemary, crushed**
- ½ **teaspoon salt**
- ½ **teaspoon pepper**
- 4 **teaspoons olive oil, divided**
- 1 **package (6 ounces) fresh baby spinach**
- 2 **garlic cloves, minced**
- 1 **can (15 ounces) white kidney or cannellini beans, rinsed and drained**

1. Drain tomatoes, reserving juice; coarsely chop tomatoes. Pound the chicken with a meat mallet to ¼-in. thickness. Rub with rosemary, salt and pepper. In a large skillet, heat 2 teaspoons oil over medium heat. Add the chicken; cook 5-6 minutes on each side or until no longer pink. Remove and keep warm.
2. In same pan, heat remaining oil over medium-high heat. Add spinach and garlic; cook and stir 2-3 minutes or until spinach is wilted. Stir in beans, tomatoes and reserved juice; heat through. Serve with chicken.

BARBECUE PORK AND
PENNE SKILLET

<FAST FIX>

BARBECUE PORK AND PENNE SKILLET

We're an active family with a busy schedule. So I appreciate simple, delicious and quick meals. A hearty pasta dish is my go-to dinner to enjoy together after errands, school activities and soccer practice.

—**JUDY ARMSTRONG** PRAIRIEVILLE, LA

START TO FINISH: 25 MIN. • **MAKES:** 8 SERVINGS

- 1 **package (16 ounces) penne pasta**
- 1 **cup chopped sweet red pepper**
- ¾ **cup chopped onion**
- 1 **tablespoon butter**
- 1 **tablespoon olive oil**
- 3 **garlic cloves, minced**
- 1 **carton (16 ounces) refrigerated fully cooked barbecued shredded pork**
- 1 **can (14½ ounces) diced tomatoes with mild green chilies, undrained**
- ½ **cup beef broth**
- 1 **teaspoon ground cumin**
- 1 **teaspoon pepper**
- ¼ **teaspoon salt**
- 1¼ **cups shredded cheddar cheese**
- ¼ **cup chopped green onions**

1. Cook pasta according to package directions. Meanwhile, in a large skillet, saute red pepper and onion in butter and oil until tender. Add garlic; saute 1 minute longer. Stir in the pork, tomatoes, broth, cumin, pepper and salt; heat through.

2. Drain pasta. Add pasta and cheese to pork mixture; stir until blended. Sprinkle with the green onions.

TOP TIP

Try one of these simple tricks to easily remove the papery skin from a fresh garlic clove.

- Using the flat side of chef's knife blade, crush garlic clove and peel away skin.
- Put the cloves in a bowl, cover with another bowl, and shake hard until the skins come off.
- Microwave cloves on high for 20 seconds (or roast briefly in a dry skillet). The heat will make the skins peel off easily.
- Put the clove in the center of a non-slip rubber jar lid opener. Fold in half and rub together until the skin peels off.

URLY NOODLE DINNER

he calendar on my kitchen wall is often full with church
ork, 4-H leader meetings and the extracurriculars of
r three daughters—and this recipe is perfect for an
-the-go family.

GWEN CLEMON SOLDIER, IA

ART TO FINISH: 25 MIN. • **MAKES:** 4-6 SERVINGS

- **1 pound ground beef**
- **1 package (3 ounces) beef ramen noodles**
- **1 can (14½ ounces) stewed tomatoes**
- **1 can (8½ ounces) whole kernel corn, drained**

a skillet, brown beef; drain. Stir in noodles with
ntents of the accompanying seasoning packet,
matoes and corn; mix well. Bring to a boil.
educe heat; cover and simmer for 10 minutes
until the noodles are tender.

REOLE SHRIMP & SAUSAGE

dd diversity to weeknight meals and get a taste of
w-country cuisine. This simple take on a Louisiana
eole classic uses whole wheat bulgur instead of rice.

TASTE OF HOME TEST KITCHEN

ART TO FINISH: 30 MIN. • **MAKES:** 4 SERVINGS

- **½ cup water**
- **½ cup chicken broth**
- **1 cup quick-cooking bulgur**
- **½ teaspoon chili powder**
- **¾ teaspoon Creole seasoning, divided**
- **½ pound smoked sausage, cut into ¼-inch slices**
- **2 teaspoons olive oil, divided**
- **1 medium onion, chopped**
- **1 medium green pepper, chopped**
- **2 garlic cloves, minced**
- **1 can (16 ounces) kidney beans, rinsed and drained**
- **1 can (14½ ounces) diced tomatoes, undrained**
- **½ pound uncooked jumbo shrimp, peeled and deveined**
- **½ teaspoon Worcestershire sauce**

. In a small saucepan, bring water and broth
a boil. Stir in the bulgur, chili powder and

¼ teaspoon Creole seasoning. Reduce heat;
cover and simmer for 15 minutes or until tender.
2. Meanwhile, in a large skillet, brown sausage
in 1 teaspoon oil. Remove and keep warm.
3. In the same skillet, saute the onion and green
pepper in remaining oil until tender. Add garlic;
cook 1 minute longer. Stir in the beans, tomatoes,
shrimp, Worcestershire sauce, sausage and the
remaining Creole seasoning. Cook for 3-5 minutes
or until shrimp turn pink. Fluff the bulgur with a
fork; serve with sausage mixture.

NOTE *The following spices may be substituted for
1 teaspoon Creole seasoning: ¼ teaspoon each salt,
garlic powder and paprika; and a pinch each of
dried thyme, ground cumin and cayenne pepper.*

CREOLE SHRIMP
& SAUSAGE

PENNE ALLA VODKA

This impressive pasta is always on the menu when my husband and I invite first-time guests over for dinner. Many friends have asked me to make the recipe again, even years after they first tried it!

—**CARA LANGER** OVERLAND PARK, KS

START TO FINISH: 30 MIN.
MAKES: 6 SERVINGS

- 1 **package (16 ounces) penne pasta**
- 3 **tablespoons butter**
- 2 **garlic cloves, minced**
- 4 **ounces thinly sliced prosciutto, cut into strips**
- 1 **can (28 ounces) whole plum tomatoes, drained and chopped**
- ¼ **cup vodka**
- ½ **teaspoon salt**
- ½ **teaspoon crushed red pepper flakes**
- ½ **cup heavy whipping cream**
- ½ **cup shredded Parmesan cheese**

1. Cook the pasta according to package directions.

2. Meanwhile, in a large skillet, heat butter over medium-high heat. Add garlic; cook and stir 1 minute. Add prosciutto; cook 2 minutes longer. Stir in the tomatoes, vodka, salt and pepper flakes. Bring to a boil. Reduce the heat; simmer mixture uncovered for 5 minutes. Stir in cream; cook 2-3 minutes longer, stirring the sauce occasionally.

3. Drain pasta. Add pasta and cheese to sauce; toss to combine.

PENNE ALLA VODKA

MOM'S SPANISH RICE

MEDITERRANEAN CHICKEN

As special as it is simple to prepare, this moist, flavorful chicken is dressed in tomatoes, olives and capers. It's a knockout main dish for dinner parties.

—MARY RELYEA CANASTOTA, NY

START TO FINISH: 25 MIN.
MAKES: 4 SERVINGS

- 4 **boneless skinless chicken breast halves (6 ounces each)**
- ¼ **teaspoon salt**
- ¼ **teaspoon pepper**
- 3 **tablespoons olive oil**
- 1 **pint grape tomatoes**
- 16 **pitted Greek or ripe olives, sliced**
- 3 **tablespoons capers, drained**

1. Sprinkle chicken with salt and pepper. In a large ovenproof skillet, cook chicken in oil over medium heat for 2-3 minutes on each side or until golden brown. Add tomatoes, olives and capers.
2. Bake, uncovered, at 475° for 10-14 minutes or until a meat thermometer reads 170°.

MOM'S SPANISH RICE

My mother is famous for her Spanish rice, the ultimate comfort food. When I want a taste of home, I pull out this cherished recipe.

—JOAN HALLFORD
NORTH RICHLAND HILLS, TX

START TO FINISH: 20 MIN.
MAKES: 4 SERVINGS

- 1 **pound lean ground beef (90% lean)**
- 1 **large onion, chopped**
- 1 **medium green pepper, chopped**
- 1 **can (15 ounces) tomato sauce**
- 1 **can (14½ ounces) no-salt-added diced tomatoes, drained**
- 1 **teaspoon ground cumin**
- 1 **teaspoon chili powder**
- ½ **teaspoon garlic powder**
- ¼ **teaspoon salt**
- 2⅔ **cups cooked brown rice**

1. In a large skillet, cook beef, onion and pepper over medium heat 6-8 minutes or until beef is no longer pink and the onion is tender, breaking up the beef into crumbles; drain.
2. Stir in tomato sauce, tomatoes and seasonings; bring to a boil. Add rice; heat through, stirring mixture occasionally.

APPLE-TOPPED HAM STEAK

When it's time to dine with friends, I serve ham with a tangy sauce of sweet and tart apples, zingy mustard and a dash of sage.
—**ELEANOR CHORE** ATHENA, OR

START TO FINISH: 30 MIN. • **MAKES:** 8 SERVINGS

- 4 fully cooked boneless ham steaks (8 ounces each)
- 1 cup chopped onion
- 3 cups apple juice
- 2 teaspoons Dijon mustard
- 2 medium green apples, thinly sliced
- 2 medium red apples, thinly sliced
- 2 tablespoons cornstarch
- ¼ cup cold water
- 1 tablespoon minced fresh sage or 1 teaspoon rubbed sage
- ¼ teaspoon pepper

1. In a large skillet coated with cooking spray, brown the ham steaks in batches over medium heat; remove and keep warm.

2. In same skillet, saute onion until tender. Stir in apple juice and mustard; bring to a boil. Add the apples. Reduce heat; cover skillet and simmer for 4 minutes or until apples are tender.

3. Combine cornstarch and water until smooth; stir into apple juice mixture. Bring to a boil; cook and stir for 2 minutes. Stir in the sage and pepper. Return steaks to skillet; heat through.

SPICY MANGO SCALLOPS

Warm up your family with this spicy-sweet seafood dish. If you prepare the recipe with smaller scallops, decrease the cooking time.
—**NICOLE FILIZETTI** STEVENS POINT, WI

START TO FINISH: 30 MIN. • **MAKES:** 4 SERVINGS

- 12 sea scallops (1½ pounds)
- 1 tablespoon peanut or canola oil
- 1 medium red onion, chopped
- 1 garlic clove, minced
- ¼ to ½ teaspoon crushed red pepper flakes
- ½ cup unsweetened pineapple juice
- ¼ cup mango chutney
- 2 cups hot cooked basmati rice
  Minced fresh cilantro

1. Pat scallops dry with paper towels. In a large skillet, heat oil over medium-high heat. Add the scallops; cook 1-2 minutes on each side or until golden brown and firm. Remove from pan.

2. Add onion to the same pan; cook and stir until tender. Add garlic and pepper flakes; cook 1 minute longer. Stir in pineapple juice. Bring to a boil; cook until liquid is reduced by half. Stir in chutney.

3. Return scallops to pan; heat through, stirring gently to coat. Serve with rice; lightly sprinkle with minced cilantro.

SPICY MANGO SCALLOPS

GREEN CHILI GRILLED CHEESE MELT

My daughter created a masterpiece with her ultimate grilled cheese and chilies. Want more heat? Use a 4-ounce can of diced jalapenos instead of chilies.

—JULIA HUNTINGTON CHEYENNE, WY

START TO FINISH: 25 MIN.
MAKES: 6 SERVINGS

- 4 ounces cream cheese, softened
- 1 cup (4 ounces) shredded Colby-Monterey Jack cheese
- 1 cup (4 ounces) shredded part-skim mozzarella cheese
- 1 can (4 ounces) chopped green chilies, drained
- 2 tablespoons mayonnaise
- ¼ teaspoon garlic powder
  Dash seasoned salt
- 12 slices white bread
- 6 slices tomato
- ¼ cup butter, melted

1. In a small bowl, mix the first seven ingredients until blended. Spread mixture over half of the bread slices. Top with tomato and remaining bread.

2. Brush outsides of sandwiches with melted butter. In a large skillet, toast the sandwiches in batches over medium-low heat 3-4 minutes on each side or until golden brown and the filling is heated through.

GREEN CHILI GRILLED CHEESE MELT

SKILLET CASSOULET

My speedy stovetop variation of a French classic is chock-full of flavor. Kielbasa, ham and cannellini beans make the stew a hearty meal-in-one.

—**BARBARA BRITTAIN** SANTEE, CA

START TO FINISH: 30 MIN.
MAKES: 3 SERVINGS

- 2 **teaspoons canola oil**
- ¼ **pound smoked turkey kielbasa, cut into ½-inch slices**
- ¼ **pound fully cooked boneless ham, cubed**
- 2 **medium carrots, sliced**
- 1 **celery rib, sliced**
- ½ **medium red onion, sliced**
- 2 **garlic cloves, minced**
- 1 **can (15 ounces) no-salt-added white kidney or cannellini beans, rinsed and drained**
- 1 **can (14½ ounces) no-salt-added diced tomatoes, undrained**
- ¾ **teaspoon dried thyme**
- ⅛ **teaspoon pepper**

1. In a large skillet, heat oil over medium-high heat. Add kielbasa, ham, carrots, celery and onion; cook and stir until the sausage is browned and the vegetables are tender. Add garlic; cook mixture 1 minute longer.
2. Stir in remaining ingredients. Bring to a boil. Reduce the heat; simmer, uncovered, 4-5 minutes or until heated through.

SAUCY SKILLET LASAGNA

Thanks to no-cook noodles, this skillet version of traditional lasagna makes a fast and filling Italian entree. It's a smart new way to make this family favorite.

—**MEGHAN CRIHFIELD** RIPLEY, WV

START TO FINISH: 30 MIN.
MAKES: 8 SERVINGS

- 1 **pound ground beef**
- 1 **can (14½ ounces) diced tomatoes, undrained**
- 2 **large eggs, lightly beaten**
- 1½ **cups ricotta cheese**
- 4 **cups marinara sauce**
- 1 **package (9 ounces) no-cook lasagna noodles**
- 1 **cup (4 ounces) shredded part-skim mozzarella cheese, optional**

1. In a large skillet, cook beef over medium heat 6-8 minutes or until no longer pink, breaking into crumbles; drain. Transfer to a large bowl; stir in tomatoes. In a small bowl, combine eggs and ricotta cheese.
2. Return 1 cup of the meat mixture to the skillet; spread evenly. Layer with 1 cup ricotta mixture, 1½ cups marinara sauce and half of the noodles, breaking the noodles to fit as necessary. Repeat the layers. Top with the remaining marinara sauce.
3. Bring to a boil. Reduce heat; simmer, covered, 15-17 minutes or until the noodles are tender. Remove from heat. If desired, sprinkle with mozzarella cheese. Let stand for 2 minutes or until cheese is melted.

SAUCY SKILLET LASAGNA

TANGY CHICKEN & PEPPERS

TANGY CHICKEN & PEPPERS

I created this tasty dish when I was pressed for time during the work week. It couldn't be easier to make. Frozen veggies and convenience items help save time. It's also great with noodles in place of the rice.

DONNA MCLEOD BENTONVILLE, AR

INGREDIENTS FAST FIX

START TO FINISH: 30 MIN.
MAKES: 6 SERVINGS

- 6 boneless skinless chicken breast halves (6 ounces each)
- ½ teaspoon salt
- ¼ teaspoon pepper
- 1 package (16 ounces) frozen pepper and onion stir-fry blend
- 1 jar (16 ounces) pineapple salsa
- 1 can (11 ounces) mandarin oranges, drained
- 4½ cups hot cooked brown rice or hot cooked rice

Sprinkle chicken with salt and pepper. Heat a large nonstick skillet coated with cooking spray over medium heat. Brown chicken in batches; remove from pan. In same pan, add stir-fry blend and salsa; bring to a boil, stirring occasionally. Return chicken to pan; reduce heat. Simmer, covered, 12-15 minutes or until a thermometer inserted in chicken reads 165°. Stir in oranges; heat through. Serve with rice.

FAST FIX

FRESH CORN & TOMATO FETTUCCINE

Combine delicious whole wheat pasta with fresh garden produce and feta cheese. Cooking the corn cobs with the pasta saves time and cleanup.

—**ANGELA SPENGLER** TAMPA, FL

START TO FINISH: 30 MIN.
MAKES: 4 SERVINGS

- 8 ounces uncooked whole wheat fettuccine
- 2 medium ears sweet corn, husks removed
- 2 teaspoons plus 2 tablespoons olive oil, divided
- ½ cup chopped sweet red pepper
- 4 green onions, chopped
- 2 medium tomatoes, chopped
- ½ teaspoon salt
- ½ teaspoon pepper
- 1 cup crumbled feta cheese
- 2 tablespoons minced fresh parsley

1. In a Dutch oven, cook the fettuccine according to package directions, adding corn during the last 8 minutes of cooking.
2. Meanwhile, in a small skillet, heat 2 teaspoons of the oil over medium-high heat. Add the red pepper and green onions; cook and stir until tender.
3. Drain pasta and corn; transfer pasta to a large bowl. Cool corn slightly; cut corn from cob and add to pasta. Add tomatoes, salt, pepper, remaining oil and the pepper mixture; toss to combine. Sprinkle with cheese and parsley.

⑤ INGREDIENTS **FAST FIX**

CHICKEN-FRIED STEAK & GRAVY

My grandmother taught me how to make her famous Texas-style chicken-fried steak. I taught my daughters, and when my granddaughters are older, I'll show them, too.

—**DONNA CATER** FORT ANN, NY

START TO FINISH: 30 MIN. • **MAKES:** 4 SERVINGS

- 1¼ cups all-purpose flour, divided
- 2 large eggs
- 1½ cups 2% milk, divided
- 4 beef cubed steaks (6 ounces each)
- 1¼ teaspoons salt, divided
- 1 teaspoon pepper, divided
   Oil for frying
- 1 cup water

1. Place 1 cup flour in a shallow bowl. In a separate shallow bowl, whisk eggs and ½ cup milk until blended. Sprinkle steaks with ¾ teaspoon each salt and pepper. Dip in flour to coat both sides; shake off excess. Dip in egg mixture, then again in flour.

2. In a large skillet, heat ¼ in. of oil over medium heat. Add steaks; cook 4-6 minutes on each side or until golden brown and a thermometer reads 160°. Remove from pan; drain on paper towels. Keep warm.

3. Remove all but 2 tablespoons oil from pan. Stir in the remaining ¼ cup flour, ½ teaspoon salt and ¼ teaspoon pepper until smooth; cook and stir over medium heat 3-4 minutes or until golden brown. Gradually whisk in water and remaining milk. Bring to a boil, stirring constantly; cook and stir 1-2 minutes or until thickened. Serve the gravy with the steaks.

CHICKEN FRIED STEAK & GRAVY

STOVETOP HAMBURGER CASSEROLE

This dish is about enjoying comfort food at its best. Not only is it loaded with ground beef, pasta, veggies and cheddar cheese, but it also comes together in a jiffy.
—EDITH LANDINGER LONGVIEW, TX

PREP/TOTAL TIME: 25 MIN.
MAKES: 6 SERVINGS

- 1 package (7 ounces) small pasta shells
- 1½ pounds ground beef
- 1 large onion, chopped
- 3 medium carrots, chopped
- 1 celery rib, chopped
- 3 garlic cloves, minced
- 3 cups cubed cooked red potatoes
- 1 can (15¼ ounces) whole kernel corn, drained
- 2 cans (8 ounces each) tomato sauce
- 1½ teaspoons salt
- ½ teaspoon pepper
- 1 cup (4 ounces) shredded cheddar cheese

1. Cook pasta according to the package directions. Meanwhile, in a large skillet, cook the beef and onion over medium heat until meat is no longer pink; drain. Add carrots and celery; cook and stir for 5 minutes or until vegetables are crisp-tender. Add the minced garlic; cook 1 minute longer.

2. Stir in the potatoes, corn, tomato sauce, salt and pepper; heat through. Drain the pasta and add to skillet; toss to coat. Sprinkle with cheese. Cover and cook until cheese is melted.

HEARTY BEEF RAVIOLI

HEARTY BEEF RAVIOLI

We add our favorite taco toppings to beef ravioli in this fun, family-friendly supper. It's easy for kids to customize their fixings for a tasty, no-fuss meal.
—*TASTE OF HOME* TEST KITCHEN

START TO FINISH: 25 MIN.
MAKES: 6 SERVINGS

- 1 package (25 ounces) frozen beef ravioli
- ½ pound extra-lean ground beef (95% lean)
- 1 medium green pepper, chopped
- 1 can (14½ ounces) no-salt-added diced tomatoes, undrained
- 1 can (8 ounces) no-salt-added tomato sauce
- 2 tablespoons reduced-sodium taco seasoning
- ¾ cup shredded reduced-fat cheddar cheese
- 1 can (2¼ ounces) sliced ripe olives, drained

1. Cook ravioli according to package directions; drain.

2. Meanwhile, in a large nonstick skillet, cook beef and pepper over medium heat 4-6 minutes or until beef is no longer pink, breaking up beef into crumbles. Stir in tomatoes, tomato sauce and taco seasoning. Bring to a boil. Reduce heat; simmer, uncovered, 5-7 minutes or until slightly thickened.

3. Serve with ravioli. Top with cheese and olives.

BACON CHEESEBURGER PASTA

My husband works long hours and often eats later than our children, so recipes that are both kid-friendly and easy to reheat are winners in my keeper pile. If you prefer a lighter version, use reduced-fat cheese and ground turkey in place of the beef.
—**MELISSA STEVENS** ELK RIVER, MN

START TO FINISH: 30 MIN.
MAKES: 4-6 SERVINGS

- 8 ounces uncooked penne pasta
- 1 pound ground beef
- 6 bacon strips, diced
- 1 can (10¾ ounces) condensed tomato soup, undiluted
- ½ cup water
- 1 cup (4 ounces) shredded cheddar cheese
  Barbecue sauce and prepared mustard, optional

1. Cook pasta according to package directions. Meanwhile, in a large skillet, cook beef over medium heat until no longer pink; drain and set aside.
2. In the same skillet, cook bacon until crisp; remove with a slotted spoon to paper towels to drain. Discard drippings. Drain pasta; add to the skillet. Stir in the soup, water, beef and bacon; heat through.
3. Remove from the heat and sprinkle with cheese. Cover and let stand for 2-3 minutes or until the cheese is melted. Serve with barbecue sauce and prepared mustard if desired.

⑤ INGREDIENTS FAST FIX

SIZZLE & SMOKE FLAT IRON STEAKS

Smoked paprika and chipotle pepper give this version of blackened steak a spicy, Southwestern flair. To temper the heat, add a crisp salad of leafy greens with fresh fruit and cheese.
—**DENISE POUNDS** HUTCHINSON, KS

START TO FINISH: 20 MIN.
MAKES: 4 SERVINGS

- 1½ teaspoons smoked paprika
- 1 teaspoon salt
- 1 teaspoon ground chipotle pepper
- ½ teaspoon pepper
- 1¼ pounds beef flat iron steaks or top sirloin steak (¾ inch thick)
- 2 tablespoons butter
  Lime wedges, optional

1. Combine the seasonings; rub over steaks. In a large skillet, cook beef in butter over medium-high heat for 30 seconds on each side. Reduce heat to medium; cook steaks for 5-7 minutes on each side or until the meat reaches desired doneness (for medium-rare, a thermometer should read 145°; medium, 160°; well-done, 170°).
2. Cut into slices; serve with lime wedges if desired.

SIZZLE & SMOKE FLAT IRON STEAKS

ASIAN BEEF NOODLES

ASIAN BEEF NOODLES

I've raised beef for most of my life, so I'm excited whenever I try new recipes that feature it. This dish is absolutely delicious.

—**MARGERY BRYAN** MOSES LAKE, WA

START TO FINISH: 30 MIN.
MAKES: 4 SERVINGS

- 1 **package (3 ounces) beef-flavored ramen noodles**
- 1 **pound beef top sirloin steak**
- 1 **jalapeno pepper, seeded and finely chopped**
- 1 **tablespoon canola oil**
- 2 **tablespoons water**
- 1 **tablespoon steak sauce**
- 1 **medium carrot, shredded**
- 2 **tablespoons sliced green onion**
- ¼ **cup salted peanuts**

1. Set aside seasoning packet from noodles. Prepare noodles according to package directions; drain and set aside.

2. Cut steak into thin strips. In a large skillet, stir-fry the beef and jalapeno in oil for 1-2 minutes or until meat is no longer pink. Remove and keep warm.

3. In the same skillet, combine the noodles, water, steak sauce, carrot, onion and contents of seasoning packet. Cook and stir until heated through. Return beef to the pan. Sprinkle with peanuts. Serve immediately.

NOTE *Wear disposable gloves when cutting hot peppers; the oils can burn skin. Avoid touching your face.*

**LINDA SCHEND'S DEEP-DISH
SAUSAGE PIZZA FRITTATA**
PAGE 60

Breakfast & Brunch

Skillet specialties like omelets and hash browns are cornerstones of morning meals. Dig in to these hearty eye-openers any day of the week.

CREAMY EGGS & MUSHROOMS AU GRATIN

When I want a brunch dish that has the crowd-pleasing appeal of scrambled eggs but a little more intrigue, I make this. The mushrooms and rich Parmesan sauce give it the unexpected flavors that make it special
—**DEBORAH WILLIAMS** PEORIA, AZ

PREP: 15 MIN. • **COOK:** 25 MIN. • **MAKES:** 8 SERVINGS

- **2 tablespoons butter**
- **1 pound sliced fresh mushrooms**
- **1 green onion, chopped**

SAUCE
- **2 tablespoons butter, melted**
- **3 tablespoons all-purpose flour**
- **½ teaspoon salt**
- **⅛ teaspoon pepper**
- **1 cup 2% milk**
- **½ cup heavy whipping cream**
- **2 tablespoons grated Parmesan cheese**

EGGS
- **16 large eggs**
- **¼ teaspoon salt**
- **⅛ teaspoon pepper**
- **¼ cup butter, cubed**
- **½ cup grated Parmesan cheese**
- **1 green onion, finely chopped**

1. In a large broiler-safe skillet, heat butter over medium-high heat. Add mushrooms; cook and stir 4-6 minutes or until browned. Add green onion; cook 1 minute longer. Remove from pan with a slotted spoon. Wipe skillet clean.
2. For sauce, in a small saucepan, melt butter over medium heat. Stir in flour, salt and pepper until smooth; whisk in milk and cream. Bring to a boil, stirring constantly; cook and stir 2-4 minutes or until thickened. Remove from heat; stir in cheese.
3. Preheat broiler. For eggs, in a large bowl, whisk eggs, salt and pepper until blended. In same skillet, heat butter over medium heat. Pour in egg mixture; cook and stir just until eggs are thickened and no liquid egg remains. Remove from heat.
4. Spoon half of the sauce over the eggs; top with mushrooms. Add remaining sauce; sprinkle with cheese. Broil 4-5 in. from heat 4-6 minutes or until top is lightly browned. Sprinkle with green onion.

HAM AND AVOCADO SCRAMBLE

Hearty ham, creamy avocado and a hint of garlic—this winning egg dish has all the makings of an outstanding breakfast, lunch or even dinner!
—**ELISABETH LARSEN**
PLEASANT GROVE, UT

START TO FINISH: 15 MIN. • **MAKES:** 4 SERVINGS

- **8 large eggs**
- **¼ cup 2% milk**
- **1 teaspoon garlic powder**
- **¼ teaspoon pepper**
- **1 cup cubed fully cooked ham**
- **1 tablespoon butter**
- **1 medium ripe avocado, peeled and cubed**
- **1 cup (4 ounces) shredded Colby-Monterey Jack cheese**

In a large bowl, whisk the eggs, milk, garlic powder and pepper; stir in ham. In a large skillet, melt butter over medium-high heat. Add egg mixture; cook and stir until almost set. Stir in avocado and cheese. Cook and stir until completely set.

CREAMY EGGS &
MUSHROOMS AU GRATIN

FARMERS BREAKFAST

(5)INGREDIENTS FAST FIX

FARMERS BREAKFAST

You're almost guaranteed to have a great day when you start it off with this hearty hash. It's a one-dish wonder that'll easily keep your family satisfied until lunch.
—**JEANNETTE WESTPHAL** GETTYSBURG, SD

START TO FINISH: 20 MIN. • **MAKES:** 4-6 SERVINGS

- 6 **bacon strips, diced**
- 2 **tablespoons diced onion**
- 3 **medium potatoes, cooked and cubed**
- 6 **large eggs, beaten**
  Salt and pepper to taste
- ½ **cup shredded cheddar cheese**

In a skillet, cook bacon until crisp. Remove to paper towel to drain. In drippings, saute onion and potatoes until potatoes are browned, about 5 minutes. Pour eggs into skillet; cook and stir gently until eggs are set and cooked to desired doneness. Season with salt and pepper. Sprinkle with cheese and bacon; let stand for 2-3 minutes or until cheese melts.

(5)INGREDIENTS FAST FIX

CURRY SCRAMBLE

I have eggs every morning, so this recipe is a great change from classic scrambled eggs. If I have sliced peppers on hand, I add them on top.
—**VALERIE BELLEY** ST. LOUIS, MO

START TO FINISH: 15 MIN. • **MAKES:** 4 SERVINGS

- 8 **large eggs**
- ¼ **cup fat-free milk**
- ½ **teaspoon curry powder**
- ¼ **teaspoon salt**
- ⅛ **teaspoon pepper**
- ⅛ **teaspoon ground cardamom, optional**
- 2 **medium tomatoes, sliced or chopped**

1. In a large bowl, whisk the eggs, milk, curry powder, salt, pepper and, if desired, cardamom until blended.
2. Place a large nonstick skillet coated with cooking spray over medium heat. Pour in egg mixture; cook and stir until eggs are thickened and no liquid egg remains. Serve with tomatoes.

CALICO SCRAMBLED EGGS

CREAM CHEESE & CHIVE OMELET

The first bite of the creamy filling lets you know this isn't any old omelet. Make it once, and I suspect you'll be fixing it often.

—ANNE TROISE MANALAPAN, NJ

START TO FINISH: 15 MIN. • **MAKES:** 2 SERVINGS

- 1 **tablespoon olive oil**
- 4 **large eggs**
- 2 **tablespoons minced chives**
- 2 **tablespoons water**
- ⅛ **teaspoon salt**
- ⅛ **teaspoon pepper**
- 2 **ounces cream cheese, cubed**
  Salsa

1. In a large nonstick skillet, heat oil over medium-high heat. Whisk the eggs, chives, water, salt and pepper. Add egg mixture to skillet (mixture should set immediately at edges).

2. As eggs set, push cooked edges toward the center, letting uncooked portion flow underneath. When the eggs are set, sprinkle cream cheese on one side; fold other side over filling. Slide omelet onto a plate; cut in half. Serve with salsa.

ALICO SCRAMBLED EGGS

hen you're short on time and scrambling to get meal on the table, this recipe is "eggs-actly" what ou need: a short ingredient list and quick cooking ne. Plus, with green pepper and tomato, it's a colorful dition to the table.

TASTE OF HOME TEST KITCHEN

ART TO FINISH: 20 MIN. • **MAKES:** 4 SERVINGS

- 8 **large eggs**
- ¼ **cup 2% milk**
- ⅛ **to ¼ teaspoon dill weed**
- ⅛ **to ¼ teaspoon salt**
- ⅛ **to ¼ teaspoon pepper**
- 1 **tablespoon butter**
- ½ **cup chopped green pepper**
- ¼ **cup chopped onion**
- ½ **cup chopped fresh tomato**

In a large bowl, whisk the first five ingredients ntil blended. In a 12-in. nonstick skillet, heat tter over medium-high heat. Add the green pper and onion; cook and stir until tender. emove from pan.

In same pan, pour in egg mixture; cook and stir er medium heat until eggs begin to thicken. Add mato and pepper mixture; cook until heated rough and no liquid egg remains, stirring gently.

CREAM CHEESE & CHIVE OMELET

HAM STEAKS WITH GRUYERE, BACON & MUSHROOMS

This meat lover's breakfast has a big wow factor. It's one of my favorites because the Gruyere, bacon and fresh mushrooms in the topping are a great combination.

—**MARY LISA SPEER** PALM BEACH, FL

START TO FINISH: 25 MIN.
MAKES: 4 SERVINGS

- 2 **tablespoons butter**
- ½ **pound sliced fresh mushrooms**
- 1 **shallot, finely chopped**
- 2 **garlic cloves, minced**
- ⅛ **teaspoon coarsely ground pepper**
- 1 **fully cooked boneless ham steak (about 1 pound), cut into four pieces**
- 1 **cup (4 ounces) shredded Gruyere cheese**
- 4 **bacon strips, cooked and crumbled**
- 1 **tablespoon minced fresh parsley, optional**

1. In a large nonstick skillet, heat butter over medium-high heat. Add mushrooms and shallot;

cook and stir 4-6 minutes or until tender. Add garlic and pepper; cook 1 minute longer. Remove from pan; keep warm. Wipe skillet clean.

2. In same skillet, cook ham over medium heat 3 minutes. Turn; sprinkle with cheese and bacon. Cook, covered, 2-4 minutes longer or until cheese is melted and ham is heated through. Serve with mushroom mixture. If desired, sprinkle with parsley.

FETA ASPARAGUS FRITTATA

Asparagus and feta cheese come together to make this frittata extra special. It's a perfect dish for a lazy Sunday morning or to serve with a tossed salad for a light lunch.

—**MILDRED SHERRER**
FORT WORTH, TX

START TO FINISH: 30 MIN.
MAKES: 2 SERVINGS

- 12 **fresh asparagus spears, trimmed**
- 2 **green onions, chopped**
- 1 **garlic clove, minced**
- 1 **tablespoon olive oil**
- 6 **large eggs**
- 2 **tablespoons heavy whippin cream**
  Dash salt and pepper
- ½ **cup crumbled feta cheese**

1. In a large skillet, cook the asparagus in a small amount of water for 6-8 minutes or until crisp-tender; drain. Finely chop two spears; set the remaining asparagus aside.

2. In an 8-in. ovenproof pan or skillet, saute the onions, garlic and chopped asparagus in oil until tender. In a bowl, whisk th eggs, cream, salt and pepper; pour into skillet. Cover and cook over medium heat for 3-5 minutes or until eggs are nearly set.

3. Arrange reserved asparagus spears so they resemble spokes of a wheel over eggs; sprinkle with feta cheese. Bake, uncovered, at 350° for 7-9 minutes or until eggs are completely set.

FETA ASPARAGUS FRITTATA

BREAKFAST
PIZZA SKILLET

BREAKFAST PIZZA SKILLET

I found the recipe for this hearty stovetop dish several years ago and changed it to fit our tastes. When I served it at a Christmas brunch, it was an instant hit.

—MARILYN HASH ENUMCLAW, WA

PREP: 35 MIN. • **COOK:** 10 MIN.
MAKES: 6 SERVINGS

- 1 **pound bulk Italian sausage**
- 5 **cups frozen shredded hash brown potatoes**
- ½ **cup chopped onion**
- ½ **cup chopped green pepper**
- ¼ **to ½ teaspoon salt**
  Pepper to taste
- ½ **cup sliced mushrooms**
- 4 **large eggs, lightly beaten**
- 1 **medium tomato, thinly sliced**
- 1 **cup (4 ounces) shredded cheddar cheese**
  Sour cream and salsa, optional

1. In a large skillet, cook sausage over medium heat until no longer pink. Add the potatoes, onion, green pepper, salt and pepper. Cook over medium-high heat for 18-20 minutes or until the potatoes are browned.
2. Stir in mushrooms. Pour eggs over the potato mixture. Arrange tomato slices on top. Sprinkle with cheese.
3. Cover and cook over medium-low heat for 10-15 minutes or until eggs are completely set (do not stir). Serve with sour cream and salsa if desired.

DEEP-DISH SAUSAGE PIZZA FRITTATA

This sunrise specialty combines the best of two worlds—breakfast and pizza! It's colorful, fresh and a cinch to make in a handy cast-iron skillet.

LINDA SCHEND KENOSHA, WI

PREP/TOTAL TIME: 30 MIN.
MAKES: 8 SERVINGS

- 8 **ounces bulk Italian sausage**
- 3 **cups sliced fresh mushrooms**
- ¼ **cup finely chopped red onion**
- ¼ **cup finely chopped green pepper**
- 12 **large eggs, beaten**
- ½ **cup marinara sauce**
- ⅔ **cup shredded part-skim mozzarella cheese**
- 3 **tablespoons grated Parmesan cheese**
- 2 **tablespoons minced fresh parsley**

1. Preheat broiler. In a 10-in. cast-iron or ovenproof skillet, cook sausage, mushrooms, onion and pepper over medium heat until sausage is no longer pink and the vegetables are tender, breaking sausage into crumbles, about 10 minutes; drain.

2. Return sausage mixture to the skillet. Pour in beaten eggs. Cook, covered, until the eggs are nearly set, about 5 minutes. Spread marinara over the top; sprinkle with cheeses.

3. Broil 3-4 in. from heat until the eggs are completely set and the cheese is melted, about 2 minutes. Let stand 5 minutes. Sprinkle with parsley; cut frittata into wedges.

TOP TIP

To prepare mushrooms for use in cooking, gently remove dirt by rubbing with a mushroom brush, or wipe them with a damp paper towel. Or quickly rinse them under cold water, drain and pat dry. Do not peel mushrooms. Trim the stems. Mushrooms can be eaten raw, marinated, sauteed, stir-fried, baked, broiled or grilled.

DEEP-DISH SAUSAGE PIZZA FRITTATA

SPARAGUS MELET TORTILLA WRAP

is omelet wrap boasts whole ains, veggies and protein, so the ly thing I have to add is a side of sh fruit for a complete, healthy eakfast. I sometimes replace the paragus with fresh spinach.

BONITA SUTER LAWRENCE, MI

ART TO FINISH: 20 MIN.
AKES: 1 SERVING

1 **large egg**
2 **large egg whites**
1 **tablespoon fat-free milk**
2 **teaspoons grated Parmesan cheese**
⅛ **teaspoon pepper**
4 **fresh asparagus spears, trimmed and sliced**
1 **teaspoon butter**
1 **green onion, chopped**
1 **whole wheat tortilla (8 inches), warmed**

In a small bowl, whisk the first e ingredients until blended. ace a small nonstick skillet ated with cooking spray over edium heat; add asparagus. ook and stir 3-4 minutes or til crisp-tender. Remove om pan.

In same skillet, heat butter er medium-high heat. Pour in g mixture. Mixture should set mediately at edges. As eggs set, ush cooked portions toward the nter, letting uncooked eggs w underneath. When eggs are ickened and no liquid egg mains, spoon green onion and paragus on one side. Fold melet in half; serve in tortilla.

ASPARAGUS OMELET TORTILLA WRAP

ITALIAN SAUSAGE BREAKFAST WRAPS

My husband leaves for work at 4 a.m., and I want him to have a healthy breakfast to start the day. I usually make half a dozen of these on Sunday and keep them in the fridge so he can grab one and go.

—**DAUNA HARWOOD** ELKHART, IN

START TO FINISH: 30 MIN.
MAKES: 6 SERVINGS

- ¾ **pound Italian turkey sausage links, casings removed**
- 1 **small green pepper, finely chopped**
- 1 **small onion, finely chopped**
- 1 **medium tomato, chopped**
- 4 **large eggs**
- 6 **large egg whites**
- 1 **cup chopped fresh spinach**
- 6 **whole wheat tortillas (8 inches)**
- 1 **cup (4 ounces) shredded reduced-fat cheddar cheese**

1. In a large skillet, cook sausage, pepper, onion and tomato over medium heat until meat is no longer pink and vegetables are tender, breaking up sausage into crumbles; drain. Return to pan.

2. In a bowl, whisk eggs and egg whites until blended. Add egg mixture to sausage. Cook and stir until eggs are thickened and no liquid egg remains. Add spinach; cook and stir just until wilted.

3. Spoon ¾ cup egg mixture across center of each tortilla; top with about 2 tablespoons cheese. Fold bottom and sides of tortilla over filling and roll up.

ITALIAN SAUSAGE BREAKFAST WRAPS

MEDITERRANEAN BROCCOLI & CHEESE OMELET

AST FIX

MEDITERRANEAN BROCCOLI & CHEESE OMELET

My Italian mother-in-law taught me to make this omelet. She would make it for breakfast, lunch or dinner and eat it on Italian bread. I often toss in leftover broccoli to keep prep simple.
—**MARY LICATA** PEMBROKE PINES, FL

START TO FINISH: 30 MIN. • **MAKES:** 4 SERVINGS

- 2½ cups fresh broccoli florets
- 6 large eggs
- ¼ cup 2% milk
- ½ teaspoon salt
- ¼ teaspoon pepper
- ⅓ cup grated Romano cheese
- ⅓ cup sliced pitted Greek olives
- 1 tablespoon olive oil
  Shaved Romano cheese and minced fresh parsley

Preheat broiler. In a large saucepan, place steamer basket over 1 in. of water. Place broccoli in basket. Bring water to a boil. Reduce heat to a simmer; steam, covered, 4-6 minutes or until broccoli is crisp-tender.

2. In a large bowl, whisk eggs, milk, salt and pepper. Stir in cooked broccoli, grated cheese and olives. In a 10-in. ovenproof skillet, heat oil over medium heat; pour in egg mixture. Cook, uncovered, 4-6 minutes or until nearly set.

3. Broil 3-4 in. from heat 2-4 minutes or until eggs are completely set. Let stand 5 minutes. Cut into wedges. Sprinkle with shaved cheese and parsley.

FAST FIX
SAUERKRAUT LATKES

Sauerkraut in potato pancakes might seem like an unusual ingredient, but it's worth trying. The apples mellow the tang for a surprisingly pleasant flavor.
—**AYSHA SCHURMAN** AMMON, ID

PREP: 20 MIN. • **COOK:** 5 MIN./BATCH • **MAKES:** 2½ DOZEN

- 3 pounds russet potatoes, peeled and shredded
- 1½ cups shredded peeled apples
- 1½ cups sauerkraut, rinsed and well drained
- 6 large eggs, lightly beaten
- 6 tablespoons all-purpose flour
- 2 teaspoons salt
- 1½ teaspoons pepper
- ¾ cup canola oil
  Sour cream and chopped green onions, optional

1. In a large bowl, combine the potatoes, apples, sauerkraut and eggs. Combine the flour, salt and pepper; stir into potato mixture.

2. Heat 2 tablespoons oil in a large nonstick skillet over medium heat. Drop batter by ¼ cupfuls into oil; press lightly to flatten. Fry in batches until golden brown on both sides, using remaining oil as needed. Drain on paper towels. Top with sour cream and green onions if desired.

DID YOU KNOW?

Sauerkraut—raw, finely shredded fermented cabbage—is actually good for you. It's fat-free and contains many nutrients, including vitamin C, iron, calcium, potassium, phosphorus, thiamin, riboflavin and niacin.

BAKED PEACH PANCAKE

1. In a small bowl, combine the sliced peaches, sugar and lemon juice; set aside. In a large bowl, beat eggs until fluffy. Add the flour, milk and salt; beat until smooth.

2. Place butter in a 10-in. ovenproof skillet in a 400° oven for 3-5 minutes or until melted. Immediately pour batter into hot skillet. Bake for 20-25 minutes or until pancake has risen and puffed all over.

3. Fill with peach slices and sprinkle with nutme[g.] Serve immediately with sour cream if desired.

HOMEMADE BREAKFAST SAUSAGE PATTIES

Buttermilk is the secret ingredient that keeps these pork patties moist, while a blend of seasonings create[s] a flavor that can't be beat.
—**HARVEY KEENEY** MANDAN, ND

PREP: 30 MIN. • **COOK:** 10 MIN./BATCH
MAKES: 20 PATTIES

- ¾ **cup buttermilk**
- 2¼ **teaspoons kosher salt**
- 1½ **teaspoons rubbed sage**
- 1½ **teaspoons brown sugar**
- 1½ **teaspoons pepper**
- ¾ **teaspoon dried marjoram**
- ¾ **teaspoon dried savory**
- ¾ **teaspoon cayenne pepper**
- ¼ **teaspoon ground nutmeg**
- 2½ **pounds ground pork**

1. In a large bowl, combine buttermilk and seasonings. Add pork; mix lightly but thoroughly. Shape into twenty 3-in. patties.

2. In a large skillet coated with cooking spray, coo[k] patties in batches over medium heat 5-6 minutes on each side or until a thermometer reads 160°. Remove to paper towels to drain.

FREEZE OPTION *Wrap each cooked, cooled patty in plastic wrap; transfer to a resealable plastic freez[er] bag. May be frozen for up to 3 months. To use, unwrap patties and place on a baking sheet coate[d] with cooking spray. Bake at 350° for 15 minutes o[n] each side or until heated through.*

BAKED PEACH PANCAKE

This dish makes for a dramatic presentation. I usually take it right from the oven to the table, fill it with peaches and sour cream and serve bacon or ham alongside. Whenever I go home, my mom—the best cook I know—asks me to make this.
—**NANCY WILKINSON** PRINCETON, NJ

PREP: 10 MIN. • **BAKE:** 25 MIN. • **MAKES:** 6 SERVINGS

- 2 **cups fresh or frozen sliced peeled peaches**
- 4 **teaspoons sugar**
- 1 **teaspoon lemon juice**
- 3 **large eggs**
- ½ **cup all-purpose flour**
- ½ **cup 2% milk**
- ½ **teaspoon salt**
- 2 **tablespoons butter**
  Ground nutmeg
  Sour cream, optional

WEET POTATO PANCAKES WITH CINNAMON CREAM

Topped with a rich cinnamon cream, these sweet pancakes are an ideal side dish for celebrating the tastes and aromas of fall.
—**TAMMY REX** NEW TRIPOLI, PA

EP: 25 MIN. • **COOK:** 5 MIN./BATCH
AKES: 12 SERVINGS (1½ CUPS TOPPING)

1 **package (8 ounces) cream cheese, softened**
¼ **cup packed brown sugar**
½ **teaspoon ground cinnamon**
½ **cup sour cream**
NCAKES
6 **large eggs**
¾ **cup all-purpose flour**
½ **teaspoon ground nutmeg**

½ **teaspoon salt**
¼ **teaspoon pepper**
6 **cups shredded sweet potatoes (about 3 large)**
3 **cups shredded peeled apples (about 3 large)**
⅓ **cup grated onion**
½ **cup canola oil**

1. In a small bowl, beat the cream cheese, brown sugar and cinnamon until blended; beat in sour cream. Set aside.

2. In a large bowl, whisk the eggs, flour, nutmeg, salt and pepper. Add the sweet potatoes, apples and onion; toss to coat.

3. In a large nonstick skillet, heat 2 tablespoons oil over medium heat. Working in batches, drop sweet potato mixture by ⅓ cupfuls into oil; press slightly to flatten. Fry for 2-3 minutes on each side until golden brown, using remaining oil as needed. Drain on paper towels. Serve with cinnamon topping.

WEET POTATO PANCAKES WITH CINNAMON CREAM

FAST FIX

ITALIAN GARDEN FRITTATA

I serve this pretty frittata with melon wedges for a delicious breakfast or brunch. It always gets rave reviews.

—**SALLY MALONEY** DALLAS, GA

START TO FINISH: 30 MIN.
MAKES: 4 SERVINGS

- 4 **large eggs**
- 6 **large egg whites**
- ½ **cup grated Romano cheese, divided**
- 1 **tablespoon minced fresh sage**
- ½ **teaspoon salt**
- ¼ **teaspoon pepper**
- 1 **teaspoon olive oil**
- 1 **small zucchini, sliced**
- 2 **green onions, sliced**
- 2 **plum tomatoes, thinly sliced**

1. Preheat broiler. In a large bowl, whisk eggs, egg whites, ¼ cup cheese, sage, salt and pepper until blended.

2. In a 10-in. broiler-safe skillet coated with cooking spray, heat oil over medium-high heat. Add zucchini and green onions; cook and stir 2 minutes. Reduce heat to medium-low. Pour in egg mixture. Cook, covered, 4-7 minutes or until eggs are nearly set.

3. Uncover; top with tomatoes and remaining cheese. Broil 3-4 in. from heat 2-3 minutes or until eggs are completely set. Let stand 5 minutes. Cut frittata into wedges.

DAD'S BLUEBERRY BUTTERMILK PANCAKES

My dad makes his famous blueberry pancakes for us every Saturday. The combination of oats, cornmeal and buttermilk in the batter gives the pancakes heartiness we can't resist.

—**GABRIELLE SHORT**
PLEASANT HILL, IA

PREP: 15 MIN. + STANDING
COOK: 10 MIN./BATCH
MAKES: 12 PANCAKES

- 1 **cup all-purpose flour**
- 3 **tablespoons cornmeal**
- 3 **tablespoons quick-cooking oats**
- 3 **tablespoons sugar**
- 1 **teaspoon baking powder**
- ½ **teaspoon baking soda**
- ½ **teaspoon salt**
  Dash ground nutmeg
- 1 **large egg**
- 1½ **cups buttermilk**
- 2 **tablespoons canola oil**
- 1 **teaspoon vanilla extract**
- 1 **cup fresh or frozen blueberries**

1. In a large bowl, whisk the firs eight ingredients. In another bowl, whisk egg, buttermilk, oil and vanilla until blended. Add to flour mixture; stir just until moistened (batter will be lumpy Let stand 15 minutes.

2. Lightly grease a griddle or large nonstick skillet; heat over medium heat. Stir blueberries into batter. Pour batter by ¼ cupfuls onto griddle or skille Cook until bubbles on top begir to pop and bottoms are golden brown. Turn; cook until second side is brown.

DAD'S BLUEBERRY BUTTERMILK PANCAKES

SPANISH OMELET

SPANISH OMELET

Wake up taste buds with the yummy, zesty flavors of warm refried beans, salsa and shredded cheese. The best part: You can whip up this satisfying hot breakfast in 15 minutes. Take it up a notch with a hot salsa, or add sizzling cooked bacon for a smoky twist.

—**TERESA GUNNELL** LOVETTSVILLE, VA

START TO FINISH: 15 MIN.
MAKES: 2 SERVINGS

   6 **large eggs**
   ¼ **cup water**
   1 **cup refried beans, warmed**
   ¼ **cup chopped red onion**
   ½ **cup shredded Mexican
        cheese blend, divided**
   ¼ **cup salsa**

1. Heat a 10-in. nonstick skillet coated with cooking spray over medium heat. Whisk eggs and water. Add half of the egg mixture to skillet (mixture should set immediately at edges).
2. As the eggs set, push the cooked edges toward the center, letting the uncooked portion flow underneath. When the eggs are set, spoon half of the beans and half of the onion on one side and sprinkle with 2 tablespoons cheese; fold other side over filling. Slide omelet onto a plate. Repeat. Garnish with salsa and remaining cheese.

BRUNCH HASH & EGG BAKE

BRUNCH HASH & EGG BAKE

When my kids were little, I cooked for eight people, all of whom loved fried eggs. I couldn't easily serve that many hot eggs at once, so I baked them with vegetable hash. I like to use feta cheese for this dish, but shredded cheddar or Parmesan work, too.

—LILY JULOW LAWRENCEVILLE, GA

PREP: 45 MIN. • **BAKE:** 15 MIN. • **MAKES:** 8 SERVINGS

- 2 **pounds Yukon Gold potatoes, peeled and cut into ¾-inch pieces**
- 1 **pound bulk Italian sausage**
- 1 **large onion, finely chopped**
- ¼ **cup olive oil**
- ¼ **teaspoon salt**
- ¼ **teaspoon pepper**
- 8 **large eggs**
- 1 **cup (4 ounces) crumbled feta cheese**
- 3 **tablespoons minced fresh parsley**

1. Preheat oven to 375°. Place the potatoes in a large saucepan; add water to cover. Bring to a boil. Reduce heat; cook, uncovered, 5-7 minutes or until almost tender. Drain.

2. Meanwhile, in a 12-in. ovenproof skillet, cook sausage and onion over medium heat 8-10 minutes or until sausage is no longer pink, breaking up sausage into crumbles. Remove with a slotted spoon. Discard drippings, wiping skillet clean.

3. In same skillet, heat the oil over medium-high heat. Add drained potatoes; sprinkle with salt and pepper. Cook 10-15 minutes or until golden brown, turning potatoes occasionally. Stir in sausage mixture. Remove from heat.

4. With the back of a spoon, make eight wells in potato mixture. Break one egg into each well. Sprinkle with cheese.

5. Bake 12-15 minutes or until egg whites are set and yolks begin to thicken but are not hard. Sprinkle with parsley.

FRENCH BANANA PANCAKES

These pancakes are a breakfast favorite in our family. They're easy, too—our daughters make them all by themselves when they have friends spend the night. Now their friends' mothers are asking for the recipe!

CHERYL SOWERS BAKERSFIELD, CA

PREP: 10 MIN. • **COOK:** 30 MIN. • **MAKES:** 5-6 SERVINGS

PANCAKES
1 cup all-purpose flour
¼ cup confectioners' sugar
1 cup milk
2 large eggs
3 tablespoons butter, melted
1 teaspoon vanilla extract
¼ teaspoon salt

FILLING
¼ cup butter
¼ cup packed brown sugar
¼ teaspoon ground cinnamon
¼ teaspoon ground nutmeg
¼ cup half-and-half cream
5 to 6 firm bananas, halved lengthwise
   Whipped cream and additional cinnamon,
     optional

Sift flour and confectioners' sugar into a bowl. Add milk, eggs, butter, vanilla and salt; beat until smooth.

Heat a lightly greased 6-in. skillet; add about tablespoons batter, spreading to almost cover bottom of skillet. Cook until lightly browned; turn and brown the other side. Remove to a wire rack. Repeat with remaining batter (make 10-12 pancakes), greasing skillet as needed.

For filling, melt butter in large skillet. Stir in brown sugar, cinnamon and nutmeg. Stir in cream and cook until slightly thickened. Add half of the bananas at a time to skillet; heat for 2-3 minutes, spooning sauce over them. Remove from the heat.

Roll a pancake around each banana half and place on a serving platter. Spoon sauce over pancakes. Top with whipped cream and dash of cinnamon if desired.

FAST FIX
BACON 'N' EGG BAGELS

Better than morning fast-food fare, these savory sandwiches with veggie cream cheese and zesty olives will have mouths watering. For a change of pace, prepare them with another cream cheese variety or speed things up by using precooked bacon warmed in the microwave.

—CHRIS AND JENNY THACKRAY CORPUS CHRISTI, TX

START TO FINISH: 20 MIN. • **MAKES:** 4 SERVINGS

4 bagels, split and toasted
½ cup garden vegetable cheese spread
½ cup sliced pimiento-stuffed olives
8 bacon strips, halved
4 large eggs
4 slices Muenster cheese

1. Spread each bagel half with cheese spread. Place olives on bagel bottoms; set aside.
2. In a large skillet, cook bacon over medium heat until crisp. Using a slotted spoon, remove to paper towels; drain, reserving 3 tablespoons drippings. Heat drippings over medium-hot heat. Add eggs; reduce heat to low. Fry until white is completely set and yolk begins to thicken but is not hard.
3. Place an egg on each bagel bottom. Layer with cheese, bacon and bagel tops.

BACON 'N' EGG BAGELS

CHEESE & RED PEPPER LATKES

These zesty latkes combine three cheeses with a handful of garlic and a colorful burst of red peppers.

—CHRISTINE MONTALVO
WINDSOR HEIGHTS, IA

PREP: 30 MIN. • **COOK:** 5 MIN./BATCH
MAKES: 3 DOZEN

- 3 **large onions, finely chopped**
- 3 **medium sweet red peppers, finely chopped**
- ⅓ **cup butter, cubed**
- 18 **medium garlic cloves, minced, divided**
- 1 **tablespoon celery salt**
- 1 **tablespoon coarsely ground pepper**
- 3 **pounds russet potatoes, peeled and shredded**
- 1½ **cups grated Parmesan cheese**
- 1½ **cups (6 ounces) shredded cheddar cheese**
- 1 **cup (4 ounces) shredded part-skim mozzarella cheese**
- 1 **cup all-purpose flour**
- ¾ **cup sour cream**
- ¾ **cup canola oil**
  Minced fresh parsley

TOP TIP

Latkes, or potato pancakes fried in oil, are one of the most popular of all Jewish foods, especially during Hanukkah. They symbolize the ancient lamps that held only enough oil for one day but magically burned for eight. There are many variations of the treats, which can be served as an appetizer or a side dish.

1. In a large skillet, saute the onions and red peppers in butter until tender. Add ¼ cup garlic, celery salt and pepper; cook 1 minute longer.

2. Transfer to a large bowl. Add the potatoes, cheeses, flour, sour cream and remaining garlic; mix well.

3. Heat 2 tablespoons oil in a large nonstick skillet over medium heat. Drop batter by ¼ cupfuls into oil; press lightly to flatten. Fry in batches until golden brown on both sides, using remaining oil as needed. Drain on paper towels. Sprinkl with parsley.

CHEESE & RED PEPPER LATKES

PINACH-MUSHROOM CRAMBLED EGGS

y husband and I enjoyed a
ushroom egg dish at a hotel
staurant. I've created a healthy
ndition with loads of hearty
ushroom flavor.

RACHELLE MCCALLA WAYNE, NE

TART TO FINISH: 15 MIN.
IAKES: 2 SERVINGS

- 2 **large eggs**
- 2 **large egg whites**
- ⅛ **teaspoon salt**
- ⅛ **teaspoon pepper**
- 1 **teaspoon butter**
- ½ **cup thinly sliced fresh mushrooms**
- ½ **cup fresh baby spinach, chopped**
- 2 **tablespoons shredded provolone cheese**

In a small bowl, whisk eggs,
gg whites, salt and pepper until
lended. In a small nonstick
killet, heat butter over medium-
igh heat. Add mushrooms; cook
nd stir 3-4 minutes or until
ender. Add the spinach; cook
nd stir until wilted. Reduce heat
o medium.

Add the egg mixture; cook and
tir just until eggs are thickened
nd no liquid egg remains. Stir in
he cheese.

SPINACH-MUSHROOM
SCRAMBLED EGGS

MUSHROOM-HERB STUFFED FRENCH TOAST

Transform ordinary French toast into a savory delight with mushrooms, cheese and rich flavors. The ooey-gooey texture is irresistible!

—**LISA HUFF** WILTON, CT

PREP: 25 MIN. • **COOK:** 5 MIN./BATCH
MAKES: 8 SERVINGS

- 1 pound thinly sliced baby portobello mushrooms
- 4 tablespoons butter, divided
- 1 package (8 ounces) reduced-fat cream cheese
- 2 cups (8 ounces) shredded Gruyere or Swiss cheese, divided
- 4 tablespoons minced chives, divided
- 1 tablespoon minced fresh tarragon or 1 teaspoon dried tarragon
- 1 garlic clove, minced
- ⅛ teaspoon salt
- ⅛ teaspoon pepper
- 16 slices Texas toast
- 4 large eggs
- 2 cups 2% milk
- 2 tablespoons butter, melted

1. In a large skillet, saute mushrooms in 1 tablespoon butter until tender; set aside.
2. In a small bowl, beat the cream cheese, 1 cup Gruyere cheese, 2 tablespoons chives, tarragon, garlic, salt and pepper until blended. Spread over

bread slices. Spoon mushrooms over half of the slices; place remaining bread slices over the top, spread side down.
3. In a shallow bowl, whisk the eggs, milk and melted butter. Dip both sides of sandwiches into egg mixture.
4. In a large skillet, toast sandwiches in remaining butter in batches for 2-3 minutes on each side or until golden brown. Sprinkle with remaining cheese and chives.

HASH BROWN & APPLE PANCAKE

Wedges of this crispy hash make a fast and fabulous side dish. Perked up with onions, chives and Swiss cheese, it takes only minutes and goes well with all kinds of brunch entrees.

—**SUSAN HEIN** BURLINGTON, WI

START TO FINISH: 20 MIN. • **MAKES:** 4 SERVINGS

- 1¼ cups frozen shredded hash brown potatoes, thawed
- ½ cup finely chopped apple
- ¼ cup finely chopped onion
- 1 large egg white
- 1 tablespoon minced fresh chives
- ¼ teaspoon salt
- ¼ teaspoon pepper
- 2 tablespoons butter, divided
- 2 tablespoons canola oil, divided
- ½ cup shredded Swiss cheese

1. In a large bowl, combine the first seven ingredients. In a large nonstick skillet, heat 1 tablespoon butter and 1 tablespoon oil over medium-high heat.
2. Spread half of the potato mixture evenly in pan; sprinkle with cheese. Top with remaining potato mixture, pressing gently into skillet. Cook 5 minutes or until bottom is browned.
3. Carefully invert pancake onto a plate. Heat remaining butter and oil in same pan. Slide pancake into skillet, browned side up. Cook 5 minutes longer or until bottom is browned and cheese is melted. Slide pancake onto a plate; cut into four wedges.

MIGAS, MY WAY

Migas is a traditional Tex-Mex scrambled egg specialty famous for the addition of corn tortillas. My family gives my version a big thumbs up. I sometimes substitute fresh corn tortillas for the chips by cutting the tortillas into strips and sauteeing them with the pepper and onion.

JOAN HALLFORD
NORTH RICHLAND HILLS, TX

START TO FINISH: 25 MIN.
MAKES: 2 SERVINGS

- ¼ cup chopped onion
- ¼ cup chopped green pepper
- 1 tablespoon bacon drippings or canola oil
- 4 large eggs
- 1 tablespoon water
- 1 tablespoon salsa
- ½ cup crushed tortilla chips
- ½ cup shredded cheddar cheese, divided
  Chopped green onions, additional salsa and warm flour tortillas, optional

1. In a large skillet, saute onion and green pepper in drippings until tender. In a small bowl, whisk the eggs, water and salsa. Add to skillet; cook and stir until set. Stir in tortilla chips and ¼ cup cheese.

2. Sprinkle with remaining cheese. If desired, top with green onions and additional salsa and serve with tortillas.

GOOD MORNING FRITTATA

Start the day right with this fast, fluffy egg dish. Egg substitute and skim milk cut down on calories, while orange bell peppers add sunshiny sweetness and crunch. You can use red or green peppers if you prefer.

—**MARY RELYEA** CANASTOTA, NY

START TO FINISH: 20 MIN.
MAKES: 2 SERVINGS

- 1 cup egg substitute
- ¼ cup fat-free milk
- ⅛ teaspoon pepper
  Dash salt
- ¼ cup chopped sweet orange pepper
- 2 green onions, thinly sliced
- ½ teaspoon canola oil
- ⅓ cup cubed fully cooked ham
- ¼ cup shredded reduced-fat cheddar cheese

1. In a small bowl, whisk the egg substitute, milk, pepper and salt; set aside. In an 8-in. ovenproof skillet, saute orange pepper and onions in oil until tender. Add ham; heat through. Reduce heat; top with egg mixture. Cover and cook for 4-6 minutes or until nearly set.

2. Uncover skillet; sprinkle with cheese. Broil 3-4 in. from the heat for 2-3 minutes or until eggs are completely set. Let stand for 5 minutes. Cut into wedges.

MIGAS, MY WAY

GRANDMOTHER'S TOAD IN A HOLE

I have fond memories of my grandmother's Yorkshire pudding wrapped around sausages, a puffy dish my kids called "The Boat."

—**SUSAN KIEBOAM** STREETSBORO, OH

PREP: 10 MIN. + STANDING
BAKE: 25 MIN. • **MAKES:** 6 SERVINGS

- 3 **large eggs**
- 1 **cup 2% milk**
- ½ **teaspoon salt**
- 1 **cup all-purpose flour**
- 1 **package (12 ounces) uncooked maple breakfast sausage links**
- 3 **tablespoons olive oil**
  Butter and maple syrup, optional

1. Preheat oven to 400°. In a small bowl, whisk eggs, milk and salt. Whisk flour into egg mixture until blended. Let stand for 30 minutes. Meanwhile, cook sausage according to package directions; cut each sausage into three pieces.

2. Place oil in a 12-in. nonstick ovenproof skillet. Place in oven 3-4 minutes or until hot. Stir batter and pour into prepared skillet; top with sausage. Bake 20-25 minutes or until golden brown and puffed. Remove from skillet; cut into wedges. If desired, serve with butter and syrup.

GRANDMOTHER'S TOAD IN A HOLE

I'M STUFFED FRENCH TOAST

successfully remade this French toast specialty I enjoyed while dining out. The banana cream cheese filling makes it out-of-this-world delicious.

—MELISSA KERRICK AUBURN, NY

PREP: 30 MIN. • **COOK:** 5 MIN.
MAKES: 4 SERVINGS

- 2 **medium ripe bananas, sliced**
- 2 **tablespoons brown sugar**
- 1 **teaspoon banana or vanilla extract**
- 1 **package (8 ounces) reduced-fat cream cheese**
- 8 **slices oat bread (½ inch thick)**
- 2 **large eggs**
- ⅔ **cup evaporated milk**
- 1¼ **teaspoons ground cinnamon**
- 1¼ **teaspoons vanilla extract**
- 1 **tablespoon butter**

- 1 **cup sliced fresh strawberries or frozen unsweetened sliced strawberries, thawed**
- ½ **cup fresh blueberries or frozen unsweetened blueberries**
- 1 **tablespoon sugar**
  Confectioners' sugar

1. In a large skillet coated with cooking spray, saute bananas with brown sugar. Stir in banana extract. In a small bowl, beat cream cheese until smooth. Add banana mixture; beat well. Spread on four slices of bread; top with remaining bread.

2. In a shallow bowl, whisk the eggs, milk, cinnamon and vanilla. Dip both sides of sandwiches in the egg mixture.

3. In a large skillet, toast the sandwiches in butter for 2-3 minutes on each side or until golden brown.

4. Meanwhile, in a small saucepan, combine the strawberries, blueberries and sugar; heat through. Serve with French toast; sprinkle with confectioners' sugar.

FAST FIX ▶

DENVER SCRAMBLE TOSTADA

My tostadas feature the ingredients of a classic Denver omelet: ham, cheddar and green pepper. I also make a zesty Mexican version with chorizo and pepper jack and a Reuben with corned beef and Swiss.

—JOI SINCLAIR ATCHISON, KS

START TO FINISH: 15 MIN.
MAKES: 6 SERVINGS

- 1 **tablespoon butter**
- ½ **cup finely chopped green pepper**
- ⅓ **cup finely chopped onion**
- ¼ **teaspoon pepper**
- ⅛ **teaspoon salt**
- 12 **large eggs, beaten**
- 1 **cup cubed fully cooked ham**
- ¾ **cup shredded cheddar cheese**
- 6 **tostada shells, warmed Additional shredded cheddar cheese**

In a large nonstick skillet, melt butter over medium heat. Add green pepper, onion, pepper and salt; cook and stir 2-3 minutes or until vegetables are crisp-tender. Add eggs, ham and cheese; cook and stir until eggs are thickened and no liquid egg remains. Serve over tostada shells; sprinkle with additional cheese.

I'M STUFFED FRENCH TOAST

**DENISE PATTERSON'S
BEEF & SPINACH LO MEIN**
PAGE 85

Beef & Ground Beef

When it comes to fast-to-fix dinners, beef and ground beef are naturals! Grab your favorite skillet and whip up a hearty meal tonight.

TENDER ROUND STEAK

This is one of my favorite recipes and, not surprisingly, I make it often. Rich and creamy mashed potatoes and a green salad round out the meal.

—**CAROL BROWN** MIDWAY, ON

PREP: 20 MIN. • **BAKE:** 65 MIN.
MAKES: 2 SERVINGS

- ½ **pound beef top round steak**
- 2 **tablespoons all-purpose flour**
- ½ **teaspoon salt**
- 1 **tablespoon canola oil**
- ¼ **cup chopped celery**
- ¼ **cup chopped carrot**
- 1 **tablespoon chopped onion**
- 1 **can (14½ ounces) stewed tomatoes, undrained**
- ¼ **teaspoon Worcestershire sauce**
- 2 **tablespoons shredded sharp cheddar cheese**

1. Trim beef; cut into two portions and flatten to ¼-in. thickness. In a large resealable plastic bag, combine flour and salt; add beef and shake to coat. In a small ovenproof skillet, brown beef in oil on both sides. Remove and keep warm.

2. In the drippings, saute the celery, carrot and onion for 3-4 minutes or until crisp-tender. Add tomatoes and Worcestershire sauce, stirring to loosen browned bits from pan. Bring to a boil. Reduce heat; simmer, uncovered, for 5 minutes. Return beef to the pan; spoon some of the vegetable mixture over the top.

3. Cover and bake at 325° for 1 hour or until meat is tender. Uncover; sprinkle with cheese. Bake 5 minutes longer or until cheese is melted.

FAST FIX ▶
WAGON WHEEL PASTA TOSS

I needed a quick one-skillet dish to put on the table. I thought if I added pizza sauce, pepperoni and mozzarella cheese to pasta, it might appeal to my daughter's selective palate. I was right!

—**LORI DANIELS** BEVERLY, WV

START TO FINISH: 30 MIN.
MAKES: 4 SERVINGS

- 1½ **cups uncooked wagon wheel pasta**
- 1 **pound ground beef**
- 1 **cup sliced fresh mushrooms**
- ½ **cup chopped green pepper**
- 1 **can (15 ounces) tomato puree**
- ½ **cup diced pepperoni**
- 4½ **teaspoons sugar**
- 1 **teaspoon Italian seasoning**
- ½ **teaspoon salt**
- ½ **teaspoon garlic powder**
- ½ **teaspoon dried oregano**
- ¼ **teaspoon onion powder**
- 2 **cups (8 ounces) shredded part-skim mozzarella cheese**

1. Cook pasta according to package directions. Meanwhile, in a large skillet, cook the beef, mushrooms and green pepper over medium heat until meat is no longer pink; drain. Add the tomato puree, pepperoni, sugar and seasonings; cook and stir for 5 minutes.

2. Drain pasta; stir into meat mixture. Heat through. Sprinkle with cheese. Remove from the heat; cover and let stand until cheese is melted.

WAGON WHEEL PASTA TOSS

GREEK BEEF PITAS

GREEK BEEF PITAS

A local pita restaurant inspired me to make my own Greek-style sandwiches at home. Add olives if you like.

—**NANCY SOUSLEY** LAFAYETTE, IN

START TO FINISH: 25 MIN.
MAKES: 4 SERVINGS

- 1 ~~pound lean ground beef~~ **(90% lean)**
- 1 small onion, chopped
- 3 garlic cloves, minced
- 1 teaspoon dried oregano
- ¾ teaspoon salt, divided
- 1 cup reduced-fat plain Greek yogurt
- 1 medium tomato, chopped
- ½ cup chopped peeled cucumber
- 1 teaspoon dill weed
- 4 whole pita breads, warmed
  Additional chopped tomatoes and cucumber, optional

1. In a large skillet, cook beef, onion and garlic over medium heat 8-10 minutes or until beef is no longer pink and vegetables are tender, breaking up beef into crumbles; drain. Stir in oregano and ½ teaspoon salt.

2. In a small bowl, mix yogurt, tomato, cucumber, dill and remaining salt. Spoon ¾ cup beef mixture over each pita bread; top with 3 tablespoons yogurt sauce. If desired, top with additional tomatoes and cucumbers. Serve with remaining yogurt sauce.

DANISH MEATBALLS
WITH PAN GRAVY

ANISH MEATBALLS WITH PAN GRAVY

My great-grandmother made these meatballs, and I'm sure her mother taught her. Six generations have enjoyed them, and one of my daughters was proud to serve them at her wedding.

KALLEE KRONG-MCCREERY ESCONDIDO, CA

EP: 25 MIN. • **COOK:** 20 MIN. • **MAKES:** 8 SERVINGS

1 **cup soft bread crumbs**
½ **cup finely chopped onion**
⅓ **cup 2% milk**
1 **large egg, lightly beaten**
3 **tablespoons minced fresh parsley**
1 **teaspoon salt**
½ **teaspoon pepper**
1 **pound ground beef**
1 **pound bulk pork sausage**
2 **tablespoons canola oil**
1 **to 3 tablespoons butter, divided**

RAVY
3 **tablespoons all-purpose flour**
¾ **teaspoon beef bouillon granules**
½ **teaspoon pepper**
¼ **teaspoon salt**
¾ **cups 2% milk**

In a large bowl, combine the first seven gredients. Add beef and sausage; mix lightly t thoroughly. Shape ¼ cupfuls of mixture into meatballs; flatten to 1-in. thickness.

In a large skillet, heat oil and 1 tablespoon butter er medium-low heat; cook meatballs in batches 9 minutes on each side or until a thermometer ads 160°. Remove from pan, reserving ¼ cup ippings in pan. (If necessary, add additional tter to the drippings to reach ¼ cup.)

For gravy, stir flour, bouillon granules, pepper d salt into drippings until smooth; whisk in milk. ing to a boil, stirring constantly; cook and stir 1-2 inutes or until thickened. Serve with meatballs.

OTE *To make soft bread crumbs, tear bread into eces and place in a food processor or blender. ver and pulse until crumbs form. One slice of ead yields ½-¾ cup crumbs.*

RAVIOLI SKILLET

Prosciutto and mozzarella dress up store-bought ravioli to make it extra special.

—*TASTE OF HOME TEST KITCHEN*

START TO FINISH: 30 MIN. • **MAKES:** 4 SERVINGS

1 **pound ground beef**
¾ **cup chopped green pepper**
1 **ounce prosciutto or deli ham, chopped**
3 **cups spaghetti sauce**
¾ **cup water**
1 **package (25 ounces) frozen cheese ravioli**
1 **cup (4 ounces) shredded part-skim mozzarella cheese**

1. In a large skillet, cook the beef, green pepper and prosciutto over medium heat until beef is no longer pink; drain.
2. Stir in spaghetti sauce and water; bring to a boil. Add ravioli. Reduce heat; cover and simmer for 7-9 minutes or until ravioli is tender, stirring once. Sprinkle with cheese. Simmer, uncovered, 1-2 minutes longer or until cheese is melted.

TENDERLOIN WITH HORSERADISH CREAM CHEESE

My husband and I both love this classic combination of beef and horseradish. He requests it often, and I look forward to it just as much as he does. It's great with baked potatoes.

—**MARY LOU COOK** WELCHES, OR

START TO FINISH: 20 MIN.
MAKES: 4 SERVINGS

- 4 **beef tenderloin steaks (4 ounces each)**
- ¼ **teaspoon salt**
- ¼ **teaspoon pepper**
- 1 **teaspoon olive oil**
- 1 **package (8 ounces) cream cheese, softened**
- 2 **tablespoons grated Parmesan cheese**
- 2 **tablespoons prepared horseradish**
- 2 **tablespoons minced fresh parsley**

1. Sprinkle steaks with salt and pepper. In a large skillet, heat oil over medium heat. Add steaks; cook 4-6 minutes on each side or until meat reaches desired doneness (for medium-rare, a thermometer should read 145°; medium, 160°; well-done, 170°).
2. Meanwhile, in a small bowl, mix cream cheese, Parmesan cheese and horseradish until blended. Serve with steaks. Sprinkle with parsley.

MERLOT FILET MIGNON

Although this filet is such a simple recipe, you can feel confident serving it to your guests. The rich sauce adds a touch of elegance. Just add a salad and rolls.

—**JAUNEEN HOSKING** WATERFORD, WI

START TO FINISH: 20 MIN.
MAKES: 2 SERVINGS

- 2 **beef tenderloin steaks (8 ounces each)**
- 3 **tablespoons butter, divided**
- 1 **tablespoon olive oil**
- 1 **cup merlot**
- 2 **tablespoons heavy whipping cream**
- ⅛ **teaspoon salt**

1. In a small skillet, cook steaks in 1 tablespoon butter and oil over medium heat for 4-6 minutes on each side or until meat reaches desired doneness (for medium-rare, a thermometer should read 145°; medium, 160°; well-done, 170°). Remove and keep warm.
2. In the same skillet, add wine stirring to loosen browned bits from pan. Bring to a boil; cook until liquid is reduced to ¼ cup. Add the cream, salt and remaining butter; bring to a boil. Cook and stir for 1-2 minutes or until slightly thickened and butter is melted. Serve with steaks.

MERLOT FILET MIGNON

MOM'S SLOPPY TACOS

Even if you have a hectic weeknight, if you've got 30 minutes, you can serve up a healthy meal. This quick, convenient recipe makes it possible.

—KAMI JONES AVONDALE, AZ

START TO FINISH: 30 MIN.
MAKES: 6 SERVINGS

- 1½ **pounds extra-lean ground beef (95% lean)**
- 1 **can (15 ounces) tomato sauce**
- ¾ **teaspoon garlic powder**
- ½ **teaspoon salt**
- ¼ **teaspoon pepper**
- ¼ **teaspoon cayenne pepper**
- 12 **taco shells, warmed**
  Optional toppings: shredded lettuce and cheese, chopped tomatoes, avocado and olives

In a large skillet, cook beef over medium heat until no longer pink. Stir in the tomato sauce, garlic powder, salt, pepper and cayenne. Bring to a boil. Reduce heat; simmer, uncovered, for 10 minutes.

Fill each taco shell with ¼ cup beef mixture and toppings of your choice.

TOP TIP

After browning the ground beef for tacos, I stir in taco seasoning mix but substitute tomato juice for the water. This gives the tacos an even richer flavor.
CATHERINE M. TULSA, OK

MOM'S SLOPPY TACOS

CASHEW CURRIED BEEF

CASHEW CURRIED BEEF

This recipe is a favorite with my whole family. The ingredients are a wonderful mix of sweet, salty and spicy. And, it's easy to make!

—JENNIFER FRIDGEN EAST GRAND FORKS, MN

PREP: 20 MIN. • **COOK:** 20 MIN. • **MAKES:** 5 SERVINGS

- 1 **pound beef top sirloin steak, thinly sliced**
- 2 **tablespoons canola oil, divided**
- 1 **can (13.66 ounces) coconut milk, divided**
- 1 **tablespoon red curry paste**
- 2 **tablespoons packed brown sugar**
- 2 **tablespoons fish sauce or soy sauce**
- 8 **cups chopped bok choy**
- 1 **small sweet red pepper, sliced**
- ½ **cup salted cashews**
- ½ **cup minced fresh cilantro**
  Hot cooked brown rice

1. In a large skillet, saute the beef in 1 tablespoon canola oil until no longer pink. Remove from skillet and set aside.

2. Spoon ½ cup cream from top of coconut milk and place in the pan. Add remaining oil; bring to a boil. Add curry paste; cook and stir for 5 minutes or until oil separates from coconut milk mixture.

3. Stir in the brown sugar, fish sauce and remaining coconut milk. Bring to a boil. Reduce heat; simmer, uncovered, 5 minutes or until slightly thickened. Add the chopped bok choy and red pepper; return to a boil. Cook and stir 2-3 minutes longer or until vegetables are tender.

4. Stir in the cashews, cilantro and beef; heat through. Serve with rice.

NOTE *This recipe was tested with regular (full-fat) coconut milk. Light coconut milk contains less fat.*

DID YOU KNOW?

Coconut milk is a sweet milky-white liquid high in oil derived from the meat of a mature coconut. It is not the naturally occurring liquid found inside a coconut. In the United States, coconut milk is usually purchased in cans and used in both savory and sweet dishes, many of which originate from tropical or Asian cuisines.

ORCUPINE MEATBALLS

These well-seasoned meatballs smothered in a rich tomato sauce are one of my mother's best main dishes. I loved this meal when I was growing up. I made it at home for my children, and now my daughters ke it for their own families.

ARLIS WILFER WEST BEND, WI

EP: 20 MIN. • **COOK:** 1 HOUR • **MAKES:** 4-6 SERVINGS

- ½ cup uncooked long grain rice
- ½ cup water
- ⅓ cup chopped onion
- 1 teaspoon salt
- ½ teaspoon celery salt
- ⅛ teaspoon pepper
- ⅛ teaspoon garlic powder
- 1 pound ground beef
- 2 tablespoons canola oil
- 1 can (15 ounces) tomato sauce
- 1 cup water
- 2 tablespoons brown sugar
- 2 teaspoons Worcestershire sauce

a bowl, combine the first seven ingredients.
ld beef and mix well. Shape into 1½-in. balls.
a large skillet, brown meatballs in oil; drain.
mbine tomato sauce, water, brown sugar and
rcestershire sauce; pour over meatballs.
duce heat; cover and simmer for 1 hour.

ST FIX

EEF & SPINACH LO MEIN

ou like good Chinese food, this dish will definitely
isfy. I discovered the recipe at an international
ncheon, and it's now in regular rotation.

DENISE PATTERSON BAINBRIDGE, OH

ART TO FINISH: 30 MIN. • **MAKES:** 5 SERVINGS

- ¼ cup hoisin sauce
- 2 tablespoons soy sauce
- 1 tablespoon water
- 2 teaspoons sesame oil
- 2 garlic cloves, minced
- ¼ teaspoon crushed red pepper flakes
- 1 pound beef top round steak, thinly sliced

- 6 ounces uncooked spaghetti
- 4 teaspoons canola oil, divided
- 1 can (8 ounces) sliced water chestnuts, drained
- 2 green onions, sliced
- 1 package (10 ounces) fresh spinach, coarsely chopped
- 1 red chili pepper, seeded and thinly sliced

1. In a small bowl, mix the first six ingredients. Remove ¼ cup mixture to a large bowl; add beef and toss to coat. Marinate at room temperature 10 minutes.

2. Cook spaghetti according to package directions. Meanwhile, in a large skillet, heat 1½ teaspoons canola oil. Add half of the beef mixture; stir-fry 1-2 minutes or until no longer pink. Remove from pan. Repeat with an additional 1½ teaspoons oil and remaining beef mixture.

3. Stir-fry water chestnuts and green onions in remaining canola oil 30 seconds. Stir in spinach and remaining hoisin mixture; cook until spinach is wilted. Return beef to pan; heat through.

4. Drain spaghetti; add to beef mixture and toss to combine. Sprinkle with chili pepper.

NOTE *Wear disposable gloves when cutting hot peppers; the oils can burn skin. Avoid touching your face.*

BEEF & SPINACH LO MEIN

FAST FIX

TENDERLOIN STEAK DIANE

I toss in extra mushrooms when I make this recipe. My son loves them, and they're fantastic with the steak.

—**CAROLYN TURNER** RENO, NV

START TO FINISH: 30 MIN.
MAKES: 4 SERVINGS

- 4 **beef tenderloin steaks (6 ounces each)**
- 1 **teaspoon steak seasoning**
- 2 **tablespoons butter**
- 1 **cup sliced fresh mushrooms**
- ½ **cup reduced-sodium beef broth**
- ¼ **cup heavy whipping cream**
- 1 **tablespoon steak sauce**
- 1 **teaspoon garlic salt with parsley**
- 1 **teaspoon minced chives**

1. Sprinkle steaks with steak seasoning. In a large skillet, heat butter over medium heat. Add steaks; cook for 4-5 minutes on each side or until meat reaches desired doneness (for medium-rare, a thermometer should read 145°; medium, 160°; well-done, 170°). Remove steaks from pan.

2. Add mushrooms to skillet; cook and stir over medium-high heat until tender. Add broth, stirring to loosen browned bits from pan. Stir in cream, steak sauce and garlic salt. Bring to a boil; cook and stir 1-2 minutes or until sauce is slightly thickened.

3. Return steaks to pan; turn to coat and heat through. Stir in minced chives.

NOTE *This recipe was tested with McCormick Montreal Steak Seasoning. Look for it in the spice aisle.*

TENDERLOIN STEAK DIANE

AJITA BURGER WRAPS

his combo gives you a tender
urger, crisp veggies and a crunchy
ell, plus fajita flavor. Kids love it.

ANTONIO SMITH
ANAL WINCHESTER, OH

TART TO FINISH: 30 MIN.
AKES: 4 SERVINGS

- 1 **pound lean ground beef (90% lean)**
- 2 **tablespoons fajita seasoning mix**
- 2 **teaspoons canola oil**
- 1 **medium green pepper, cut into thin strips**
- 1 **medium red sweet pepper, cut into thin strips**
- 1 **medium onion, halved and sliced**
- 4 **flour tortillas (10 inches)**
- ¾ **cup shredded cheddar cheese**

1. In a large bowl, combine beef and seasoning mix, mixing lightly but thoroughly. Shape into four ½-in.-thick patties.
2. In a large skillet, heat oil over medium heat. Add burgers; cook 4 minutes on each side. Remove from pan. In same skillet, add peppers and onion; cook and stir 5-7 minutes or until lightly browned and tender.
3. On the center of each tortilla, place ½ cup pepper mixture, one burger and 3 tablespoons cheese. Fold sides of tortilla over burger; fold top and bottom to close, forming a square.
4. Wipe skillet clean. Place wraps in skillet, seam side down. Cook wraps on medium heat 1-2 minutes on each side or until golden brown and a thermometer inserted in beef reads 160°.

CHILI BEEF NOODLE SKILLET

A friend gave me this recipe. My husband likes this entree's hearty blend of beef, onion and tomatoes. I like it because I can get it to the table so quickly.

—DEBORAH ELLIOTT
RIDGE SPRING, SC

START TO FINISH: 30 MIN.
MAKES: 8 SERVINGS

- 1 **package (8 ounces) egg noodles**
- 2 **pounds ground beef**
- 1 **medium onion, chopped**
- ¼ **cup chopped celery**
- 2 **garlic cloves, minced**
- 1 **can (28 ounces) diced tomatoes, undrained**
- 1 **tablespoon chili powder**
- ¼ to ½ **teaspoon salt**
- ⅛ **teaspoon pepper**
- ½ to 1 **cup shredded cheddar cheese**

1. Cook noodles according to package directions. Meanwhile, in a large skillet, cook the beef, onion, celery and garlic over medium heat until meat is no longer pink and vegetables are tender; drain. Add the tomatoes, chili powder, salt and pepper. Cook and stir for 2 minutes or until heated through.
2. Drain the noodles; stir into beef mixture and heat through. Remove from the heat. Sprinkle with cheddar cheese; cover and let stand for 5 minutes or until cheese is melted.

FAJITA BURGER WRAPS

⟨5⟩INGREDIENTS FAST FIX⟩
BEEF TIP STEW OVER FUSILLI

Fire-roasted tomatoes add bright color and delightful flair to this hearty entree that boasts a well-seasoned vegetable blend.

—TASTE OF HOME TEST KITCHEN

START TO FINISH: 25 MIN. • **MAKES:** 4 SERVINGS

- 2½ cups uncooked fusilli pasta
- 1 package (17 ounces) refrigerated beef tips with gravy
- 1 package (12 ounces) frozen garlic baby peas and mushrooms blend
- 1 can (14½ ounces) fire-roasted diced tomatoes, undrained
- ½ teaspoon dried thyme
- ¼ teaspoon pepper

Cook the pasta according to package directions. Meanwhile, in a large skillet, combine the beef tips with gravy, vegetable blend, tomatoes, thyme and pepper; heat through. Drain the pasta. Serve with the beef mixture.

**BEEF TIP STEW
OVER FUSILLI**

MOM'S SWEDISH MEATBALLS

Mom fixed these meatballs for family dinners, potluck suppers and PTA meetings. After smelling the aromas of browning meat and caramelized onions, everyone will be ready to eat.

—MARYBETH MANK MESQUITE, TX

PREP: 30 MIN. • **COOK:** 40 MIN. • **MAKES:** 6 SERVINGS

- ¾ cup seasoned bread crumbs
- 1 medium onion, chopped
- 2 large eggs, lightly beaten
- ⅓ cup minced fresh parsley
- 1 teaspoon coarsely ground pepper
- ¾ teaspoon salt
- 2 pounds ground beef

GRAVY
- ½ cup all-purpose flour
- 2¾ cups 2% milk
- 2 cans (10½ ounces each) condensed beef consomme, undiluted
- 1 tablespoon Worcestershire sauce
- 1 teaspoon coarsely ground pepper
- ¾ teaspoon salt

NOODLES
- 1 package (16 ounces) egg noodles
- ¼ cup butter, cubed
- ¼ cup minced fresh parsley

1. In a bowl, combine the first six ingredients. Add beef; mix lightly but thoroughly. Shape into 1½-in. meatballs (about 36). In a large skillet, brown meatballs in batches. Using a slotted spoon, remove to paper towels to drain, reserving the drippings in pan.

2. For gravy, stir the flour into drippings; cook and stir until light brown (do not burn). Gradually whisk in milk until smooth. Stir in the consomme, Worcestershire sauce, pepper and salt. Bring to a boil; cook and stir for 2 minutes or until thickened.

3. Return meatballs to pan. Cook, uncovered, for 15-20 minutes longer or until meatballs are cooked through, stirring occasionally.

4. Meanwhile, cook noodles according to package directions. Drain; toss with butter. Serve with meatball mixture; sprinkle with parsley.

1. In a small bowl, mix the first eight ingredients. In a large nonstick skillet, heat 1 teaspoon oil over medium-high heat. Add beef; stir-fry 1-2 minutes or until no longer pink. Remove from pan.

2. Stir-fry broccoli in remaining oil 4-5 minutes or until crisp-tender. Add green onions; cook 1-2 minutes longer or just until tender.

3. Stir cornstarch mixture and add to pan. Bring to a boil; cook and stir for 2-3 minutes or until thickened. Return beef to pan; heat through.

CABBAGE ROLL SKILLET

Have a happy helping of this modern take on traditional cabbage roll casserole. I serve it over brown rice. It's also a great make-ahead dish, as it freezes well.
—**SUSAN CHICKNESS** PICTOU COUNTY, NS

PREP: 15 MIN. • **COOK:** 20 MIN. • **MAKES:** 6 SERVINGS

- 1 **can (28 ounces) whole plum tomatoes, undrained**
- 1 **pound extra-lean ground beef (95% lean)**
- 1 **large onion, chopped**
- 1 **can (8 ounces) tomato sauce**
- 2 **tablespoons cider vinegar**
- 1 **tablespoon brown sugar**
- 1 **teaspoon dried oregano**
- 1 **teaspoon dried thyme**
- ½ **teaspoon pepper**
- 1 **small head cabbage, thinly sliced (about 6 cups)**
- 1 **medium green pepper, cut into thin strips**
- 4 **cups hot cooked brown rice**

1. Drain the plum tomatoes, reserving liquid; coarsely chop tomatoes. In a large nonstick skillet, cook beef and onion over medium-high heat for 6-8 minutes or until the beef is no longer pink, breaking up beef into crumbles. Stir in tomato sauce, vinegar, brown sugar, seasonings and the tomatoes and reserved liquid.

2. Add cabbage and green pepper; cook, covered, 6 minutes, stirring occasionally. Cook, uncovered, 6-8 minutes longer or until cabbage is tender. Serve with rice.

SAUCY BEEF & BROCCOLI

AST FIX

AUCY BEEF & BROCCOLI

hen I want hearty flavor fast, I know it's time for my mous beef and broccoli stir-fry. It's extra delicious th chow mein noodles.
ROSA EVANS ODESSA, MO

TART TO FINISH: 30 MIN. • **MAKES:** 2 SERVINGS

- 1 **tablespoon cornstarch**
- ½ **cup water**
- ½ **teaspoon beef stock concentrate**
- ¼ **cup sherry or additional beef broth**
- 2 **tablespoons reduced-sodium soy sauce**
- 1 **tablespoon brown sugar**
- 1 **garlic clove, minced**
- 1 **teaspoon minced fresh gingerroot**
- 2 **teaspoons canola oil, divided**
- ½ **pound beef top sirloin steak, cut into ¼-inch strips**
- 2 **cups fresh broccoli florets**
- 8 **green onions, cut into 1-inch pieces**

⑤ INGREDIENTS · FAST FIX ▶
DIJON BEEF TENDERLOIN

I like having an ace recipe up my sleeve. This tenderloin with Dijon is my go-to for birthdays, buffets, holidays and other celebrations.
—**DONNA LINDECAMP** MORGANTON, NC

START TO FINISH: 20 MIN.
MAKES: 4 SERVINGS

- 4 **beef tenderloin steaks (1 inch thick and 4 ounces each)**
- ½ **teaspoon salt**
- ¼ **teaspoon pepper**
- 5 **tablespoons butter, divided**
- 1 **large onion, halved and thinly sliced**
- 1 **cup beef stock**
- 1 **tablespoon Dijon mustard**

1. Sprinkle steaks with salt and pepper. In a large skillet, heat 2 tablespoons butter over medium-high heat. Add steaks; cook 4-6 minutes on each side or until meat reaches desired doneness (for medium-rare, a thermometer should read 145°; medium, 160°; well-done, 170°). Remove from pan; keep warm.
2. In same pan, heat 1 tablespoon butter over medium heat. Add onion; cook and stir 4-6 minutes or until tender. Stir in stock; bring to a boil. Cook 1-2 minutes or until liquid is reduced by half. Stir in mustard; remove from heat. Cube remaining butter; stir into sauce just until blended. Serve with steaks.

BBQ HOEDOWN TACOS

Here's a yummy twist on traditional tacos that will bring out the cowboy in young and old alike. They're easy to make after a busy day.
—**DENISE POUNDS** HUTCHINSON, KS

PREP: 20 MIN. • **COOK:** 15 MIN.
MAKES: 4 SERVINGS

- 1 **pound ground beef**
- 1 **small onion, chopped**
- ¾ **cup barbecue sauce**
- 1 **can (4 ounces) chopped green chilies**
- 1 **teaspoon ground coriander**
- 1 **teaspoon ground cumin**
- ½ **teaspoon salt**
- 2 **cups angel hair coleslaw mix**
- ¼ **cup green goddess salad dressing**
- 8 **flour tortillas (6 inches), warmed**
- 8 **slices pepper jack cheese**

1. In a large nonstick skillet, cook beef and onion over medium heat until meat is no longer pink; drain. Stir in the barbecue sauce, chilies, coriander, cumin and salt. Bring to a boil. Reduce heat; simmer, uncovered, for 5-7 minutes to allow flavors to blend.
2. In a small bowl, combine coleslaw mix and salad dressing; toss to coat. On each tortilla, layer cheese, beef mixture and coleslaw; fold to close.

BBQ HOEDOWN TACOS

CONTEST-WINNING GERMAN PIZZA

I serve this fun take on German "pizza" when our family visits from Pennsylvania. Even if it's just my husband, our son and me around the table, this skillet sensation is always a favorite.

—AUDREY NOLT VERSAILLES, MO

PREP: 20 MIN. • **COOK:** 40 MIN.
MAKES: 4-6 SERVINGS

- **1 pound ground beef**
- **½ medium onion, chopped**
- **½ green pepper, diced**
- **1½ teaspoon salt, divided**
- **½ teaspoon pepper**
- **2 tablespoons butter**
- **6 medium potatoes (about 2¼ pounds), peeled and finely shredded**
- **3 large eggs, lightly beaten**
- **⅓ cup milk**
- **2 cups (8 ounces) shredded cheddar or part-skim mozzarella cheese**

1. In a large skillet over medium heat, cook and stir ground beef, onion, green pepper, ½ teaspoon salt and pepper until meat is no longer pink; drain. Remove and keep warm.

2. Reduce heat to low; melt butter in pan. Spread potatoes over butter and sprinkle with remaining salt. Top with beef mixture. Combine eggs and milk; pour over all.

3. Cover and cook 30 minutes or until set in the center. Sprinkle with mozzarella cheese; cover and cook until cheese is melted. Cut into wedges.

CONTEST-WINNING GERMAN PIZZA

CHUCK WAGON TORTILLA STACK

CHUCK WAGON TORTILLA STACK

Piling on loads of hearty flavor at mealtime is easy when I roll out this skillet specialty. I layer the meat mixture with tortillas in a deep skillet and let it simmer. It's easy to cut and spoon out of the pan.

—BERNICE JANOWSKI STEVENS POINT, WI

PREP: 15 MIN. • **COOK:** 40 MIN. • **MAKES:** 4-6 SERVINGS

- 1 **pound ground beef**
- 2 **to 3 garlic cloves, minced**
- 1 **can (16 ounces) baked beans**
- 1 **can (14½ ounces) stewed tomatoes, undrained**
- 1 **can (11 ounces) whole kernel corn, drained**
- 1 **can (4 ounces) chopped green chilies**
- ¼ **cup barbecue sauce**
- 4½ **teaspoons chili powder**
- 1½ **teaspoons ground cumin**
- 4 **flour tortillas (10 inches)**
- 1⅓ **cups (about 5 ounces) shredded pepper jack cheese**
  Shredded lettuce, chopped red onion, sour cream and/or chopped tomatoes, optional

1. In a large skillet, cook beef until no longer pink; drain. Add garlic, beans, tomatoes, corn, chilies, barbecue sauce, chili powder and cumin. Bring to a boil. Reduce heat; simmer, uncovered, for 10-12 minutes or until liquid is reduced.

2. Coat a large deep skillet with cooking spray. Place one tortilla in skillet; spread with 1½ cups meat mixture. Sprinkle with ⅓ cup cheese. Repeat layers three times. Cover and cook on low for 15 minutes or until cheese is melted and tortillas are heated through. Cut into wedges. Serve with toppings of your choice.

TOP TIP

Have a few leftover tortillas in the fridge? Here are three fun ways to use them up.

- Brush the tortillas with butter and sprinkle with herbs or cinnamon sugar. Bake until crisp.
- Spread peanut butter, apple butter and cream cheese on a tortilla, and roll it up for a quick snack.
- Let tortillas dry on racks until brittle, then crumble into small pieces to use on soups or salads in place of croutons.

ULTIMATE STEAK DE BURGO

3. In same skillet, melt ½ cup butter over medium heat. Whisk in garlic paste, cream and wine; heat through. Serve over steaks; sprinkle with herbs.

SPICY BEEF & PEPPER STIR-FRY

Looking for a recipe that lets you play with heat and spice? Give this quick stir-fry a try. I balance the beef with coconut milk and a spritz of lime. If you like, serve it alongside cooked rice or chow mein noodles.
—**JOY ZACHARIA** CLEARWATER, FL

PREP: 20 MIN. + STANDING • **COOK:** 10 MIN.
MAKES: 4 SERVINGS

- 1 **pound beef top sirloin steak, cut into thin strips**
- 1 **tablespoon minced fresh gingerroot**
- 3 **garlic cloves, minced, divided**
- ¼ **teaspoon pepper**
- ¾ **teaspoon salt, divided**
- 1 **cup light coconut milk**
- 2 **tablespoons sugar**
- 1 **tablespoon Sriracha Asian hot chili sauce**
- ½ **teaspoon grated lime peel**
- 2 **tablespoons lime juice**
- 2 **tablespoons canola oil, divided**
- 1 **large sweet red pepper, cut into thin strips**
- ½ **medium red onion, thinly sliced**
- 1 **jalapeno pepper, seeded and thinly sliced**
- 4 **cups fresh baby spinach**
- 2 **green onions, thinly sliced**
- 2 **tablespoons chopped fresh cilantro**

1. In a large bowl, toss beef with ginger, 2 garlic cloves, pepper and ½ teaspoon salt; let stand 15 minutes. In a small bowl, whisk coconut milk, sugar, chili sauce, lime peel, lime juice and remaining salt until blended.
2. In a large skillet, heat 1 tablespoon oil over medium-high heat. Add beef; stir-fry 2-3 minutes or until no longer pink. Remove from pan.
3. Stir-fry red pepper, red onion, jalapeno and remaining garlic in remaining oil 2-3 minutes or just until vegetables are crisp-tender. Stir in coconut milk mixture; heat through. Add spinach and beef; cook until spinach is wilted and beef is heated through, stirring occasionally. Sprinkle with green onions and cilantro.

ULTIMATE STEAK DE BURGO

ou'll love this traditional beef entree seasoned with utter, herbs and garlic. There's lots of gravy, so serve it ith mashed potatoes or crusty bread for dipping. rench onion soup is also a delicious accompaniment.
—HOLLIS MONROE AMES, IA

TART TO FINISH: 30 MIN. • **MAKES:** 4 SERVINGS

- 1 **garlic clove, minced**
- ¾ **teaspoon salt, divided**
- 4 **beef tenderloin steaks (1-inch thick and 4 ounces each)**
- ¼ **teaspoon pepper**
- 1 **tablespoon butter**
- ½ **cup butter, cubed**
- ½ **cup half-and-half cream**
- 2 **tablespoons sweet white wine**
- ½ **teaspoon minced fresh oregano or ⅛ teaspoon dried oregano**
- ½ **teaspoon minced fresh basil or ⅛ teaspoon dried basil**

Place garlic on a cutting board; sprinkle with 4 teaspoon salt. Mash garlic with flat side of the nife blade, forming a smooth paste. Sprinkle eaks with pepper and remaining salt.

In a large skillet, heat 1 tablespoon butter over edium heat. Add steaks; cook 4-6 minutes on ach side or until meat reaches desired doneness or medium-rare, a thermometer should read 5°; medium, 160°; well-done, 170°). Remove om pan; keep warm.

**SUZEE KREBS'
GOBBLER CAKES**
PAGE 97

Chicken & Turkey

Longtime dinner classics, chicken and turkey remain surefire winners for today's family cooks. Sizzle up a new favorite with these savory dishes.

GORGONZOLA & ORANGE
CHICKEN TENDERS

⑤ INGREDIENTS FAST FIX ▶

GORGONZOLA & ORANGE CHICKEN TENDERS

My mom makes this for family gatherings, and we can't get enough. The marmalade and Gorgonzola might sound like an unusual combo, but you'll be pleasantly surprised to see they make a great pair.
—YVETTE GORMAN DENVER, PA

START TO FINISH: 25 MIN.
MAKES: 4 SERVINGS

- 1 **large egg**
- ¼ **teaspoon salt**
- ¾ **cup seasoned bread crumbs**
- 1 **pound chicken tenderloins**
- 2 **tablespoons olive oil**
- ¼ **cup orange marmalade, warmed**
- ¼ **cup crumbled Gorgonzola cheese**

1. In a shallow bowl, whisk egg and salt. Place bread crumbs in another shallow bowl. Dip chicken in egg, then in bread crumbs, patting to help coating adhere to the tenderloins.
2. In a large skillet, heat oil over medium heat. Add chicken; cook 3-4 minutes on each side or until chicken is no longer pink. Drizzle with warm marmalade; top with cheese. Remove from heat; let stand, covered, until cheese begins to melt.

URKEY SLOPPY OES WITH VOCADO SLAW

Sloppy joes are a suppertime staple, but my friends always say this avocado slaw gives them new e. Try them—you'll agree! The eamy slaw is wonderful with the ngy sandwich filling.

JACYN SIEBERT SAN FRANCISCO, CA

REP: 15 MIN. • **COOK:** 20 MIN.
AKES: 6 SERVINGS

- 1 **pound ground turkey**
- 1 **medium onion, chopped**
- 1 **envelope sloppy joe mix**
- 1 **can (6 ounces) tomato paste**
- 1¼ **cups water**

LAW
- 1 **medium ripe avocado, peeled and cubed**
- 1 **tablespoon olive oil**
- 2 **teaspoons lemon juice**
- ½ **teaspoon ground cumin**
- ¼ **teaspoon salt**
- ¼ **teaspoon pepper**
- 2½ **cups coleslaw mix**
- 6 **hamburger buns, split**

1. In a large skillet, cook turkey and onion over medium heat 7-8 minutes or until the turkey is no longer pink and the onion is tender, breaking up turkey into crumbles; drain.

2. Stir in sloppy joe mix, tomato paste and water. Bring to a boil. Reduce heat; simmer, uncovered, 8-10 minutes or until thickened, stirring occasionally.

3. Meanwhile, place avocado, oil, lemon juice, cumin, salt and pepper in a blender; cover and process until smooth. Transfer to a small bowl; stir in coleslaw mix. Spoon meat mixture onto bun bottoms and top with slaw. Replace tops.

TURKEY SLOPPY JOES WITH AVOCADO SLAW

GOBBLER CAKES

I watched a chef make crab cakes and decided to try it with turkey and stuffing. Now my kids request them year-round.

—SUZEE KREBS BRIELLE, NJ

PREP: 25 MIN. • **COOK:** 10 MIN./BATCH
MAKES: 4 SERVINGS

- 1 **large egg**
- 2 **cups cooked stuffing**
- 1¼ **cups finely chopped cooked turkey**
- ½ **cup dried cranberries**
- ¼ **cup mayonnaise**
- ½ **cup crushed cornflakes**
- 1 **tablespoon canola oil**
  Cranberry sauce and turkey gravy, optional

1. In a large bowl, mix egg, stuffing, turkey, cranberries and mayonnaise. Shape into eight ½-in.-thick patties. Coat with crushed cornflakes.

2. In a large skillet, heat oil over medium heat. Add patties in batches; cook 3-4 minutes on each side or until golden brown. Serve warm, with cranberry sauce and gravy if desired.

BACON & ROSEMARY
CHICKEN

FAST FIX

BACON & ROSEMARY CHICKEN

Simple ingredients add up to simply fantastic flavor in this fast recipe that everyone raves over. It will become a new family favorite at your house.

—YVONNE STARLIN WESTMORELAND, TN

START TO FINISH: 30 MIN. • **MAKES:** 4 SERVINGS

- 4 **boneless skinless chicken breast halves (5 ounces each)**
- ½ **teaspoon salt**
- ¼ **teaspoon pepper**
- ¼ **cup all-purpose flour**
- 5 **bacon strips, chopped**
- 1 **tablespoon butter**
- 4 **garlic cloves, thinly sliced**
- 1 **tablespoon minced fresh rosemary or 1 teaspoon dried rosemary, crushed**
- ⅛ **teaspoon crushed red pepper flakes**
- 1 **cup reduced-sodium chicken broth**
- 2 **tablespoons lemon juice**

1. Pound chicken breasts slightly with a meat mallet to uniform thickness; sprinkle with salt and pepper. Place flour in a shallow bowl. Dip chicken in flour to coat both sides; shake off excess.

2. In a large skillet, cook bacon over medium heat until crisp, stirring occasionally. Remove with a slotted spoon; drain on paper towels. Discard drippings, reserving 2 tablespoons in pan. Cook chicken in butter and reserved drippings 4-6 minutes on each side or until a thermometer reads 165°. Remove and keep warm.

3. Add garlic, rosemary and pepper flakes to skillet; cook and stir 1 minute. Add broth and lemon juice; bring to a boil. Cook until liquid is reduced by half. Return chicken and bacon to skillet; heat through.

CLASSIC ITALIAN CHICKEN

Simmer breaded chicken in a tomatoey sauce
seasoned with garlic, oregano and basil. A sprinkling
of cheeses gives it a fast final touch.
—BOBBY TAYLOR LAPORTE, IN

PREP: 10 MIN. • **COOK:** 45 MIN. • **MAKES:** 4 SERVINGS

- 1 large egg
- 1 tablespoon plus ¼ cup water, divided
- ½ cup seasoned bread crumbs
- 1 broiler/fryer chicken (2 to 3 pounds), cut up
- 2 tablespoons canola oil
- 1 can (10¾ ounces) condensed tomato soup, undiluted
- ¼ cup chopped onion
- ½ teaspoon garlic powder
- ½ teaspoon dried basil
- ½ teaspoon dried oregano
- 1 cup (4 ounces) shredded part-skim mozzarella cheese
  Shredded Parmesan cheese

In a shallow bowl, beat egg and 1 tablespoon
water. Place the bread crumbs in another shallow
bowl. Dip chicken in egg mixture, then coat with
crumbs. In a large skillet, cook chicken in oil over
medium heat for 4-5 minutes or until browned;
drain. Remove and keep warm.

In the same skillet, combine the soup, onion,
garlic powder, basil, oregano and remaining water.
Return chicken to pan. Cover and simmer for
40-45 minutes or until chicken juices run clear.
Sprinkle with mozzarella cheese; cover and cook
for 1-2 minutes or until cheese is melted. Sprinkle
with Parmesan cheese.

MEXICAN CORN BREAD PIZZA

Sweet corn bread and spicy taco flavors combine for a
fun take on "pizza." I use ground turkey instead of beef
and other reduced-fat ingredients to keep it light. Now
I can enjoy a delicious dinner guilt-free!
—CHRISTY WEST GREENFIELD, IN

PREP: 25 MIN. • **BAKE:** 20 MIN. • **MAKES:** 6 SERVINGS

- 1 package (8½ ounces) corn bread/muffin mix
- ⅓ cup fat-free milk
- 1 large egg, lightly beaten
- 1 cup frozen corn, thawed
- ¾ pound extra-lean ground turkey
- 1 small onion, chopped
- 1 small sweet red pepper, chopped
- 2 jalapeno peppers, seeded and chopped
- 3 tablespoons reduced-sodium taco seasoning
- ½ cup water
- ¾ cup shredded reduced-fat Mexican cheese blend
- 1 small tomato, chopped
- ¼ cup sliced ripe olives
- 2 green onions, chopped
- 6 tablespoons reduced-fat sour cream

1. In a small bowl, combine the corn bread mix,
milk and egg. Stir in corn just until blended. Spread
evenly into a 10-in. ovenproof skillet coated with
cooking spray. Bake at 400° for 14-18 minutes or
until a toothpick inserted near the center comes
out clean.

2. Meanwhile, in a large nonstick skillet, cook the
turkey, onion, red pepper and jalapenos over
medium heat until meat is no longer pink; drain.
Stir in taco seasoning and water; bring to a boil.
Reduce heat; simmer, uncovered, for 5 minutes.

3. Spoon turkey mixture over corn bread; sprinkle
with cheese. Bake for 5-10 minutes or until cheese
is melted. Sprinkle with tomato, olives and green
onions. Cut into six wedges; top each with sour
cream.

NOTE *Wear disposable gloves when cutting hot
peppers; the oils can burn skin. Avoid touching
your face.*

MEXICAN CORN
BREAD PIZZA

TURKEY CURRY

I'm always looking for new and interesting ways to use leftover turkey, especially around the holidays. This is a zesty entree you can make as spicy as you like by varying the amount of curry powder.
—**MARTHA BALSER** CINCINNATI, OH

START TO FINISH: 20 MIN. • **MAKES:** 4 SERVINGS

- 1 cup sliced celery
- ½ cup sliced carrots
- 1 cup fat-free milk, divided
- 2 tablespoons cornstarch
- ¾ cup reduced-sodium chicken broth
- 2 cups diced cooked turkey or chicken
- 2 tablespoons dried minced onion
- ½ teaspoon garlic powder
- 1 to 4 teaspoons curry powder
  Hot cooked rice, optional

1. Lightly coat a skillet with cooking spray; saute celery and carrots until tender. In a bowl, mix ¼ cup milk and cornstarch until smooth. Add broth and remaining milk; mix until smooth.
2. Pour over vegetables. Bring to a boil; cook and stir for 2 minutes or until thickened. Add the turkey, onion, garlic powder and curry powder; heat through, stirring occasionally. Serve with rice if desired.

FLAVORFUL CHICKEN FAJITAS

No one will love fajita night more tha you after you get a taste of these. Th best part is it takes only 25 minutes t make this sizzling dinner.
—**JULIE STERCHI** CAMPBELLSVILLE, KY

PREP: 20 MIN. + MARINATING • **COOK:** 5 MIN.
MAKES: 6 SERVINGS

- 4 tablespoons canola oil, divided
- 2 tablespoons lemon juice
- 1½ teaspoons seasoned salt
- 1½ teaspoons dried oregano
- 1½ teaspoons ground cumin
- 1 teaspoon garlic powder
- ½ teaspoon chili powder
- ½ teaspoon paprika
- ½ teaspoon crushed red pepper flakes, optional
- 1½ pounds boneless skinless chicken breast, cut into thin strips
- ½ medium sweet red pepper, julienned
- ½ medium green pepper, julienned
- 4 green onions, thinly sliced
- ½ cup chopped onion
- 6 flour tortillas (8 inches), warmed
  Shredded cheddar cheese, taco sauce, salsa, guacamole and sour cream

1. In a large resealable plastic bag, combine 2 tablespoons oil, lemon juice and seasonings; add the chicken. Seal and turn to coat; refrigerate for 1-4 hours.
2. In a large skillet, saute peppers and onions in remaining oil until crisp-tender. Remove and keep warm.
3. Discard marinade. In the same skillet, cook chicken over medium-high heat for 5-6 minutes o until no longer pink. Return pepper mixture to pa heat through.
4. Spoon filling down the center of tortillas; fold in half. Serve with cheese, taco sauce, salsa, guacamole and sour cream.

FLAVORFUL CHICKEN FAJITAS

FAST FIX ▶

QUICK CHICKEN & BROCCOLI STIR-FRY

This Asian stir-fry is a surefire winner. The spicy sauce works with chicken, seafood, pork or beef. Add whatever veggies you have on hand.

—KRISTIN RIMKUS SNOHOMISH, WA

START TO FINISH: 25 MIN.
MAKES: 4 SERVINGS

- 2 **tablespoons rice vinegar**
- 2 **tablespoons mirin (sweet rice wine)**
- 2 **tablespoons chili garlic sauce**
- 1 **tablespoon cornstarch**
- 1 **tablespoon reduced-sodium soy sauce**
- 2 **teaspoons fish sauce or additional soy sauce**
- ½ **cup reduced-sodium chicken broth, divided**
- 2 **cups instant brown rice**
- 2 **teaspoons sesame oil**
- 4 **cups fresh broccoli florets**
- 2 **cups cubed cooked chicken**
- 2 **green onions, sliced**

1. In a small bowl, mix the first six ingredients and ¼ cup chicken broth until smooth. Cook the rice according to the package directions.

2. Meanwhile, in a large skillet, heat oil over medium-high heat. Add broccoli; stir-fry 2 minutes. Add remaining broth; cook 1-2 minutes or until broccoli is crisp-tender. Stir sauce mixture and add to pan. Bring to a boil; cook and stir 1-2 minutes or until sauce is thickened.

3. Stir in chicken and green onions; heat through. Serve with rice.

QUICK CHICKEN & BROCCOLI STIR-FRY

CHICKEN 'N' SWEET POTATO STEW

HICKEN 'N' SWEET OTATO STEW

Tired of the same old dinnertime fare? Spice it up with my Malaysian-inspired stew. Served on a bed of hot couscous, this flavorful dish is as good as it gets.

—AGNES WARD STRATFORD, ON

ART TO FINISH: 30 MIN. **MAKES:** 2 SERVINGS

- ⅔ **pound boneless skinless chicken breasts, cut into 1-inch cubes**
- ½ **teaspoon minced fresh gingerroot**
- 1 **garlic clove, minced**
- ½ **teaspoon olive oil**
- ½ **cup chopped onion**
- ½ **cup chopped sweet red pepper**
- ½ **teaspoon ground coriander**
- ½ **teaspoon ground cumin**
- ½ **teaspoon curry powder**
  Dash ground cinnamon
- ½ **cups cubed peeled sweet potatoes**
- ¾ **cup reduced-sodium chicken broth**
- 1 **cup water**
- 1 **tablespoon thawed orange juice concentrate**
- ½ **cup uncooked couscous**
- 1 **tablespoon cornstarch**
- 6 **tablespoons light coconut milk**
- 1 **tablespoon minced fresh cilantro**

1. In a large skillet, saute the chicken, ginger and garlic in oil until chicken juices run clear. Add the onion, pepper and seasonings; saute 4-5 minutes longer. Add sweet potatoes and broth. Bring to a boil. Reduce heat; cover and simmer mixture for 10-12 minutes or until tender.

2. Meanwhile, in a small saucepan, bring water and orange juice concentrate to a boil. Stir in couscous. Cover and remove from the heat; let stand for 5-10 minutes or until water is absorbed. Fluff with a fork.

3. Combine cornstarch and coconut milk until smooth. Stir into chicken mixture. Bring to a boil; cook and stir for 2 minutes or until thickened. Stir in cilantro. Serve with couscous.

TORTELLINI PRIMAVERA

This was a family favorite when my kids were teenagers. It's so tasty and easy to whip up.
—TINA GREEN ALBANY, OR

PREP: 20 MIN. • **COOK:** 15 MIN. • **MAKES:** 2 SERVINGS

- 1 cup frozen cheese tortellini
- 2 tablespoons olive oil, divided
- 3 tablespoons prepared pesto, divided
- ¼ pound boneless skinless chicken breast, cut into 1-inch cubes
- 1 cup cut fresh asparagus (1-inch pieces)
- ¼ cup each chopped sweet yellow pepper, green pepper and sweet onion
- ¼ cup sliced fresh carrot
- ¼ cup fresh or frozen snow peas
- ¼ cup fresh broccoli florets
- ¼ teaspoon garlic powder
- ⅛ teaspoon salt
- ⅛ teaspoon pepper
- 2 plum tomatoes, cut into wedges
- 3 tablespoons grated Parmesan cheese, divided
- 1 tablespoon water

1. Cook tortellini according to package directions. Meanwhile, in a small bowl, combine 4½ teaspoons oil and 4½ teaspoons pesto. Add chicken and toss to coat. Let stand at room temperature while cooking the vegetables.
2. In a large skillet, saute the asparagus, peppers, onion, carrot, peas, broccoli, garlic powder, salt and pepper in remaining oil until crisp-tender. Drain tortellini and return to saucepan; add vegetables.
3. In the same skillet, cook and stir the chicken for 4-5 minutes or until juices run clear. Stir in the tomatoes, 2 tablespoons Parmesan cheese, water and remaining pesto; simmer for 2 minutes. Add tortellini mixture; toss. Sprinkle with remaining Parmesan cheese.

BOW TIES WITH CHICKEN & SHRIMP

Serve your clan this nourishing stovetop supper to keep them warm and satisfied when the weather turns cold.
—JAN ARCHER KANSAS CITY, MO

PREP: 20 MIN. • **COOK:** 15 MIN. • **MAKES:** 7 SERVINGS

- 5¼ cups uncooked bow tie pasta
- ¾ pound boneless skinless chicken breasts, cubed
- 1 tablespoon butter
- 1 tablespoon olive oil
- 2 green onions, chopped
- 2 garlic cloves, minced
- 2 cans (14½ ounces each) Italian diced tomatoes, undrained
- 2 tablespoons minced fresh parsley, divided
- 1 tablespoon each minced fresh basil, thyme and oregano or 1 teaspoon each dried basil, thyme and oregano
- ¼ teaspoon pepper
- 2 teaspoons cornstarch
- ½ cup reduced-sodium chicken broth
- ¾ pound cooked large shrimp, peeled and deveined
- 3 plum tomatoes, diced
- 10 large pitted ripe olives, sliced
   Minced fresh parsley

1. Cook pasta according to package directions. Meanwhile, in a large nonstick skillet, saute chicken in butter and oil until no longer pink. Add onions and garlic; cook 1 minute longer. Stir in the canned tomatoes, herbs and pepper.
2. Combine cornstarch and broth until smooth; stir into the pan. Bring to a boil; cook and stir for 2 minutes or until thickened. Add the shrimp, plum tomatoes and olives; heat through. Drain pasta; serve with chicken mixture. Sprinkle with parsley.

TURKEY MOLE TACOS

In contrast to traditional tacos, these taste complete as is without need for further garnishes or sauces. I've also made this using bite-sized pieces of chicken thighs and increased the cooking time accordingly.

HELEN GLAZIER SEATTLE, WA

PREP: 25 MIN. • **COOK:** 20 MIN. • **MAKES:** 6 SERVINGS

- 1¼ pounds lean ground turkey
- 1 celery rib, chopped
- 4 green onions, chopped
- 2 garlic cloves, minced
- 1 can (14½ ounces) diced tomatoes, undrained
- 1 jar (7 ounces) roasted sweet red peppers, drained and chopped
- 2 ounces 53% cacao dark baking chocolate, chopped
- 4 teaspoons chili powder
- 1 teaspoon ground cumin
- ½ teaspoon salt
- ¼ teaspoon ground cinnamon
- ¼ cup lightly salted mixed nuts, coarsely chopped
- 12 corn tortillas (6 inches), warmed

1. In a large nonstick skillet coated with cooking spray, cook the turkey, celery, green onions and garlic over medium heat until meat is no longer pink and vegetables are tender; drain.

2. Stir in the tomatoes, red peppers, chocolate, chili powder, cumin, salt and cinnamon. Bring to a boil. Reduce heat; cover and simmer for 10 minutes, stirring occasionally.

3. Remove from the heat; stir in nuts. Place about ⅓ cup filling on each tortilla.

FREEZE OPTION *Freeze cooled meat mixture in freezer containers. To use, partially thaw in refrigerator overnight. Heat through in a saucepan, stirring occasionally and adding a little water if necessary.*

TURKEY MOLE TACOS

FAST FIX

ITALIAN TURKEY SKILLET

I always have leftover turkey on hand, so I like creative ways to use it up that taste just as good, if not better, as the original. This pasta toss lightly coated with tomato sauce and accented with fresh mushrooms does the trick.

—**PATRICIA KILE** ELIZABETHTOWN, PA

START TO FINISH: 20 MIN.
MAKES: 8 SERVINGS

- 1 **package (16 ounces) linguine**
- 2 **tablespoons canola oil**
- ¾ **cup sliced fresh mushrooms**
- 1 **medium onion, chopped**
- 1 **celery rib, chopped**
- 1 **small green pepper, chopped**
- 2 **cups cubed cooked turkey**
- 1 **can (14½ ounces) diced tomatoes, drained**
- 1 **can (10¾ ounces) condensed tomato soup, undiluted**
- 1 **tablespoon Italian seasoning**
- 1 **tablespoon minced fresh parsley**
- ¼ **teaspoon pepper**
- ⅛ **teaspoon salt**
- 1 **cup (4 ounces) shredded cheddar cheese, optional**

1. Cook linguine according to package directions. Meanwhile, in a large skillet, heat oil over medium-high heat. Add the mushrooms, onion, celery and green pepper; cook and stir until tender. Stir in turkey, tomatoes, soup and the seasonings; heat through.

2. Drain linguine; add to turkey mixture and toss to combine. If desired, sprinkle with cheese and let stand, covered, until cheese is melted.

ITALIAN TURKEY SKILLET

~~F~~AVORITE SKILLET ~~L~~ASAGNA

~~W~~hole wheat noodles and zucchini ~~pu~~mp up the nutrition in this easy ~~din~~ner, while fat-free ricotta makes ~~it lo~~ok and taste indulgent.

—~~L~~ORIE MINER KAMAS, UT

~~ST~~ART TO FINISH: 30 MIN.
~~M~~AKES: 5 SERVINGS

- ~~1/~~2 **pound Italian turkey sausage links, casings removed**
- 1 **small onion, chopped**
- 1 **jar (14 ounces) spaghetti sauce**
- 2 **cups uncooked whole wheat egg noodles**
- 1 **cup water**
- ~~1/~~2 **cup chopped zucchini**
- ~~1/~~2 **cup fat-free ricotta cheese**
- 2 **tablespoons grated Parmesan cheese**
- 1 **tablespoon minced fresh parsley or 1 teaspoon dried parsley flakes**
- ½ **cup shredded part-skim mozzarella cheese**

1. In a large nonstick skillet, cook sausage and onion over medium heat until no longer pink, breaking up sausage into crumbles; drain. Stir in spaghetti sauce, noodles, water and the zucchini. Bring mixture to a boil. Reduce heat; simmer, covered, 8-10 minutes or until noodles are tender, stirring occasionally.

2. In a small bowl, combine ricotta cheese, Parmesan cheese and parsley. Drop by tablespoonfuls over pasta mixture. Sprinkle with the mozzarella cheese; cook, covered, 3-5 minutes longer or until cheese is melted.

FAVORITE SKILLET LASAGNA

MANGO CHUTNEY CHICKEN CURRY

My father dreamed up this curry and chutney combination. Now my family cooks it on road trips—in rain and sun, in the mountains, even on the beach. Adjust the curry for taste and heat.

—**DINA MORENO** SEATTLE, WA

START TO FINISH: 25 MIN.
MAKES: 4 SERVINGS

- 1 **tablespoon canola oil**
- 1 **pound boneless skinless chicken breasts, cubed**
- 1 **tablespoon curry powder**
- 2 **garlic cloves, minced**
- ¼ **teaspoon salt**
- ¼ **teaspoon pepper**
- ½ **cup mango chutney**
- ½ **cup half-and-half cream**

1. In a large skillet, heat oil over medium-high heat; brown chicken. Stir in curry powder, garlic, salt and pepper; cook 1-2 minutes longer or until aromatic.

2. Stir in chutney and cream. Bring to boil. Reduce heat; simmer, uncovered, 4-6 minutes or until chicken is no longer pink, stirring occasionally.

QUICK CHICKEN PARMESAN

My mother inspired me to develop my first pasta sauce. It's tangy, simple and really satisfying. The longer it simmers, the better it gets, so keep that in mind if you have time to spare.

—DANIELLE GROCHOWSKI
MILWAUKEE, WI

PREP: 10 MIN. • **COOK:** 25 MIN.
MAKES: 4 SERVINGS

- 12 **ounces frozen grilled chicken breast strips (about 3 cups)**
- 1 **can (14½ ounces) diced tomatoes, undrained**
- 1 **can (6 ounces) tomato paste**
- 2 **tablespoons dry red wine or chicken broth**
- 1 **tablespoon olive oil**
- 1½ **teaspoons Italian seasoning**
- 1 **garlic clove, minced**
- ½ **teaspoon sugar**
- ⅓ **cup shredded Parmesan cheese**
- ⅓ **cup shredded part-skim mozzarella cheese**
  Hot cooked pasta

1. Heat a large skillet over medium heat. Add chicken strips; cook and stir 5-8 minutes or until heated through. Remove from pan.

2. In same skillet, combine tomatoes, tomato paste, wine, oil, Italian seasoning, garlic and sugar; bring to a boil, stirring occasionally. Reduce the heat; simmer mixture, uncovered, 10-15 minutes to allow flavors to blend, stirring occasionally.

3. Stir in the chicken. Sprinkle with cheeses; cook, covered, for another 1-2 minutes or until cheese melts. Serve with pasta.

FAST FIX

TURKEY PENNE WITH LEMON CREAM SAUCE

You'll please every palate at the table with this colorful pasta. Creamy, satisfying and loaded with lively flavors, it's the perfect way to sneak fresh veggies into little tummies.

—TASTE OF HOME TEST KITCHEN

START TO FINISH: 30 MIN.
MAKES: 4 SERVINGS

- 2 **cups uncooked penne pasta**
- ½ **pound turkey breast cutlets, cut into ¾-inch pieces**
- 3 **tablespoons butter, divided**
- 2 **cups fresh broccoli florets**
- 3 **small carrots, thinly sliced**
- 2 **garlic cloves, minced**
- 2 **tablespoons all-purpose flour**
- 1½ **teaspoons chicken bouillon granules**
- ½ **teaspoon dried thyme**
- ¼ **teaspoon pepper**
- ⅛ **teaspoon salt**
- 2½ **cups half-and-half cream**
- ¼ **cup lemon juice**
- 2 **plum tomatoes, seeded and chopped**

1. Cook pasta according to package directions. Meanwhile, in a large skillet, saute turkey in 1 tablespoon butter until no longer pink. Remove from skillet and keep warm.

2. In the same skillet, saute broccoli and carrots in remaining butter until crisp-tender. Add garlic; cook 1 minute longer. Stir in the flour, bouillon granules, thyme, pepper and salt until blended. Combine cream and lemon juice; gradually stir into broccoli mixture. Bring to a boil; cook and stir for 2-3 minutes or until thickened.

3. Drain pasta; add to the skillet. Stir in turkey and tomatoes and heat through.

TURKEY PENNE WITH LEMON CREAM SAUCE

CARIBBEAN CHICKEN STIR-FRY

Fruit cocktail in stir-fry? You might be surprised how good this dish is. It's a promising go-to option anytime time is tight.

—JEANNE HOLT
MENDOTA HEIGHTS, MN

START TO FINISH: 25 MIN.
MAKES: 4 SERVINGS

- 2 **teaspoons cornstarch**
- ¼ **cup water**
- 1 **pound boneless skinless chicken breasts, cut into ½-inch strips**
- 2 **teaspoons Caribbean jerk seasoning**
- 1 **can (15 ounces) mixed tropical fruit, drained and coarsely chopped**
- 2 **packages (8.8 ounces each) ready-to-serve brown rice**

In a small bowl, mix the cornstarch and water until smooth.

Coat a large skillet with cooking spray and heat over medium-high heat. Add chicken; sprinkle with jerk seasoning. Stir-fry 3-5 minutes or until no longer pink. Stir cornstarch mixture and add to pan with fruit. Bring to a boil; cook and stir 1-2 minutes or until sauce is thickened.

Meanwhile, heat the rice according to package directions. Serve with chicken.

CARIBBEAN CHICKEN STIR-FRY

cheese, salt and ½ cup sour cream mixture. Spoon ½ cup chicken mixture on each tortilla. Fold sides and ends over filling and roll up. Spritz both sides with cooking spray.

2. In a large nonstick skillet or griddle coated with cooking spray, cook the burritos in batches over medium heat for 3-4 minutes on each side or until golden brown. Serve with remaining sour cream mixture and salsa if desired.

TURKEY FETTUCCINE SKILLET

Forget ho-hum turkey sandwiches. I created this simple skillet as a tasty way to use up the leftover bird from holiday dinners. It's become a family tradition to enjoy it the day after Thanksgiving and Christmas.
—**KARI JOHNSTON** MARWAYNE, AB

PREP: 10 MIN. • **COOK:** 30 MIN. • **MAKES:** 6 SERVINGS

- 8 **ounces uncooked fettuccine**
- ½ **cup chopped onion**
- ½ **cup chopped celery**
- 4 **garlic cloves, minced**
- 1 **teaspoon canola oil**
- 1 **cup sliced fresh mushrooms**
- 2 **cups fat-free milk**
- 1 **teaspoon salt-free seasoning blend**
- ¼ **teaspoon salt**
- 2 **tablespoons cornstarch**
- ½ **cup fat-free half-and-half**
- ⅓ **cup grated Parmesan cheese**
- 3 **cups cubed cooked turkey breast**
- ¾ **cup shredded part-skim mozzarella cheese**

1. Cook fettuccine according to package direction. Meanwhile, in a large ovenproof skillet coated with cooking spray, saute the onion, celery and garlic in oil for 3 minutes. Add mushrooms; cook and stir until vegetables are tender. Stir in milk, seasoning blend and salt. Bring to a boil.

2. Combine the cornstarch and half-and-half until smooth; stir into skillet. Cook and stir for 2 minutes or until thickened and bubbly. Stir in Parmesan cheese just until melted.

3. Stir in turkey. Drain fettuccine; add to turkey mixture. Heat through. Sprinkle with mozzarella cheese. Broil 4-6 in. from the heat for 2-3 minutes or until cheese is melted.

FAST FIX
SKILLET CHICKEN BURRITOS

Here's one of my favorite go-to dishes when I'm in a rush to make dinner. Preparing the burritos in the skillet not only saves time, it gives the them a crispy outside and ooey-gooey inside.
—**SCARLETT ELROD** NEWNAN, GA

START TO FINISH: 30 MIN. • **MAKES:** 8 SERVINGS

- 1 **cup (8 ounces) reduced-fat sour cream**
- ¼ **cup chopped fresh cilantro**
- 2 **tablespoons chopped pickled jalapeno slices**
- 2 **teaspoons chopped onion**
- 2 **teaspoons Dijon mustard**
- 1 **teaspoon grated lime peel**

BURRITOS

- 2 **cups cubed cooked chicken breast**
- 1 **can (15 ounces) black beans, rinsed and drained**
- 1 **can (11 ounces) Mexicorn, drained**
- 1 **cup (4 ounces) shredded reduced-fat cheddar cheese**
- ¼ **teaspoon salt**
- 8 **whole wheat tortillas (8 inches), warmed**
  Cooking spray
  Salsa, optional

1. In a small bowl, combine the first six ingredients. In a large bowl, combine the chicken, beans, corn,

PEEDY CHICKEN MARSALA

This is one of my favorite dishes to order in restaurants, so I created a version that I could make flash on a weeknight at home.

—RISHA KRUSE EAGLE, ID

ART TO FINISH: 30 MIN.
KES: 4 SERVINGS

- ounces uncooked whole wheat or multigrain angel hair pasta
- boneless skinless chicken breast halves (5 ounces each)
- cup all-purpose flour
- teaspoon lemon-pepper seasoning
- teaspoon salt
- tablespoons olive oil, divided
- cups sliced fresh mushrooms
- garlic clove, minced
- cup dry Marsala wine

1. Cook pasta according to package directions. Pound chicken with a meat mallet to ¼-in. thickness. In a large resealable plastic bag, mix the flour, lemon pepper and salt. Add chicken, one piece at a time; close bag and shake to coat.
2. In a large skillet, heat 1 tablespoon oil over medium heat. Add chicken; cook for 4-5 minutes on each side or until no longer pink. Remove from pan.
3. In the same skillet, heat the remaining oil over medium-high heat. Add mushrooms; cook and stir until tender. Add garlic; cook 1 minute longer. Add wine; bring to a boil. Cook for 5-6 minutes or until liquid is reduced by half, stirring to loosen browned bits from pan. Return chicken to pan, turning to coat with the sauce; heat through.
4. Drain the pasta; serve with chicken mixture.

BLUEBERRY-DIJON CHICKEN

Blueberries and chicken may seem like a strange combination, but prepare to be dazzled. I add a sprinkling of minced fresh basil as the finishing touch.

—SUSAN MARSHALL
COLORADO SPRINGS, CO

START TO FINISH: 30 MIN.
MAKES: 4 SERVINGS

- 4 boneless skinless chicken breast halves (6 ounces each)
- ¼ teaspoon salt
- ¼ teaspoon pepper
- 1 tablespoon butter
- ½ cup blueberry preserves
- ⅓ cup raspberry vinegar
- ¼ cup fresh or frozen blueberries
- 3 tablespoons Dijon mustard
  Minced fresh basil or tarragon, optional

1. Sprinkle chicken with salt and pepper. In a large skillet, cook chicken in butter over medium heat for 6-8 minutes on each side or until a thermometer reads 170°. Remove and keep warm.
2. In the same skillet, combine preserves, vinegar, blueberries and mustard, stirring to loosen browned bits from pan. Bring to a boil; cook and stir until thickened. Serve with chicken. Sprinkle with basil if desired.

SPEEDY CHICKEN MARSALA

CHICKEN PORTOBELLO STROGANOFF

My chicken and portobello version of the classic beef dish is the result of my opening the fridge for dinner one night and improvising with what I had on hand. It's a keeper!

—KATIE ROSE PEWAUKEE, WI

PREP: 15 MIN. • **COOK:** 25 MIN.
MAKES: 4 SERVINGS

- 1 **pound ground chicken**
- 12 **ounces baby portobello mushrooms, halved**
- 1 **medium onion, chopped**
- 1 **tablespoon olive oil**
- 2 **garlic cloves, minced**
- 3 **tablespoons white wine or chicken broth**
- 2 **cups chicken broth**
- ½ **cup heavy whipping cream**
- 2 **tablespoons lemon juice**
- ¼ **teaspoon salt**
- ⅛ **teaspoon white pepper**
- 1 **cup (8 ounces) sour cream Hot cooked egg noodles or pasta**

1. In a large skillet, cook the chicken, mushrooms and onion in oil over medium-high heat until meat is no longer pink. Add garlic; cook 1 minute longer.
2. Stir in wine. Bring to a boil; cook until the liquid is almost evaporated. Add the broth, cream, lemon juice, salt and pepper. Bring to a boil; cook until liquid is reduced by half.
3. Reduce heat. Gradually stir in sour cream; heat through (do not boil). Serve with noodles.

CHICKEN PORTOBELLO STROGANOFF

SKILLET-ROASTED LEMON CHICKEN WITH POTATOES

I teach home economics and have my students prepare this skillet sensation in our nutrition unit. It h a delicious lemon-herb flavor and simple to make.

—MINDY ROTTMUND LANCASTER,

PREP: 20 MIN. • **BAKE:** 25 MIN.
MAKES: 4 SERVINGS

- 1 **tablespoon olive oil, divide**
- 1 **medium lemon, thinly slice**
- 4 **garlic cloves, minced and divided**
- ¼ **teaspoon grated lemon pe**
- ½ **teaspoon salt, divided**
- ¼ **teaspoon pepper, divided**
- 8 **boneless skinless chicken thighs (4 ounces each)**
- ¼ **teaspoon dried rosemary, crushed**
- 1 **pound fingerling potatoes, halved lengthwise**
- 8 **cherry tomatoes**

1. Preheat oven to 450°. Greas a 10-inch cast-iron skillet with 1 teaspoon oil. Arrange lemon slices in a single layer in skillet
2. Combine 1 teaspoon oil, 2 minced garlic cloves, lemon peel, ¼ teaspoon salt and ⅛ teaspoon pepper; rub over chicken. Place over lemon.
3. In a large bowl, combine rosemary and the remaining o' garlic, salt and pepper. Add the potatoes and tomatoes; toss to coat. Arrange over chicken. Ba uncovered, 25-30 minutes or until chicken is no longer pink and potatoes are tender.

GOAT CHEESE-STUFFED
CHICKEN WITH APRICOT GLAZE

GOAT CHEESE-STUFFED
CHICKEN WITH APRICOT GLAZE

My original version of this recipe used several tablespoons of butter versus the one tablespoon of oil. With a few more tweaks, this rich and filling entree is under 350 calories.

—**DAVID DAHLMAN** CHATSWORTH, CA

PREP: 20 MIN. • **COOK:** 20 MIN. • **MAKES:** 2 SERVINGS

2 **boneless skinless chicken breast halves
   (6 ounces each)**
¼ **teaspoon salt**
¼ **teaspoon pepper**
2 **tablespoons goat cheese**
2 **tablespoons part-skim ricotta cheese**
4 **tablespoons chopped shallots, divided**
1 **teaspoon olive oil**
⅔ **cup reduced-sodium chicken broth**
2 **tablespoons apricot spreadable fruit**
1 **tablespoon lemon juice**
1 **teaspoon spicy brown mustard**
1 **teaspoon minced fresh parsley**

1. Flatten chicken to ¼-in. thickness; sprinkle with salt and pepper. Combine the goat cheese, ricotta and 1 tablespoon shallots; spread over the center of each chicken breast. Roll up and secure with toothpicks.

2. In a small nonstick skillet, brown chicken in oil on all sides. Remove and keep warm.

3. In the same skillet, saute remaining shallots until tender. Stir in the broth, spreadable fruit, lemon juice and mustard. Bring to a boil; cook until liquid is reduced by half.

4. Return chicken to the pan; cover and cook for 6-7 minutes or until no longer pink. Discard toothpicks. Serve chicken with cooking liquid. Sprinkle with parsley.

DID YOU KNOW?

Goat cheese is a soft, easily spread cheese with a distinctively tangy flavor made from the milk of goats. Goat cheese is often found in Middle Eastern or Mediterranean cuisines. Common varieties include chevre, a very soft cheese, and feta, a semi-soft cheese.

**ASPARAGUS
TURKEY STIR-FRY**

FAST FIX

ASPARAGUS TURKEY STIR-FRY

It's no surprise folks ask for the recipe after they sample this dish, just as I did when I first tasted it a friend's house. Coated with a delicious lemon sauce, this simple skillet medley is sure to satisfy on the busiest of nights. It's great in spring when fresh asparagus is in season.
—**MAY EVANS** CORINTH, KY

START TO FINISH: 20 MIN.
MAKES: 4 SERVINGS

- 2 **teaspoons cornstarch**
- ¼ **cup chicken broth**
- 1 **tablespoon lemon juice**
- 1 **teaspoon soy sauce**
- 1 **pound turkey breast tenderloin, cut into ½-inch strips**
- 1 **garlic clove, minced**
- 2 **tablespoons canola oil, divided**
- 1 **pound fresh asparagus, trimmed and cut into 1½-inch pieces**
- 1 **jar (2 ounces) sliced pimientos, drained**

1. In a small bowl, combine the cornstarch, broth, lemon juice and soy sauce until smooth; set aside. In a large skillet or wok, stir-fry the turkey and garlic in 1 tablespoon of the oil until meat is no longer pink; remove and keep warm.

2. Stir-fry asparagus in the remaining oil until crisp-tender. Add the pimientos. Stir broth mixture and add to the pan; cook and stir for 1 minute or until thickened. Return the turkey to the pan; heat through.

THAI CHICKEN PEANUT NOODLES

My husband loves the spicy Thai flavors in this speedy, simple dish. Break out the chopsticks for a more authentic experience.
JENNIFER FISHER AUSTIN, TX

START TO FINISH: 30 MIN.
MAKES: 6 SERVINGS

¼ cup creamy peanut butter
½ cup reduced-sodium chicken broth
¼ cup lemon juice
¼ cup reduced-sodium soy sauce
4 teaspoons Sriracha Asian hot chili sauce
¼ teaspoon crushed red pepper flakes
12 ounces uncooked multigrain spaghetti

1 pound lean ground chicken
1½ cups julienned carrots
1 medium sweet red pepper, chopped
1 garlic clove, minced
½ cup finely chopped unsalted peanuts
4 green onions, chopped

1. In a small bowl, whisk the first six ingredients until blended. Cook spaghetti according to package directions; drain.
2. Meanwhile, in a large skillet, cook chicken, carrots, pepper and garlic over medium heat 5-6 minutes or until chicken is no longer pink, breaking up chicken into crumbles; drain.
3. Stir in peanut butter mixture; bring to a boil. Reduce the heat; simmer, uncovered, 3-5 minutes or until the sauce is slightly thickened. Serve with spaghetti. Top with peanuts and green onions.

THAI CHICKEN PEANUT NOODLES

CHEESY ONION CHICKEN SKILLET

My zesty chicken with peppers and onions is so versatile, it works when you serve it over rice, potatoes, noodles—even a hoagie bun!
—**KIM JOHNSON** SIBLEY, IA

START TO FINISH: 20 MIN.
MAKES: 4 SERVINGS

1 pound boneless skinless chicken breasts, cubed
2 teaspoons Mrs. Dash Garlic & Herb seasoning blend
2 tablespoons olive oil, divided
1 medium green pepper, cut into strips
½ medium onion, sliced
1 cup (4 ounces) shredded Colby-Monterey Jack cheese

1. Toss chicken with seasoning blend. In a large nonstick skillet, heat 1 tablespoon of the oil over medium-high heat. Add chicken; cook and stir 5-7 minutes or until no longer pink. Remove from pan. In same pan, add remaining oil, pepper and onion; cook and stir 3-4 minutes or until onions are crisp-tender.
2. Stir in the chicken; sprinkle with cheese. Remove from the heat; let stand, covered, until the cheese is melted.

FAVORITE COLA CHICKEN

Everyone who tries this chicken asks for the recipe. They're always surprised to hear that cola is my secret ingredient.

—JEAN JARVIS WAUTOMA, WI

PREP: 5 MIN. • **COOK:** 70 MIN.
MAKES: 4 SERVINGS

- 1 can (12 ounces) diet cola
- ½ cup ketchup
- 2 to 4 tablespoons finely chopped onion
- ¼ teaspoon dried oregano
- ¼ teaspoon garlic powder
- 8 bone-in chicken thighs, skin removed

1. In a large skillet, combine first five ingredients. Bring to a boil; boil for 1 minute. Add chicken; stir to coat. Reduce the heat to medium; cover and simmer for 20 minutes.

2. Uncover skillet; simmer the mixture 45 minutes or until a thermometer reads 180°.

FAST FIX

CHICKEN SAUSAGE & GNOCCHI SKILLET

One night I needed a quick dinner. I combined a handful of fresh veggies with goat cheese, sausage and gnocchi for a satisfying meal. Feel free to mix and match other ingredients to suit your tastes.

—DAHLIA ABRAMS DETROIT, MI

START TO FINISH: 30 MIN.
MAKES: 4 SERVINGS

- 1 package (16 ounces) potato gnocchi
- 1 tablespoon butter
- 1 tablespoon olive oil
- 2 fully cooked Italian chicken sausage links (3 ounces each), sliced
- ½ pound sliced baby portobello mushrooms
- 1 medium onion, finely chopped
- 1 pound fresh asparagus, trimmed and cut into ½-inch pieces
- 2 garlic cloves, minced
- 2 tablespoons white wine or chicken broth
- 2 ounces herbed fresh goat cheese
- 2 tablespoons minced fresh basil or 2 teaspoons dried basil
- 1 tablespoon lemon juice
- ¼ teaspoon salt
- ⅛ teaspoon pepper
  Grated Parmesan cheese

1. Cook the gnocchi according to package directions; drain. Meanwhile, in a large skillet, heat butter and oil over medium-high heat. Add sausage, mushrooms and onion; cook and stir until the sausage is browned and the vegetables are tender. Add the asparagus and garlic; cook and stir 2-3 minutes longer.

2. Stir in wine. Bring to a boil; cook until the liquid is almost evaporated. Add goat cheese, basil, lemon juice, salt and pepper. Stir in gnocchi; heat through. Sprinkle mixture with Parmesan cheese.

CHICKEN SAUSAGE & GNOCCHI SKILLET

SOUTHWEST TURKEY
BULGUR DINNER

SOUTHWEST TURKEY BULGUR DINNER

In the past few years, I've incorporated more whole grains into our diet. Bulgur is one of my favorite grains to use because of its quick cooking time. In addition to being high in fiber and rich in minerals, it has a mild, nutty flavor that my kids enjoy.

MARIA VASSEUR VALENCIA, CA

PREP: 15 MIN. • **COOK:** 30 MIN. • **MAKES:** 4 SERVINGS

- 8 **ounces lean ground turkey**
- 1 **small onion, chopped**
- 1 **garlic clove, minced**
- 1 **can (16 ounces) kidney beans, rinsed and drained**
- 1 **can (14½ ounces) diced tomatoes with mild green chilies**
- 1½ **cups water**
- ½ **cup frozen corn**
- 1 **tablespoon chili powder**
- 1 **teaspoon ground cumin**
- ¼ **teaspoon pepper**
- ⅛ **teaspoon salt**
- 1 **cup bulgur**

TOPPING
- ½ **cup fat-free plain Greek yogurt**
- 1 **tablespoon finely chopped green onion**
- 1 **tablespoon minced fresh cilantro**

1. In a large nonstick skillet coated with cooking spray, cook turkey and onion over medium heat until meat is no longer pink. Add garlic; cook 1 minute longer.

2. Stir in the beans, tomatoes, water, corn, chili powder, cumin, pepper and salt. Bring to a boil. Stir in bulgur. Reduce heat; cover and simmer for 13-18 minutes or until bulgur is tender.

3. Remove from the heat; let stand 5 minutes. Fluff with a fork. Meanwhile, in a small bowl, combine the yogurt, green onion and cilantro. Serve with turkey mixture.

**TRACEY KARST'S
SKILLET PORK CHOPS WITH
APPLES & ONION** *PAGE 131*

Pork, Ham & Sausage

There's always time for bacon, sausages and ham steaks bursting with flavor. Look here for savory pork dishes sure to have mouths watering.

FRESH CORN FETTUCCINE

FAST FIX

FRESH CORN FETTUCCINE

I really love corn so it wasn't much of a leap to figure out that with the help of my food processor, I could turn fresh corn kernels into a best-of-the-season sauce that's ideal over pasta.

—LILY JULOW LAWRENCEVILLE, GA

START TO FINISH: 30 MIN. • **MAKES:** 6 SERVINGS

- 12 **ounces uncooked fettuccine**
- 4 **thick-sliced bacon strips, chopped**
- 4 **cups fresh or frozen corn, thawed**
- 3 **garlic cloves, minced**
- ¼ **teaspoon salt**
- ⅛ **teaspoon pepper**
- ½ **cup grated Parmesan cheese**
- ⅓ **cup blanched almonds**
- ⅓ **cup olive oil**
- 1 **cup thinly sliced fresh basil, divided**

Halved grape tomatoes and additional grated Parmesan cheese, optional

1. Cook fettuccine according to package direction

2. Meanwhile, in a large skillet, cook bacon over medium heat until crisp. Remove with a slotted spoon; drain on paper towels. Discard drippings, reserving 2 teaspoons.

3. Add corn, garlic, salt and pepper to drippings; cook and stir over medium-high heat until corn is tender. Remove ¾ cup corn from pan. Transfer remaining corn to a food processor; add cheese, almonds and oil. Process until blended. Return to skillet; add reserved corn and heat through.

4. Drain fettuccine, reserving ½ cup pasta water. Add pasta, three-fourths of the bacon and ¾ cup basil to corn mixture. Add enough reserved pasta water to reach desired consistency, tossing to coat Sprinkle with the remaining bacon and basil. If desired, top with tomatoes and additional cheese.

AM SLICE WITH PINEAPPLE

husband is so fond of this dish that I often have to uble the recipe. I mix any leftovers with macaroni d cheese and add a can of cheddar cheese soup for uick casserole.

DONNA WARNER TAVARES, FL

ART TO FINISH: 20 MIN. • **MAKES:** 2 SERVINGS

1 can (8¼ ounces) sliced pineapple
1 boneless fully cooked ham slice (6 ounces), cut in half
1 tablespoon butter
½ teaspoons cornstarch
¼ teaspoon ground mustard
3 tablespoons sherry or apple juice

Drain pineapple, reserving juice. Add enough ter to juice to measure ½ cup; set aside. In a ge nonstick skillet, lightly brown the pineapple d ham. Remove and keep warm.

In the same skillet, melt the butter. Whisk in rnstarch and mustard until smooth. Stir in the erry or apple juice and reserved pineapple juice. ing to a boil; cook and stir for 2 minutes or until ickened. Serve with ham and pineapple.

AM SLICE WITH INEAPPLE

PORK AND WAFFLES WITH MAPLE-PEAR TOPPING

PORK AND WAFFLES WITH MAPLE-PEAR TOPPING

Maple syrup and Dijon mustard come through beautifully in these upscale, crowd-pleasing waffles.
—*TASTE OF HOME* TEST KITCHEN

START TO FINISH: 25 MIN. • **MAKES:** 4 SERVINGS

½ cup seasoned bread crumbs
1 teaspoon dried thyme
1 pork tenderloin (1 pound), cut into 12 slices
2 tablespoons olive oil
2 medium pears, thinly sliced
½ cup maple syrup
2 tablespoons Dijon mustard
½ teaspoon salt
8 frozen waffles, toasted
2 tablespoons minced chives

1. In a large resealable plastic bag, combine bread crumbs and thyme. Add the pork, a few pieces at a time, and shake to coat. In a large skillet, cook pork in oil in batches over medium heat for 2-4 minutes on each side or until tender. Remove from the pan and keep warm.
2. Add the pears, syrup, mustard and salt to the skillet; cook and stir for 1-2 minutes or until pears are tender. Serve the pork slices and pear mixture over waffles. Sprinkle with chives.

GRILLED BACON-TOMATO SANDWICHES

My family loves to eat these , and they are so easy to prepare. Fresh basil, tangy Italian dressing and melted cheese blend perfectly in this toasty sandwich.

—**BETTY SNODDY** FRANKLIN, MO

START TO FINISH: 20 MIN.
MAKES: 2 SERVINGS

- 4 slices Italian bread (½ inch thick)
- 4 slices provolone cheese (1 ounce each)
- 4 slices tomato
- 4 bacon strips, cooked and halved
- 2 teaspoons minced fresh basil or ½ teaspoon dried basil
- 2 tablespoons Italian salad dressing

1. Top two slices of bread with a slice of cheese; layer with the tomato, bacon, basil and the remaining cheese. Top with remaining bread. Brush dressing over outsides of sandwiches.
2. In a large skillet over medium heat, toast the sandwiches for 2-3 minutes on each side or until the cheese is melted.

(5) INGREDIENTS FAST FIX

BAVARIAN SAUSAGE SUPPER

My mom, who's a great cook, shared the recipe for this easy skillet meal. Spicy kielbasa makes a flavored noodle-and-sauce mix delicious.

—**PAT FRANKOVICH**
NORTH OLMSTED, OH

START TO FINISH: 20 MIN.
MAKES: 5 SERVINGS

- 2 cups coleslaw mix
- 1 cup thinly sliced carrots
- 2 tablespoons butter
- 2¼ cups water
- ¾ pound smoked kielbasa or Polish sausage, sliced into ¼-inch pieces
- 1 package (4.9 ounces) quick-cooking noodles and sour cream and chive sauce mix
- ½ teaspoon caraway seeds, optional

In a large skillet, saute coleslaw mix and carrots in butter until crisp-tender. Add water; bring to a boil. Stir in the remaining ingredients. Return to a boil. Reduce heat; cover and cook for 8 minutes or until the noodles are tender, stirring occasionally.

GRILLED BACON-TOMATO SANDWICHES

HAM WITH MUSTARD-CREAM SAUCE

This recipe is really too simple to taste so good! It's hard to believe three common ingredients can turn a ham slice into something so special. Microwave some potatoes and open a bag of salad mix for a fuss-free meal.

—LISA NELSON BROKEN ARROW, OK

START TO FINISH: 20 MIN.
MAKES: 4 SERVINGS

- **4 boneless fully cooked ham steaks (about 5 ounces each)**
- **¼ cup water**
- **¼ cup honey mustard**
- **½ cup sour cream**
- **¼ cup thinly sliced green onions**

Place the ham steaks in a large skillet. In a small bowl, combine water and mustard; pour over ham. Bring to a boil. Reduce heat; cover and simmer for 3-4 minutes on each side or until heated through. Remove from the heat; stir in the sour cream and onions.

TOP TIP

Out of sour cream? Plain yogurt can be substituted in equal amounts for sour cream in most skillet dishes and sauces. You may notice that sauces have a slightly thinner consistency, but overall, yogurt makes a great replacement. You can also use yogurt in baked dishes, but avoid the nonfat variety.

HAM WITH MUSTARD-CREAM SAUCE

RHODE ISLAND HOT WIENERS

HODE ISLAND HOT WIENERS

Many Rhode Islanders serve their state's official food with this meat sauce, mustard, onion and a sprinkle of celery salt.

—**KAREN BARROS** BRISTOL, RI

EP: 15 MIN. • **COOK:** 50 MIN. • **MAKES:** 8 SERVINGS

- ⁴ **cup butter, cubed**
- **medium onion, finely chopped**
- **tablespoons Worcestershire sauce**
- **tablespoons paprika**
- **tablespoons chili powder**
- **teaspoons ground cumin**
- **teaspoon ground mustard**
- ⁴ **teaspoon ground cinnamon**
- ² **teaspoon ground allspice**
- **pound ground beef**
- ⁴ **cup water**
- **hot dogs**
- **hot dog buns, split and warmed**
  Toppings: yellow mustard, finely chopped onion and celery salt

In a large skillet, heat butter over medium heat.
d the onion; cook and stir 3-4 minutes or until
der. Stir in the Worcestershire sauce and the
sonings. Add beef; cook 6-8 minutes or until no
ger pink, breaking into crumbles. Stir in water;
ng to a boil. Reduce heat; simmer, uncovered,
minutes.
In a large skillet, cook hot dogs over medium
at 8-10 minutes or until lightly browned, turning
asionally. Serve in buns with meat sauce and
opings as desired.

ST FIX

ALIAN CHOPS WITH PASTA

anks to an Italian makeover, this pork is perfection
pan! Tender chops, red wine, fire-roasted tomatoes
d penne pasta make a complete meal in minutes.

ASTE OF HOME **TEST KITCHEN**

ART TO FINISH: 30 MIN. • **MAKES:** 4 SERVINGS

- ⁴ **bone-in pork loin chops (8 ounces each)**
- ² **teaspoon salt**
- ² **teaspoon pepper**

- 1 **tablespoon olive oil**
- 1 **medium green pepper, chopped**
- 1 **medium red onion, chopped**
- 3 **garlic cloves, minced**
- ⅓ **cup dry red wine or chicken broth**
- 2 **cans (14½ ounces each) fire-roasted diced tomatoes, undrained**
- 1½ **teaspoons Italian seasoning**
  Hot cooked penne pasta
  Shredded Parmesan cheese, optional

1. Sprinkle the pork chops with salt and pepper. Brown chops in oil in a large skillet. Remove and keep warm. Saute green pepper and onion in the same skillet until crisp-tender. Add garlic; cook 1 minute longer.

2. Add wine, stirring to loosen browned bits from pan. Bring to a boil; cook until liquid is almost evaporated. Add tomatoes and Italian seasoning. Cook and stir for 2-3 minutes or until the sauce is slightly thickened.

3. Return chops to the skillet. Cover and simmer for 3-5 minutes or until a meat thermometer reads 145°. Let stand for 5 minutes before serving. Serve with pasta. Sprinkle with cheese if desired.

PARMESAN PORK CUTLETS

As it cooks, the aroma of this dinner always has my kids running to the table. The easy-to-make cutlets are truly a family favorite with everyone at my home.

—**JULIE AHERN** WAUKEGAN, IL

PREP: 25 MIN. • **COOK:** 15 MIN.
MAKES: 4 SERVINGS

- 1 **pork tenderloin (1 pound)**
- ⅓ **cup all-purpose flour**
- 2 **large eggs, lightly beaten**
- 1 **cup dry bread crumbs**
- ¼ **cup grated Parmesan cheese**
- 1 **teaspoon salt**
- ¼ **cup olive oil**
  Lemon wedges

1. Cut pork diagonally into eight slices; pound each to ¼-in. thickness. Place flour and eggs in separate shallow bowls. In another shallow bowl, combine the bread crumbs, cheese and salt. Dip pork in the flour, eggs, then bread crumb mixture.
2. In a large skillet, cook pork in oil in batches over medium heat for 2-3 minutes on each side or until crisp and the meat juices run clear. Remove and keep warm. Serve with lemon wedges.

FAST FIX

APRICOT PORK MEDALLIONS

There's nothing we love more than a great pork dish for supper, and here's a recipe that's right up there with the best of them. The apricot preserves give the pork the right amount of sweetness without being overwhelming.

—**CRYSTAL JO BRUNS** ILIFF, CO

START TO FINISH: 20 MIN.
MAKES: 4 SERVINGS

- 1 **pork tenderloin (1 pound), cut into eight slices**
- 1 **tablespoon plus 1 teaspoon butter, divided**
- ½ **cup apricot preserves**
- 2 **green onions, sliced**
- 1 **tablespoon cider vinegar**
- ¼ **teaspoon ground mustard**

1. Pound pork slices with a me[at] mallet to ½-in. thickness. In a large skillet, heat 1 tablespoon butter over medium heat. Brow[n] pork on each side. Remove por[k] from pan, reserving drippings.
2. Add preserves, green onion[s,] vinegar, mustard and remainin[g] butter to pan; bring just to a bo[il,] stirring to loosen browned bits from pan. Reduce heat; simme[r,] covered, for 3-4 minutes to allo[w] flavors to blend.
3. Return pork to the pan; coo[k] until the pork is tender. Let sta[nd] 5 minutes before serving.

APRICOT PORK MEDALLIONS

PRETTY PENNE HAM SKILLET

FAST FIX ▶

PRETTY PENNE HAM SKILLET

I'm a busy nurse, so fast meals are a must. This stovetop pasta is a tasty change of pace from casseroles.

—**KATHY STEPHAN** WEST SENECA, NY

START TO FINISH: 30 MIN.
MAKES: 6 SERVINGS

- 1 package (16 ounces) penne pasta
- ¼ cup olive oil
- 3 tablespoons butter
- 3 cups cubed fully cooked ham
- 1 large sweet red pepper, finely chopped
- 1 medium onion, chopped
- 2 garlic cloves, minced
- ¼ cup minced fresh parsley
- 1½ teaspoons minced fresh basil or ½ teaspoon dried basil
- 1½ teaspoons minced fresh oregano or ½ teaspoon dried oregano
- 1 can (14½ ounces) chicken broth
- 1 tablespoon lemon juice
- ½ cup shredded Parmesan cheese

1. Cook pasta according to the package directions; drain. Meanwhile, in a large skillet, heat oil and butter over medium-high heat. Add ham, red pepper and onion; cook and stir 4-6 minutes or until the ham is browned and vegetables are tender. Add garlic and herbs; cook the mixture for 1-2 minutes longer.

2. Stir in the broth and the lemon juice. Bring to a boil. Reduce heat; simmer, uncovered, for 10-15 minutes or until liquid is reduced by half. Add the pasta; toss to combine. Sprinkle with the cheese.

**QUICK HOMEMADE
SWEET-AND-SOUR PORK**

QUICK HOMEMADE
SWEET-AND-SOUR PORK

I stir up a fast sweet-and-sour sauce to enhance the colorful combination of tender pork, crunchy vegetables and tangy pineapple. Serve it with rice, chow mein noodles or both!

—**ELEANOR DUNBAR** PEORIA, IL

PREP: 25 MIN. + MARINATING • **COOK:** 10 MIN.
MAKES: 4 SERVINGS

- ⅔ **cup packed brown sugar**
- ⅔ **cup cider vinegar**
- ⅔ **cup ketchup**
- 2 **teaspoons reduced-sodium soy sauce**
- 1 **pound boneless pork loin, cut into 1-inch cubes**
- 1 **tablespoon canola oil**
- 1 **medium onion, cut into chunks**
- 2 **medium carrots, sliced**
- 1 **medium green pepper, cut into 1-inch pieces**
- ¼ **teaspoon ground ginger**
- ½ **teaspoon minced garlic**
- 1 **can (8 ounces) pineapple chunks, drained**
  Hot cooked rice, optional

1. In a small bowl, combine the brown sugar, vinegar, ketchup, and soy sauce. Pour half into a large resealable plastic bag; add pork. Seal bag and turn to coat; refrigerate for 30 minutes. Set remaining marinade aside.

2. Drain and discard marinade from the pork. In a large skillet, cook pork in oil over medium heat for 2-3 minutes on all sides or until the meat is lightly browned; drain. Add the onion, carrots, green pepper, and ginger. Add garlic; cook 1 minute longer.

3. Cover and simmer for 6-8 minutes or until pork is tender. Add reserved marinade. Bring to a boil; cook for 1 minute or until heated through. Stir in pineapple. Serve with rice if desired.

TOP TIP

Pork loins are tender cuts of meat, as are pork chops. Tender cuts are ideal for pan-frying, stir-frying and other skillet-based cooking methods. They don't need moist-heat cooking like tougher cuts such as pork shoulder do.

ISTRO HERB-RUBBED
ORK TENDERLOIN

A mouthwatering rub featuring fresh herbs—tarragon, thyme and rosemary—releases rich, bold flavor as this pork entree sizzles. Served with a delectable thickened sauce, it's crazy good!

NAYLET LAROCHELLE MIAMI, FL

EP: 20 MIN. + MARINATING • **COOK:** 20 MIN.
AKES: 4 SERVINGS

- 3 tablespoons minced fresh tarragon
- 2 tablespoons minced fresh thyme
- 1 tablespoon minced fresh rosemary
- 2 garlic cloves, minced
- 2 teaspoons smoked paprika
- 1 teaspoon kosher salt
- ¼ teaspoon coarsely ground pepper
- 6 tablespoons olive oil, divided
- 1 pork tenderloin (1 pound), cut into 12 slices
- 1 tablespoon all-purpose flour
- ½ cup beef broth
- 2 tablespoons minced fresh chives

1. In a small bowl, combine tarragon, thyme, rosemary, garlic, paprika, salt, pepper and 4 tablespoons oil. Flatten the pork slices to ¼-in. thickness. Rub slices with herb mixture; cover and refrigerate 15 minutes.

2. In a large skillet, cook pork in remaining oil in batches over medium-high heat 1-2 minutes on each side or until browned. Remove the pork and keep warm.

3. Stir the flour into pan until blended; gradually add broth. Bring to a boil; cook and stir 2 minutes or until thickened. Serve with pork and sprinkle with chives.

ISTRO HERB-RUBBED
ORK TENDERLOIN

SMOKY SAUSAGE & PEPPER SKILLET

My family loves this combination of sausage, green peppers and onions. Everyone asks for it for their birthday meal!

—**CELINDA KULP** HUMMELSTOWN, PA

START TO FINISH: 30 MIN.
MAKES: 4 SERVINGS

SMOKY SAUSAGE
& PEPPER SKILLE

- 1 pound smoked sausage, sliced
- 2 large green peppers, thinly sliced
- 1 medium onion, thinly sliced
- 1 garlic clove, minced
- 4 teaspoons cornstarch
- 2 cups whole milk
- ¼ cup minced fresh parsley
- ¾ teaspoon dried marjoram
- ½ teaspoon pepper
- ½ cup shredded Parmesan cheese
  Hot cooked rice or pasta

1. In a large skillet, brown the sausage over medium heat. Remove with a slotted spoon; drain on paper towels.

2. Add green peppers and onion to same skillet; cook and stir until vegetables are crisp-tender. Add garlic; cook 1 minute longer. In a small bowl, mix cornstarch, milk, parsley, marjoram and pepper until blended; stir into pan. Bring to a boil; cook and stir 2 minutes or until sauce is thickened.

3. Return sausage to pan; heat through. Stir in the cheese until blended. Serve with rice.

BACON-SWISS PORK CHOPS

SKILLET PORK CHOPS WITH APPLES & ONION

Simple recipes that hit the table fast are always lifesavers. I serve skillet pork chops with veggies and sometimes, when my husband lobbies for it, cornbread stuffing.

—**TRACEY KARST** PONDERAY, ID

START TO FINISH: 20 MIN.
MAKES: 4 SERVINGS

- 4 **boneless pork loin chops (6 ounces each)**
- 3 **medium apples, cut into wedges**
- 1 **large onion, cut into thin wedges**
- ¼ **cup water**
- ⅓ **cup balsamic vinaigrette**
- ½ **teaspoon salt**
- ¼ **teaspoon pepper**

1. Place a large nonstick skillet over medium heat; brown pork chops on both sides, about 4 minutes. Remove from pan.
2. In same skillet, combine apples, onion and water. Place pork chops over apple mixture; drizzle chops with vinaigrette. Sprinkle with salt and pepper. Reduce heat; simmer, covered, 3-5 minutes or until a meat thermometer inserted in the chops reads 145°.

ACON-SWISS ORK CHOPS

always looking for quick and easy cipes that are impressive enough serve company. These pork ops smothered in bacon and viss cheese certainly deliver.

KEITH MILLER FORT GRATIOT, MI

ART TO FINISH: 25 MIN.
AKES: 4 SERVINGS

- 2 **bacon strips, chopped**
- 1 **medium onion, chopped**
- 4 **boneless pork loin chops (4 ounces each)**
- ½ **teaspoon garlic powder**
- ¼ **teaspoon salt**
- 2 **slices reduced-fat Swiss cheese, halved**

1. In a nonstick skillet coated with cooking spray, cook bacon and onion over medium heat until the bacon is crisp, stirring occasionally. Drain on paper towels; discard drippings.
2. Sprinkle the pork chops with garlic powder and salt. Add pork chops to the same pan; cook over medium heat for 3-4 minutes on each side or until a thermometer reads 145°. Top the pork with the bacon mixture and cheese. Cook, covered, on low heat 1-2 minutes or until the cheese is melted. Let stand 5 minutes before serving.

FAST FIX

BLT SKILLET

This speedy weeknight meal with chunks of bacon and tomato is reminiscent of a BLT. Whole wheat linguine gives the skillet dish extra flavor and texture.

—EDRIE O'BRIEN DENVER, CO

START TO FINISH: 25 MIN. • **MAKES:** 2 SERVINGS

- 4 ounces uncooked whole wheat linguine
- 4 bacon strips, cut into 1½-inch pieces
- 1 plum tomato, cut into 1-inch pieces
- 1 garlic clove, minced
- 1½ teaspoons lemon juice
- ¼ teaspoon salt
- ¼ teaspoon pepper
- 2 tablespoons grated Parmesan cheese
- 1 tablespoon minced fresh parsley

1. Cook linguine according to package directions. Meanwhile, in a large skillet, cook the bacon over medium heat until crisp. Remove to paper towels; drain, reserving 1 teaspoon drippings.

2. In the drippings, saute the tomato and garlic for 1-2 minutes or until heated through. Stir in the bacon, lemon juice, salt and pepper.

3. Drain the linguine; add to the skillet. Sprinkle with cheese and parsley; toss to coat.

FAST FIX

MUFFULETTA PASTA

A friend gave me this recipe when she learned that I love muffuletta sandwiches. Very rich and filling, it's an easy skillet supper that goes together quickly on a busy night. Serve it with cheesy garlic bread.

—JAN HOLLINGSWORTH HOUSTON, MS

START TO FINISH: 25 MIN. • **MAKES:** 8 SERVINGS

- 1 package (16 ounces) bow tie pasta
- 1 bunch green onions, chopped
- 2 teaspoons plus ¼ cup butter, divided
- 1 tablespoon minced garlic
- 1 package (16 ounces) cubed fully cooked ham
- 1 jar (12.36 ounces) tapenade or ripe olive bruschetta topping, drained
- 1 package (3½ ounces) sliced pepperoni
- 1 cup heavy whipping cream
- 2 cups (8 ounces) shredded Italian cheese blend

1. Cook pasta according to package directions. Meanwhile, in a large skillet, saute the onions in 2 teaspoons butter until tender. Add garlic; cook for 1 minute longer. Add the ham, tapenade and pepperoni; saute 2 minutes longer.

2. Cube remaining butter; stir butter and cream into the skillet. Bring to a boil over medium heat. Reduce heat; simmer, uncovered, for 3 minutes.

3. Drain pasta; toss with ham mixture. Sprinkle with cheese.

MUFFULETTA PASTA

TORTELLINI AND HAM

A couple of convenience items are the basis for a 25-minute meal. It's sure to become a colorful staple when you need a great last-minute weeknight supper.

—TASTE OF HOME TEST KITCHEN

START TO FINISH: 25 MIN.
MAKES: 4 SERVINGS

- 1 **package (19 ounces) frozen cheese tortellini**
- 1 **cup frozen pepper strips, thawed**
- 3 **tablespoons butter**
- 1¼ **cups cubed fully cooked ham**
- 1 **teaspoon minced garlic**
- 1½ **teaspoons cornstarch**
- ½ **cup chicken broth**
- 1 **teaspoon dried basil**
- ½ **teaspoon dried parsley flakes**
- ¼ **teaspoon pepper**
- 4 **tablespoons grated Parmesan cheese, divided**

Cook tortellini according to package directions. Meanwhile, in a large skillet, saute the pepper strips in the butter until crisp-tender. Add the ham and garlic; saute 1 minute longer.

Combine the cornstarch, broth, basil, parsley and pepper; stir into pepper mixture. Bring to a boil; cook and stir mixture for 2 minutes or until thickened.

Add 2 tablespoons cheese. Drain the tortellini; toss with the ham mixture. Sprinkle with the remaining cheese.

TORTELLINI AND HAM

MAPLE-DIJON SPROUTS & SAUSAGE

You can substitute any vegetables that you have on hand or that you prefer in this recipe. Just make sure to test them to be certain they are cooked through.

—*TASTE OF HOME* TEST KITCHEN

START TO FINISH: 30 MIN.
MAKES: 4 SERVINGS

- 4 **Italian sausage links, casings removed**
- 1 **package (16 ounces) frozen Brussels sprouts**
- ½ **pound sliced fresh mushrooms**
- 1 **cup fresh baby carrots, halved**
- 1 **medium onion, chopped**
- 2 **tablespoons maple syrup**
- 2 **tablespoons Dijon mustard**
- ½ **teaspoon dried sage leaves**
- ½ **teaspoon pepper**
- 1 **package (5.8 ounces) roasted garlic and olive oil couscous**
- ¼ **cup grated Parmesan cheese**

1. Cook sausage in a large skillet until no longer pink; drain. Add Brussels sprouts, mushrooms, carrots and onion; cook until the vegetables are crisp-tender. Add the syrup, mustard, sage and pepper; cover and cook for 4-6 minutes longer or until Brussels sprouts are tender.

2. Meanwhile, prepare couscous according to package directions. Serve with the sausage mixture and sprinkle with cheese.

CONFETTI KIELBASA SKILLET

Here's one of my husband's favorite dishes. When corn is in season, I substitute fresh kernels for frozen ones. Add a dash of cayenne pepper if you like a little heat.

—**SHEILA GOMEZ** SHAWNEE, KS

START TO FINISH: 30 MIN.
MAKES: 4 SERVINGS

- 1 **tablespoon canola oil**
- 7 **ounces smoked turkey kielbasa, cut into ¼-inch slices**
- 1 **medium onion, halved and sliced**
- ½ **cup sliced baby portobello mushrooms**
- 2 **garlic cloves, minced**
- ½ **cup reduced-sodium chicken broth**
- ¾ **teaspoon garlic and herb seasoning blend**
- 1 **can (15 ounces) no-salt-added black beans, rinsed and drained**
- 1 **package (8.8 ounces) ready-to-serve brown rice**
- 1 **cup frozen corn**
- ½ **cup chopped roasted sweet red peppers**
- 4 **teaspoons minced fresh cilantro**

1. In a large skillet, heat the oil over medium-high heat. Add the kielbasa, onion and mushroom; cook and stir for 4-6 minutes or until vegetables are tender. Add garlic; cook 1 minute longer.

2. Add the broth and seasoning blend, stirring to loosen browned bits from pan. Bring to a boil; cook 2-3 minutes or until liquid is almost evaporated. Stir in the remaining ingredients; heat the mixture through.

CONFETTI KIELBASA SKILLET

BALSAMIC PORK SCALLOPINE

BALSAMIC PORK SCALLOPINE

I developed a delightful dish by tweaking my veal scallopine recipe. I found that thinly sliced pork is an economical alternative to veal and a tasty substitute!

—**MARY COKENOUR** MONTICELLO, UT

PREP: 25 MIN. • **COOK:** 30 MIN.
MAKES: 12 SERVINGS

- 3 **pounds pork sirloin cutlets**
- 1½ **cups all-purpose flour**
- ½ **cup olive oil**
- 2 **tablespoons butter**
- 1 **medium onion, chopped**
- ½ **cup chopped roasted sweet red peppers**
- 6 **garlic cloves, minced**
- 1 **can (14½ ounces) reduced-sodium chicken broth**
- ½ **cup minced fresh basil or 2 tablespoons dried basil**
- ½ **cup balsamic vinegar**
- ½ **teaspoon pepper**

NOODLES
- 1 **package (16 ounces) egg noodles**
- ½ **cup half-and-half cream**
- ¼ **cup grated Romano cheese**
- ¼ **cup butter, cubed**
- ½ **teaspoon pepper**
- ¼ **teaspoon garlic powder**

1. Dredge pork cutlets in flour. Heat the oil and butter in a large skillet over medium-high heat; add pork and brown in batches. Set aside.

2. Add onion and red peppers to the pan; saute until onion is tender. Add garlic; cook 1 minute longer. Add broth, basil, vinegar and pepper. Return pork to the pan, layering if necessary.

3. Cover and cook over low heat for 15-20 minutes or until meat is tender.

4. Meanwhile, in a Dutch oven, cook noodles according to the package directions. Drain; stir in the cream, cheese, butter, pepper and garlic powder. Serve with the pork cutlets.

(5)INGREDIENTS | FAST FIX

PORK TENDERLOIN WITH ZESTY ITALIAN SAUCE

We like to serve this entree with garlic mashed potatoes and fresh green beans or corn on the cob.

—**JOE VINCE** PORT HURON, MI

START TO FINISH: 25 MIN.
MAKES: 4 SERVINGS

- 1 **pork tenderloin (1 pound), cut into 8 slices**
- ½ **teaspoon salt**
- ¼ **teaspoon pepper**
- 1 **tablespoon canola oil**
- ½ **cup white wine or chicken broth**
- ½ **cup zesty Italian salad dressing**
- 1 **tablespoon butter**

1. Sprinkle pork with salt and pepper. In a large skillet, heat oil over medium-high heat. Brown pork, about 2 minutes on each side; remove from the pan.

2. Add wine to pan, stirring to loosen browned bits from the bottom. Bring to a boil; cook until liquid is reduced by about half. Stir in the dressing. Reduce the heat; simmer, uncovered, for 1-2 minutes or until mixture is slightly thickened.

3. Return pork to pan; simmer, covered, for 3-5 minutes or until a thermometer inserted in meat reads 145°. Stir in the butter. Let pork rest for 5 minutes before serving with sauce.

FAST FIX

PROSCIUTTO PASTA TOSS

I love quick, simple pasta dishes, and here's one of my favorites. I fix a tossed green salad while the pasta cooks and serve up a lovely light supper in minutes. It's great for a casual spring or summer meal.

—LAURA MURPHY-OGDEN
CHARLOTTE, NC

START TO FINISH: 20 MIN.
MAKES: 6 SERVINGS

- 1 **package (16 ounces) linguine**
- ½ **cup frozen peas**
- 2 **tablespoons minced garlic**
- 1 **tablespoon Italian seasoning**
- 1 **teaspoon pepper**
- ¼ **cup olive oil**
- ½ **pound thinly sliced prosciutto or deli ham, chopped**
- ¼ **cup shredded Parmesan cheese**

1. Cook linguine according to package directions, adding peas during the last 3 minutes.
2. In a large skillet, saute the garlic, Italian seasoning and pepper in oil for 1 minute or until garlic is tender. Stir in prosciutto. Drain linguine; add to the skillet and toss to coat. Sprinkle with cheese.

PROSCIUTTO PASTA TOSS

SAUCY PORK CHOP SKILLET

Skillet pork chops make easy comfort food. We have them with a salad and fruit. If you've c fresh green beans or steamed occoli for sides, go for it.

DONNA ROBERTS MANHATTAN, KS

START TO FINISH: 30 MIN.
MAKES: 6 SERVINGS

- 3 cups uncooked instant brown rice
- 2 teaspoons canola oil
- 6 boneless pork loin chops (6 ounces each)
- 1 small onion, sliced
- 1 cup canned diced tomatoes
- 1 cup reduced-sodium beef broth
- 1 tablespoon dried parsley flakes
- ½ teaspoon salt
- ¼ teaspoon pepper
- ⅛ teaspoon dried basil
- ⅛ teaspoon dried oregano
- 2 tablespoons all-purpose flour
- ½ cup water

1. Cook rice according to the package directions. Meanwhile, in a large nonstick skillet coated with cooking spray, heat oil over medium-high heat. Brown pork chops on both sides; remove from pan.

2. Add onion to the drippings; cook and stir until tender. Stir in the tomatoes, broth, parsley and seasonings; bring to a boil.

Return pork to pan. Reduce heat; simmer, covered, 6-8 minutes or until a thermometer inserted in pork reads 145°.

3. Remove pork to a serving plate; keep warm. In a small bowl, mix flour and water until smooth; stir into sauce. Bring to a boil, stirring constantly; cook and stir 2 minutes or until thickened. Spoon over pork; serve with rice.

SPAGHETTI SKILLET

No matter who is at your table, this sausage-and-beef supper can't miss. I like the recipe's step-saver: you don't have to precook the pasta before adding it to the skillet.

—MARGERY BRYAN MOSES LAKE, WA

START TO FINISH: 25 MIN.
MAKES: 4-6 SERVINGS

- ½ pound ground beef
- ¼ pound bulk Italian sausage
- 1 can (15 ounces) tomato sauce
- 1 can (14½ ounces) stewed tomatoes
- 1 cup water
- 1 can (4 ounces) mushroom stems and pieces, drained
- 2 celery ribs, sliced
- 4 ounces uncooked spaghetti, broken in half
- ¼ teaspoon dried oregano
  Salt and pepper to taste

In a large skillet, cook beef and sausage over medium heat until no longer pink; drain. Add the remaining ingredients. Bring to a boil. Reduce the heat; cover and simmer 14-16 minutes or until the spaghetti is tender.

SAUCY PORK CHOP SKILLET

WAFFLED MONTE CRISTOS

WAFFLED MONTE CRISTOS

My husband and I enjoy Monte Cristos so much that I created a non-fried version to cut down on the fat. The unique addition of orange peel and pecans makes these beautiful sandwiches absolutely delicious!

—**MARY SHIVERS** ADA, OK

START TO FINISH: 25 MIN. • **MAKES:** 2 SERVINGS

- 1 large egg
- ¼ cup 2% milk
- 1 teaspoon sugar
- 1 teaspoon grated orange peel
- 4 slices white bread
- 2 tablespoons finely chopped pecans
- 4 slices process American cheese (⅔ ounce each)
- 2 thin slices deli turkey (½ ounce each)
- 2 slices Swiss cheese (¾ ounce each)
- 2 thin slices deli ham (½ ounce each)
- 2 teaspoons butter
- 2 teaspoons confectioners' sugar
- ¼ cup seedless raspberry jam

1. In a shallow bowl, combine the egg, milk, sugar and orange peel. Dip bread into egg mixture. Place on a preheated waffle iron; sprinkle each slice of bread with pecans. Bake according to waffle iron manufacturer's directions until golden brown.

2. Place an American cheese slice on two bread slices; layer with turkey, Swiss cheese, ham and remaining American cheese. Top with remaining bread; butter outsides of sandwiches.

3. Toast sandwiches in a skillet for 1-2 minutes on each side or until the cheese is melted. Dust with confectioners' sugar; serve with jam.

DID YOU KNOW?

While there are many variations, Monte Cristo sandwiches generally involve ham, turkey or chicken, and cheese. The bread is usually dipped in beaten eggs yolks before the sandwich is toasted Many varieties call for the entire sandwich to be dipped in a batter before deep frying. Monte Cristos are often topped with confectioners' sugar and served with jam or honey.

VEN-BARBECUED ORK CHOPS

mother has made this recipe for years, and now
epare it for my family. The chops are delicious with
lloped potatoes and home-baked bread.

ERESA KING WHITTIER, CA

EP: 10 MIN. • **BAKE:** 1 HOUR • **MAKES:** 6-8 SERVINGS

- to 8 loin or rib pork chops (¾ inch thick)
- tablespoon Worcestershire sauce
- tablespoons vinegar
- teaspoons brown sugar
- teaspoon pepper
- teaspoon chili powder
- teaspoon paprika
- cup ketchup
- cup hot water

ice chops in a heavy cast-iron skillet. Combine
remaining ingredients; pour over chops. Bake,
covered, at 375° for 1 hour.

ARMHOUSE PORK ND APPLE PIE

e always loved pork and apples together, and this
cipe combines them nicely to create a comforting
ain dish. It calls for a bit of preparation, but my family
d I agree that the wonderful flavor makes it well
orth the extra effort.

SUZANNE STROCSHER BOTHELL, WA

EP: 70 MIN. • **BAKE:** 2 HOURS • **MAKES:** 10 SERVINGS

- 1 pound sliced bacon, cut into 2-inch pieces
- 3 medium onions, chopped
- 3 pounds boneless pork, cut into 1-inch cubes
- ¾ cup all-purpose flour
  Canola oil, optional
- 3 medium tart apples, peeled and chopped
- 1 teaspoon rubbed sage
- ½ teaspoon ground nutmeg
- 1 teaspoon salt
- ¼ teaspoon pepper
- 1 cup apple cider
- ½ cup water
- 4 medium potatoes, peeled and cubed
- ½ cup milk
- 5 tablespoons butter, divided

Additional salt and pepper
Minced fresh parsley, optional

1. Cook bacon in an ovenproof 12-in. skillet until
crisp. Remove with a slotted spoon to paper towels
to drain. In drippings, saute onions until tender;
remove with slotted spoon and set aside. Dust the
pork lightly with flour. Brown a third at a time in
drippings, adding oil if needed. Remove from
the heat and drain.

2. To the pork, add the bacon, onions, apples, sage,
nutmeg, salt and pepper. Stir in cider and water.
Cover and bake at 325° for 2 hours or until pork
is tender.

3. Place potatoes in a large saucepan and cover
with water. Bring to a boil. Reduce the heat; cover
and cook for 10-15 minutes or until tender.

4. Drain and mash with milk and 3 tablespoons
butter. Add salt and pepper to taste. Remove the
skillet from the oven and spread potatoes over
pork mixture.

5. Melt remaining butter; brush over potatoes.
Broil 6 in. from the heat for 5 minutes or until
topping is browned. Sprinkle dish with parsley
if desired.

**FARMHOUSE PORK
AND APPLE PIE**

2. Reduce heat to low; add the eggs to the skillet. Cook and stir until egg mixture coats a metal spoon and reaches 160° (mixture will look like a soft frothy egg). Drain spaghetti and place in a bowl. Add eggs; toss to coat. Add the vegetable mixture, cheese, bacon, basil, oregano, salt and pepper; toss gently to coat.

FAST FIX

PUMPKIN & SAUSAGE PENNE

I once made this dish for my Italian father-in-law, who swears he'll eat pasta only with red sauce. He loved it!
—**KAREN CAMBIOTTI** STROUDSBURG, PA

START TO FINISH: 30 MIN. • **MAKES:** 2 SERVINGS

- ¾ **cup uncooked penne pasta**
- 2 **Italian sausage links, casings removed**
- ½ **cup chopped sweet onion**
- 1 **garlic clove, minced**
- 1 **teaspoon olive oil**
- ⅓ **cup white wine or chicken broth**
- 1 **bay leaf**
- ¾ **cup chicken broth**
- ⅓ **cup canned pumpkin**
- 3 **teaspoons minced fresh sage, divided**
- ⅛ **teaspoon each salt, pepper and ground cinnamon**
  Dash ground nutmeg
- 3 **tablespoons half-and-half cream**
- 2 **tablespoons shredded Romano cheese**

1. Cook pasta according to package directions. Meanwhile, in a large skillet, cook sausage over medium heat until no longer pink, breaking into crumbles. Remove with a slotted spoon; drain on paper towels. Discard drippings, reserving 1 teaspoon.
2. Cook and stir onion and garlic in oil and the reserved drippings over medium-high heat until tender. Add wine and bay leaf. Bring to a boil; cook until liquid is reduced by half. Stir in broth, pumpkin, 1½ teaspoons sage and the remaining seasonings; cook 1 minute longer. Add the cream and sausage; heat through. Remove bay leaf.
3. Drain pasta; transfer to a large bowl. Add the sausage mixture; toss to coat. Sprinkle with cheese and remaining sage.

SUMMER CARBONARA

Basil and bacon make best summer buds in a smoky-sweet pasta dish. I pair it with a simple spring mix salad with balsamic dressing and a good Chardonnay wine or a glass of cold iced tea.
—**CATHY DUDDERAR** LEXINGTON, KY

PREP: 25 MIN. • **COOK:** 10 MIN. • **MAKES:** 6 SERVINGS

- 1 **package (16 ounces) spaghetti**
- 1 **large sweet onion, finely chopped**
- 1 **medium yellow summer squash, finely chopped**
- 1 **medium zucchini, finely chopped**
- 2 **garlic cloves, minced**
- 2 **tablespoons olive oil**
- 4 **plum tomatoes, seeded and chopped**
- 2 **large eggs, beaten**
- 1 **cup grated Parmesan cheese**
- 12 **bacon strips, cooked and crumbled**
- ¼ **cup fresh basil leaves, thinly sliced**
- 1 **teaspoon minced fresh oregano or ½ teaspoon dried oregano**
- ½ **teaspoon salt**
- ¼ **teaspoon pepper**

1. Cook spaghetti according to package directions. Meanwhile, in a large skillet, saute the onion, squash, zucchini and garlic in oil until tender. Add tomatoes; heat through. Remove and keep warm.

SKILLET PORK CHOPS WITH ZUCCHINI

We live on a small farm where we're always blessed with zucchini from our garden. I try lots of different zucchini recipes, and this one is a family favorite.

—DIANE BANASZAK WEST BEND, WI

PREP: 15 MIN. • **COOK:** 35 MIN.
MAKES: 6 SERVINGS

- 3 tablespoons all-purpose flour
- 2 tablespoons plus ¼ cup grated Parmesan cheese, divided
- 1½ teaspoons salt
- ½ teaspoon dill weed
- ¼ teaspoon pepper
- 6 boneless pork loin chops (4 ounces each)
- 1 tablespoon canola oil
- 2 medium onions, sliced
- ¼ cup warm water
- 3 medium zucchini (about 1 pound), sliced
- ½ teaspoon paprika

In a shallow dish, combine the flour, 2 tablespoons cheese, salt, dill and pepper. Dip pork chops in the flour mixture to coat both sides; shake off excess.

In a large skillet, brown chops on both sides in oil. Top with the onions; add water. Bring to a boil. Reduce heat; cover and simmer for 15 minutes.

Place the zucchini over the onions. Sprinkle the remaining cheese over zucchini. Sprinkle with paprika. Cover and simmer for 10-15 minutes or until the vegetables are tender and a thermometer inserted in pork reads 145°. Let stand 5 minutes.

SKILLET PORK CHOPS WITH ZUCCHINI

**TRISHA KRUSE'S PINEAPPLE
SHRIMP STIR-FRY**
PAGE 150

Fish & Seafood

Need a few change-of-pace meal ideas?
Look no further! These stovetop dishes put
a fresh new spin on dinnertime routines.

FAST FIX

TUNA CAKES WITH MUSTARD MAYO

These patties take the cake! The recipe starts off simple with canned tuna. If you'd like, add more kick to the creamy mustard-mayo sauce with prepared horseradish.

—*TASTE OF HOME* TEST KITCHEN

START TO FINISH: 30 MIN.
MAKES: 4 SERVINGS

- 2 **large eggs**
- 3 **tablespoons minced fresh parsley, divided**
- ½ **teaspoon seafood seasoning**
- 2 **cans (5 ounces each) light water-packed tuna, drained and flaked**
- ½ **cup seasoned bread crumbs**
- ½ **cup shredded carrots**
- 2 **tablespoons butter, divided**
- 1 **package (12 ounces) frozen peas**
- ¼ **teaspoon pepper**
- ⅓ **cup mayonnaise**
- 1 **tablespoon Dijon mustard**
- 1 **teaspoon 2% milk**

1. In a large bowl, combine the eggs, 2 tablespoons parsley and seafood seasoning. Stir in the tuna, bread crumbs and carrot. Shape into eight patties.

2. In a large skillet, brown patties in 1 tablespoon butter for 3-4 minutes on each side or until golden brown.

3. Meanwhile, microwave peas according to package directions. Stir in the pepper and remaining butter and parsley. Combine the mayonnaise, mustard and milk. Serve with tuna cakes and peas.

TUNA CAKES WITH MUSTARD MAYO

ETA SHRIMP KILLET

husband and I tried a dish similar
this one on our honeymoon in
eece. I re-created the flavors in
s recipe when we got home.
hen I make it now, it brings back
ppy memories.

SONALI RUDER NEW YORK, NY

ART TO FINISH: 30 MIN.
AKES: 4 SERVINGS

- 1 tablespoon olive oil
- 1 medium onion, finely chopped
- 3 garlic cloves, minced
- 1 teaspoon dried oregano
- ½ teaspoon pepper
- ¼ teaspoon salt
- 2 cans (14½ ounces each) diced tomatoes, undrained
- ¾ cup white wine, optional
- 1 pound uncooked medium shrimp, peeled and deveined
- 2 tablespoons minced fresh parsley
- ¾ cup crumbled feta cheese

1. In a large nonstick skillet, heat oil over medium-high heat. Add onion; cook and stir 4-6 minutes or until tender. Add garlic and seasonings; cook 1 minute longer. Stir in tomatoes and, if desired, wine. Bring to a boil. Reduce the heat; simmer, uncovered, for 5-7 minutes or until the sauce is slightly thickened.
2. Add the shrimp and parsley; cook 5-6 minutes or until shrimp turn pink, stirring occasionally. Remove from heat; sprinkle with cheese. Let stand, covered, until cheese is softened.

FETA SHRIMP
SKILLET

LEMON-PEPPER TILAPIA WITH MUSHROOMS

Lemon-pepper seasoning adds a
burst of flavor to an otherwise
mild-tasting fish. This is one meal
where nobody complains about
leftovers—because there are none!

—DONNA MCDONALD
LAKE ELSINORE, CA

START TO FINISH: 25 MIN.
MAKES: 4 SERVINGS

- 2 tablespoons butter
- ½ pound sliced fresh mushrooms
- ¾ teaspoon lemon-pepper seasoning, divided
- 3 garlic cloves, minced
- 4 tilapia fillets (6 ounces each)
- ¼ teaspoon paprika
- ⅛ teaspoon cayenne pepper
- 1 medium tomato, chopped
- 3 green onions, thinly sliced

1. In a 12-in. skillet, heat the butter over medium heat. Add mushrooms and ¼ teaspoon lemon pepper; cook and stir 3-5 minutes or until mushrooms are tender. Add the garlic; cook 30 seconds longer.
2. Place fillets over mushrooms; sprinkle with paprika, cayenne and remaining lemon pepper. Cook, covered, 5-7 minutes or until fish just begins to flake easily with a fork. Top with tomato and green onions.

SNAPPER WITH ZUCCHINI
& MUSHROOM

SNAPPER WITH ZUCCHINI & MUSHROOMS

Try my snapper recipe if you're looking for a light meal that's full of fresh veggies. Colorful tomatoes, mushrooms and zucchini make a surprisingly filling topping. It's yummy with pork, too.
—**LISA GLOGOW** ALISO VIEJO, CA

PREP: 25 MIN. • **COOK:** 10 MIN. • **MAKES:** 4 SERVINGS

- 3 **cups diced zucchini**
- 2 **cups halved fresh mushrooms**
- ¾ **cup chopped sweet onion**
- 2 **tablespoons olive oil, divided**
- 3 **garlic cloves, minced**
- 1 **can (14½ ounces) diced tomatoes, undrained**
- 2 **teaspoons minced fresh basil or ½ teaspoon dried basil**
- 2 **teaspoons minced fresh oregano or ½ teaspoon dried oregano**
- ¼ **teaspoon salt**
- ¼ **teaspoon pepper**
- ¼ **teaspoon crushed red pepper flakes, optional**
- 4 **red snapper or orange roughy fillets (6 ounces each)**

1. In a large nonstick skillet coated with cooking spray, saute the zucchini, mushrooms and onion in 1 tablespoon oil until crisp-tender. Add the garlic; cook 1 minute longer. Stir in the tomatoes, basil, oregano, salt, pepper and, if desired, pepper flakes. Bring to a boil. Reduce heat; cover and simmer for 12-15 minutes or until vegetables are tender.

2. Meanwhile, in another large nonstick skillet coated with cooking spray, cook fillets in remaining oil over medium heat for 4-6 minutes on each side or until fish flakes easily with a fork. Serve with vegetable mixture.

ALIBUT STEAKS WITH APAYA MINT SALSA

The combination of zesty fruit salsa and tender halibut makes this dish the catch of the day! Even better, it's packed with nutrients.

—SONYA LABBE WEST HOLLYWOOD, CA

ART TO FINISH: 20 MIN. • **MAKES:** 4 SERVINGS

- 1 medium papaya, peeled, seeded and chopped
- ¼ cup chopped red onion
- ¼ cup fresh mint leaves
- 1 teaspoon finely chopped chipotle pepper in adobo sauce
- 2 tablespoons olive oil, divided
- 1 tablespoon honey
- 4 halibut steaks (6 ounces each)

In a small bowl, combine the papaya, onion, int, chipotle pepper, 1 tablespoon oil and honey. over and refrigerate until serving.

In a large skillet, cook halibut in remaining oil r 4-6 minutes on each side or until fish flakes sily with a fork. Serve with salsa.

ALIBUT STEAKS WITH APAYA MINT SALSA

SUMMER FISH SKILLET

SUMMER FISH SKILLET

On crazy nights when you have other proverbial fish to fry, this fresh Mediterranean medley will be the perfect dinnertime solution.

—TASTE OF HOME TEST KITCHEN

START TO FINISH: 30 MIN. • **MAKES:** 4 SERVINGS

- 2 packages (7.6 ounces each) frozen lemon butter grilled fish fillets
- 1 tablespoon olive oil
- 2 medium yellow summer squash, halved and sliced
- 2 medium sweet orange peppers, chopped
- ½ cup chopped red onion
- 2 cups fresh salsa, drained
- 4 ounces feta cheese, cubed
- 2 packages (8.8 ounces each) ready-to-serve rice pilaf with orzo pasta

1. In a large skillet, cook fish fillets in oil over medium heat for 15-20 minutes, turning once or until the fish flakes easily with a fork; remove fillets and keep warm.

2. In the same skillet, saute the squash, peppers and onion until tender. Add salsa; cook 2 minutes longer. Return fish to skillet. Add the cheese and heat through.

3. Prepare rice pilaf according to the package directions. Serve with the fish and vegetables.

(5) INGREDIENTS FAST FIX

SOUTHWESTERN FRIED PERCH

This is my favorite way to prepare perch because it's easy and tastes delicious every time. My family loves the zesty cornmeal coating.

—JIM LORD MANCHESTER, NH

START TO FINISH: 30 MIN.
MAKES: 4 SERVINGS

- 1 **envelope taco seasoning**
- 1 **pound lake perch fillets**
- 1 **large egg, lightly beaten**
- ½ **cup yellow cornmeal**
- ¼ **cup all-purpose flour**
- 3 **tablespoons canola oil**

1. Place taco seasoning in a large resealable bag; add perch fillets, one at a time, and shake to coat.
2. Place the egg in a shallow bowl. In another shallow bowl, combine cornmeal and flour. Dip fillets in egg, then coat with cornmeal mixture. Place in a single layer on a plate; refrigerate for 15 minutes.
3. In a large skillet, heat oil over medium-high heat. Fry fillets for 2-3 minutes on each side or until fish flakes easily with a fork.

DID YOU KNOW?

Overcooking dries out fish, so it's important to know how to tell when it's done. For fillets, check doneness by inserting a fork at an angle into the thickest portion of the fish and gently parting the flesh. When it's opaque and flakes into sections, it is cooked completely. A translucent appearance means it needs to cook a little longer.

SOUTHWESTERN
FRIED PERCH

FAST FIX

POACHED SALMON WITH
DILL & TURMERIC

This is among my husband's favorites because it's always tender, juicy and delicious. It's a quick, simple way to prepare salmon, and the robust turmeric doesn't overpower the taste of the fish.

EVELYN BANKER ELMHURST, NY

START TO FINISH: 30 MIN. • **MAKES:** 4 SERVINGS

- 1 tablespoon canola oil
- ¾ teaspoon cumin seeds
- 1 pound Yukon Gold potatoes (about 2 medium), finely chopped
- 1¼ teaspoons salt, divided
- ⅛ teaspoon plus ¼ teaspoon ground turmeric, divided
- 2 tablespoons chopped fresh dill, divided
- 4 salmon fillets (1 inch thick and 4 ounces each)
- 8 fresh dill sprigs

- 2 teaspoons grated lemon peel
- 2 tablespoons lemon juice
- 1 cup (8 ounces) reduced-fat plain yogurt
- ¼ teaspoon pepper

1. In a large skillet, heat oil and cumin over medium heat 1-2 minutes or until seeds are toasted, stirring occasionally. Stir in potatoes, ½ teaspoon salt and ⅛ teaspoon turmeric. Cook, covered, on medium-low 10-12 minutes or until tender. Stir in 1 tablespoon chopped dill; cook, uncovered, 1 minute. Remove from heat.

2. Meanwhile, place salmon, skin side down, in a large skillet with high sides. Add dill sprigs, lemon peel, lemon juice, ½ teaspoon salt, remaining turmeric and enough water to cover salmon. Bring just to a boil. Adjust heat to maintain a gentle simmer. Cook, uncovered, 7-9 minutes or until fish just begins to flake easily with a fork.

3. In a small bowl, mix the yogurt, pepper and the remaining 1 tablespoon chopped dill and ¼ teaspoon salt. Serve with salmon and potatoes.

soy sauce and reserved pineapple juice until the mixture is smooth.

2. In a large skillet, heat oil over medium-high he Add peppers and onion; stir-fry 1-2 minutes or jus until crisp-tender. Add shrimp; stir-fry 2-3 minut longer or until shrimp turn pink. Remove from pa

3. Place pineapple in skillet. Stir the cornstarch mixture and add to pan. Bring to a boil; cook and s 4-5 minutes or until sauce is thickened. Return shrimp mixture to pan; heat through, stirring to combine. Sprinkle with coconut; serve with rice.

FAST FIX

MEDITERRANEAN-STYLE RED SNAPPER

This entree is a nutritious time-saver. Seasoned with spices and served with a zesty sauce, it's a favorite at our house.

—JOSEPHINE PIRO EASTON, PA

START TO FINISH: 30 MIN. **• MAKES:** 4 SERVINGS

 1 **teaspoon lemon-pepper seasoning**
 ½ **teaspoon garlic powder**
 ½ **teaspoon dried thyme**
 ⅛ **teaspoon cayenne pepper**
 4 **red snapper fillets (6 ounces each)**
 2 **teaspoons olive oil, divided**
 ½ **medium sweet red pepper, julienned**
 3 **green onions, chopped**
 1 **garlic clove, minced**
 1 **can (14½ ounces) diced tomatoes, undrained**
 ½ **cup chopped pimiento-stuffed olives**
 ¼ **cup chopped ripe olives**
 ¼ **cup minced chives**

1. Combine the lemon pepper, garlic powder, thyme and cayenne; rub over fillets. In a large nonstick skillet coated with cooking spray, cook fillets in 1 teaspoon oil over medium heat for 4-5 minutes on each side or until fish flakes easily with a fork. Remove and keep warm.

2. In the same pan, saute the red pepper and onions in remaining oil until crisp-tender. Add garlic; cook 1 minute longer. Stir in tomatoes. Brin to a boil. Reduce heat; simmer, uncovered, for 3 minutes or until liquid has evaporated. Serve with snapper. Sprinkle with olives and chives.

FAST FIX

PINEAPPLE SHRIMP STIR-FRY

I came up with this recipe for a luau-themed party and served it with sliced papaya, mango and avocado. Delish! If you don't care for coconut, sprinkle with chopped macadamia nuts instead.

—TRISHA KRUSE EAGLE, ID

START TO FINISH: 30 MIN. **• MAKES:** 4 SERVINGS

 1 **can (20 ounces) unsweetened pineapple tidbits**
 2 **tablespoons cornstarch**
 1 **cup chicken broth**
 1 **tablespoon brown sugar**
 1 **tablespoon orange juice**
 1 **tablespoon reduced-sodium soy sauce**
 1 **tablespoon sesame or canola oil**
 1 **medium sweet red pepper, thinly sliced**
 1 **medium green pepper, thinly sliced**
 1 **medium sweet onion, thinly sliced**
 1 **pound uncooked shrimp (31-40 per pound), peeled and deveined**
 ¼ **cup flaked coconut, toasted**
    Hot cooked rice

1. Drain pineapple, reserving juice. In a small bowl, mix cornstarch, broth, brown sugar, orange juice,

BAJA FISH TACOS

Crisp mahi mahi will pan out beautifully when dressed up with fresh lime, cilantro and a smoky adobo sauce. One bite, and you'll be hooked!
—**BROOKE KELLER** LEXINGTON, KY

PREP: 30 MIN. • **COOK:** 5 MIN./BATCH
MAKES: 8 SERVINGS

- 1 cup reduced-fat ranch salad dressing
- 3 tablespoons adobo sauce
- 2 tablespoons minced fresh cilantro
- 2 tablespoons lime juice
- 2 pounds mahi mahi, cut into 1-inch strips
- ¼ teaspoon salt
- ¼ teaspoon pepper
- ⅔ cup all-purpose flour
- 3 large eggs, beaten
- 2 cups panko (Japanese) bread crumbs
- 1 cup canola oil
- 3 cups shredded cabbage
- 16 corn tortillas (6 inches), warmed
  Additional minced fresh cilantro and lime wedges

1. In a small bowl, combine the salad dressing, adobo sauce, cilantro and lime juice. Chill sauce until serving.

2. Sprinkle mahi mahi with salt and pepper. Place the flour, eggs and bread crumbs in separate shallow bowls. Coat mahi mahi with flour, then dip in eggs and coat with bread crumbs. In a large skillet, heat oil over medium heat; cook fish in batches for 2-3 minutes on each side or until golden brown. Drain on paper towels.

3. Place cabbage in tortillas; top with fish strips, sauce and additional cilantro. Serve tacos with lime wedges.

BAJA FISH TACOS

FAST FIX

CILANTRO SHRIMP & RICE

The aroma of fresh herbs in this one-dish wonder is so appetizing, even my young son can't resist!

—**NIBEDITA DAS** FORT WORTH, TX

START TO FINISH: 30 MIN.
MAKES: 8 SERVINGS

- 2 **packages (8½ ounces each) ready-to-serve basmati rice**
- 2 **tablespoons olive oil**
- 2 **cups frozen corn, thawed**
- 2 **medium zucchini, quartered and sliced**
- 1 **large sweet red pepper, chopped**
- ½ **teaspoon crushed red pepper flakes**
- 3 **garlic cloves, minced**
- 1 **pound peeled and deveined cooked large shrimp, tails removed**
- ½ **cup chopped fresh cilantro**
- 1 **tablespoon grated lime peel**
- 2 **tablespoons lime juice**
- ¾ **teaspoon salt**
  Lime wedges, optional

1. Prepare rice according to package directions.

2. Meanwhile, in a large skillet, heat oil over medium-high heat. Add corn, zucchini, red pepper and pepper flakes; cook and stir 3-5 minutes or until zucchini is crisp-tender. Add garlic; cook 1 minute longer. Add shrimp; cook and stir 3-5 minutes or until heated through.

3. Stir in rice, cilantro, lime peel, lime juice and salt. If desired, serve with lime wedges.

CILANTRO SHRIMP & RICE

AHI MAHI &
EGGIE SKILLET

oking mahi mahi and ratatouille
y seem complicated, but I've
veloped a simple skillet recipe
t brings out the wow factor
hout any of the fuss.

SOLOMON WANG ARLINGTON, TX

ART TO FINISH: 30 MIN.
AKES: 4 SERVINGS

- 3 **tablespoons olive oil, divided**
- 4 **mahi mahi or salmon fillets (6 ounces each)**
- 3 **medium sweet red peppers, cut into thick strips**
- ½ **pound sliced baby portobello mushrooms**
- 1 **large sweet onion, cut into thick rings and separated**
- ⅓ **cup lemon juice**
- ¾ **teaspoon salt, divided**
- ½ **teaspoon pepper**
- ¼ **cup minced fresh chives**
- ⅓ **cup pine nuts, optional**

1. In a large skillet, heat 2 tablespoons oil over medium-high heat. Add fillets; cook for 4-5 minutes on each side or until fish just begins to flake easily with a fork. Remove from pan.
2. Add remaining oil, peppers, mushrooms, onion, lemon juice and ¼ teaspoon salt. Cook, covered, over medium heat 6-8 minutes or until vegetables are tender, stirring occasionally.
3. Place fish over vegetables; sprinkle with pepper and remaining salt. Cook, covered, 2 minutes longer or until heated through. Sprinkle fish with chives and, if desired, pine nuts before serving.

MAHI MAHI &
VEGGIE SKILLET

BLACKENED CATFISH WITH MANGO AVOCADO SALSA

A delightful and tasty rub makes this quick recipe fantastic. While the fish is sitting to allow the flavors to blend, you can easily assemble the salsa. My family thinks this meal is simply marvelous.

—**LAURA FISHER** WESTFIELD, MA

PREP: 20 MIN. + CHILLING
COOK: 10 MIN. • **MAKES:** 4 SERVINGS
(2 CUPS SALSA)

- 2 **teaspoons dried oregano**
- 2 **teaspoons ground cumin**
- 2 **teaspoons paprika**
- 2¼ **teaspoons pepper, divided**
- ¾ **teaspoon salt, divided**
- 4 **catfish fillets (6 ounces each)**
- 1 **medium mango, peeled and cubed**
- 1 **medium ripe avocado, peeled and cubed**
- ⅓ **cup finely chopped red onion**
- 2 **tablespoons minced fresh cilantro**
- 2 **tablespoons lime juice**
- 2 **teaspoons olive oil**

1. Combine the oregano, cumin, paprika, 2 teaspoons pepper and ½ teaspoon salt; rub over fillets. Refrigerate for at least 30 minutes.
2. Meanwhile, in a small bowl, combine the mango, avocado, red onion, cilantro, lime juice and remaining salt and pepper. Chill until serving.
3. In a large cast-iron skillet, cook fillets in oil over medium heat for 5-7 minutes on each side or until fish flakes easily with a fork. Serve with salsa.

CORNMEAL CATFISH WITH AVOCADO SAUCE

My mother often made catfish while I was growing up in California. Now I cook it with my own special twist. When only frozen catfish fillets are available, I simply thaw them in the refrigerator overnight, and they work just as well as fresh.

—**MARY LOU COOK** WELCHES, OR

START TO FINISH: 25 MIN.
MAKES: 4 SERVINGS (¾ CUP SAUCE)

- 1 medium ripe avocado, peeled and cubed
- ⅓ cup reduced-fat mayonnaise
- ¼ cup fresh cilantro leaves
- 2 tablespoons lime juice
- ½ teaspoon garlic salt
- ¼ cup cornmeal
- 1 teaspoon seafood seasoning
- 4 catfish fillets (6 ounces each)
- 3 tablespoons canola oil
- 1 medium tomato, chopped

1. Place the first five ingredients in a food processor; process until blended.
2. In a shallow bowl, mix the cornmeal and seafood seasoning. Dip the catfish in the cornmeal mixture to coat both sides; shake off excess.
3. In a large skillet, heat oil over medium heat. Add catfish in batches; cook 4-5 minutes on each side or until fish flakes easily with a fork. Top with avocado sauce and tomato.

SCALLOPS WITH CHIPOTLE-ORANGE SAUCE

Tender scallops sprinkled with paprika and ground chipotle make this recipe a surefire way to warm up at dinnertime. Scallops are great because they're available year-round and are budget-friendly.

—**JAN JUSTICE** CATLETTSBURG, KY

START TO FINISH: 15 MIN.
MAKES: 2 SERVINGS

- ¾ pound sea scallops
- ¼ teaspoon paprika
- ¼ teaspoon salt, divided
- 2 teaspoons butter
- ¼ cup orange juice
- ¼ teaspoon ground chipotle pepper
  Hot cooked linguine, option
- 2 tablespoons thinly sliced green onion

1. Sprinkle the scallops with paprika and ⅛ teaspoon salt. In a nonstick skillet coated with cooking spray, melt butter over medium heat. Add scallops; cook for 3-4 minutes on each side or until firm and opaque.
2. Add the orange juice and remaining salt to the pan; bring to a boil. Remove from the heat; stir in chipotle pepper.
3. Serve over linguine if desired. Garnish with green onion.

SCALLOPS WITH CHIPOTLE-ORANGE SAUCE

EPPERED SOLE

asoned sole cooked with
shrooms is the only way my
ughter will eat fish. It's good for
, too, so we're both happy.
EANNETTE BAYE AGASSIZ, BC

ART TO FINISH: 25 MIN.
KES: 4 SERVINGS

- **tablespoons butter**
- **cups sliced fresh mushrooms**
- **garlic cloves, minced**
- **sole fillets (4 ounces each)**
- **teaspoon paprika**
- **teaspoon lemon-pepper
  seasoning**
- **teaspoon cayenne pepper**
- **medium tomato, chopped**
- **green onions, thinly sliced**

In a large skillet, heat the
tter over medium-high heat.
d mushrooms; cook and stir
til tender. Add garlic; cook
inute longer. Place the fillets
er the mushrooms. Sprinkle
h the paprika, lemon pepper
d cayenne.

Cook, covered, over medium
at 5-10 minutes or until fish
t begins to flake easily with a
k. Sprinkle with tomato and
en onions.

OP TIP

Fresh fish is highly perishable
and should be prepared within
a day or two after it is caught
or purchased. Freshly caught
fish should be pan-dressed,
washed in cold water, blotted
dry with paper towels, placed
in an airtight container or
heavy-duty plastic bag and
refrigerated.

PEPPERED SOLE

OFT FISH TACOS

husband, Bill, and I were cooking together in the
hen one day, and these tasty fish tacos were our
ation. The combination of tilapia, cabbage and a
of cumin is fun and different. We think it'll be
e at first bite.

—ARRIE BILLUPS FLORENCE, OR

ART TO FINISH: 25 MIN. • **MAKES:** 5 SERVINGS

- cups coleslaw mix
- cup fat-free tartar sauce
- teaspoon salt
- teaspoon ground cumin
- teaspoon pepper
- ½ pounds tilapia fillets
- tablespoons olive oil
- tablespoon lemon juice
- corn tortillas (6 inches), warmed
- Shredded cheddar cheese, chopped tomato
  and sliced avocado, optional

In a large bowl, toss the coleslaw mix, tartar
ce, salt, cumin and pepper; set aside. In a large
nstick skillet coated with cooking spray, cook
pia in oil and lemon juice over medium heat for
minutes on each side or until fish flakes easily
h a fork.
Place tilapia on tortillas; top with coleslaw
xture. Serve with cheese, tomato and avocado
esired.

HAI LIME SHRIMP & NOODLES

The flavors pop in this fast-to-fix
Thai-inspired dinner. You can add
more or less lime peel and chili paste,
depending on your personal taste.
My family loves spicy foods, but I keep
the heat moderate in this version.

—ERI RASEY CADILLAC, MI

ART TO FINISH: 25 MIN. • **MAKES:** 6 SERVINGS

- cup minced fresh basil
- tablespoons lime juice
- teaspoons Thai red chili paste
- garlic clove, minced

- 1 teaspoon minced fresh gingerroot
- 1½ pounds uncooked shrimp (26-30 per pound),
  peeled and deveined
- 12 ounces cooked angel hair pasta
- 4 teaspoons olive oil, divided
- 1 can (14½ ounces) chicken broth
- 1 can (13.66 ounces) coconut milk
- 1 teaspoon salt
- 1 tablespoon cornstarch
- 2 tablespoons cold water
- 2 tablespoons grated lime peel

1. Place the first five ingredients in a blender; cover
and process until blended. Remove 1 tablespoon
mixture; toss with shrimp.
2. Cook pasta according to package directions.
Meanwhile, in a large nonstick skillet, heat
2 teaspoons oil over medium-high heat. Add half
of the shrimp mixture; stir-fry 2-4 minutes or until
shrimp turn pink. Remove from pan; keep warm.
Repeat with remaining oil and shrimp mixture.
3. Add broth, coconut milk, salt and remaining
basil mixture to same pan. In a small bowl, mix
cornstarch and water until smooth. Stir into broth
mixture. Bring to a boil; cook and stir 1-2 minutes
or until slightly thickened. Stir in lime peel.
4. Drain pasta; add pasta and shrimp to sauce,
tossing to coat.

FAST FIX

SPICY TILAPIA RICE BOWL

I embrace healthy living, so tilapia and other fish are staples in my kitchen. Fresh vegetables are always good but take more time to prep, so I rely on a frozen veggie blend.
—**ROSALIN JOHNSON** TUPELO, MS

START TO FINISH: 30 MIN.
MAKES: 4 SERVINGS

- **4 tilapia fillets (4 ounces each)**
- **1¼ teaspoons Cajun seasoning**
- **3 tablespoons olive oil, divided**
- **1 medium yellow summer squash, halved lengthwise and sliced**
- **1 package (16 ounces) frozen pepper and onion stir-fry blend**
- **1 can (14½ ounces) diced tomatoes, drained**
- **1 envelope fajita seasoning mix**
- **1 can (15 ounces) black beans, rinsed and drained**
- **⅛ teaspoon salt**
- **⅛ teaspoon pepper**
- **3 cups hot cooked brown rice**
  Optional toppings: cubed avocado, sour cream and salsa

1. Sprinkle fillets with Cajun seasoning. In a large skillet, heat 2 tablespoons oil over medium heat. Add fillets; cook 4-6 minutes on each side or until fish just begins to flake easily with a fork. Remove and keep warm. Wipe pan clean.
2. In the same skillet, heat the remaining oil. Add squash; cook and stir 3 minutes. Add stir-fry blend and tomatoes; cook 6-8 minutes longer or until vegetables are tender. Stir in fajita seasoning mix; cook and stir 1-2 minutes longer or until slightly thickened.
3. In a small bowl, mix beans, salt and pepper. Divide rice among four serving bowls; lay[er] with beans, vegetables and fill[ets] Serve with toppings as desired[.]

(5) INGREDIENTS FAST FIX

TUNA NOODLE SKILLET

Enjoy the comforting flavor of tu[na] noodle casserole in minutes with this creamy stovetop version. It's easy to make with convenient ingredients like frozen peas and bottled Alfredo sauce.
—**RUTH SIMON** BUFFALO, NY

START TO FINISH: 30 MIN.
MAKES: 6 SERVINGS

- **2 jars (16 ounces each) Alfr[edo] sauce**
- **1 can (14½ ounces) chicken broth**
- **1 package (16 ounces) wide egg noodles**
- **1 package (10 ounces) froz[en] peas**
- **¼ teaspoon pepper**
- **1 can (12 ounces) albacore white tuna in water**

1. In a large skillet over mediu[m] heat, bring Alfredo sauce and broth to a boil. Add noodles; cover and cook for 7-8 minute[s.]
2. Reduce the heat; stir in the peas and pepper. Cover and co[ok] 4 minutes longer or until the noodles are tender. Stir in tun[a;] heat through.

SPICY TILAPIA
RICE BOWL

ΓEAMED MUSSELS
ΊTH PEPPERS

ve this dish with toasted French bread to soak up the
ciously seasoned broth. If you like food with a little
toss in the jalapeno seeds.

ASTE OF HOME TEST KITCHEN

ΞP: 30 MIN. • **COOK:** 10 MIN. • **MAKES:** 4 SERVINGS

- **pounds fresh mussels, scrubbed and beards removed**
- **jalapeno pepper, seeded and chopped**
- **tablespoons olive oil**
- **garlic cloves, minced**
- **bottle (8 ounces) clam juice**
- **cup white wine or additional clam juice**
- **cup chopped sweet red pepper**
- **green onions, sliced**
- **teaspoon dried oregano**
- **bay leaf**
- **tablespoons minced fresh parsley**
- **teaspoon salt**
- **teaspoon pepper**
- **French bread baguette, sliced, optional**

1. Tap mussels; discard any that do not close.
Set aside. In a large skillet, saute jalapeno in oil
until tender. Add garlic; cook 1 minute longer.
Stir in the clam juice, wine, red pepper, green
onions, oregano and bay leaf.

2. Bring to a boil. Reduce heat; add mussels. Cover
and simmer for 5-6 minutes or until mussels open.
Discard the bay leaf and any unopened mussels.
Sprinkle with parsley, salt and pepper. Serve with
baguette slices if desired.

NOTE *Wear disposable gloves when cutting hot
peppers; the oils can burn skin. Avoid touching
your face.*

TOP TIP

Always clean the sand and grit off of mussels
before cooking by scrubbing them on both sides
with a stiff brush under running cold water. The
beard is inedible and needs to be removed prior to
cooking. Do not debeard mussels more than 1 hour
before cooking, as this shortens their shelf life.

FAST FIX

EASY CRAB CAKES

Canned crabmeat makes these delicate patties the ideal dish when your clan is hungry and you're pressed for time. You can also form the crab mixture into four thick patties instead of eight cakes.

—CHARLENE SPELOCK APOLLO, PA

START TO FINISH: 25 MIN.
MAKES: 4 SERVINGS

- 1 **cup seasoned bread crumbs, divided**
- 2 **green onions, finely chopped**
- ¼ **cup finely chopped sweet red pepper**
- 1 **large egg, lightly beaten**
- ¼ **cup reduced-fat mayonnaise**
- 1 **tablespoon lemon juice**
- ½ **teaspoon garlic powder**
- ⅛ **teaspoon cayenne pepper**
- 2 **cans (6 ounces each) crabmeat, drained, flaked and cartilage removed**
- 1 **tablespoon butter**

1. In a large bowl, combine ⅓ cup bread crumbs, green onions, chopped red pepper, egg, mayonnaise, lemon juice, garlic powder and cayenne; fold in crab.

2. Place the remaining bread crumbs in a shallow bowl. Divide the mixture into eight portions; shape into 2-in. balls. Gently coat in bread crumbs and shape into a ½-in.-thick patty.

3. In a large nonstick skillet, heat butter over medium-high heat. Add crab cakes; cook for 3-4 minutes on each side or until golden brown.

EASY CRAB CAKES

TUNA WITH CITRUS PONZU SAUCE

I like this Asian-inspired tuna because it's easy to prepare, delicious and healthy, too.

DIANE HALFERTY
CORPUS CHRISTI, TX

START TO FINISH: 20 MIN.
MAKES: 4 SERVINGS

- ¼ teaspoon Chinese five-spice powder
- ¼ teaspoon salt
- ¼ teaspoon cayenne pepper
- 4 tuna steaks (6 ounces each)
- 1 tablespoon canola oil
- ¼ cup orange juice
- 2 green onions, thinly sliced
- 1 tablespoon lemon juice
- 1 tablespoon reduced-sodium soy sauce
- 2 teaspoons rice vinegar
- 1 teaspoon brown sugar
- ¼ teaspoon minced fresh gingerroot

1. Combine the five-spice powder, salt and cayenne; sprinkle over tuna steaks. In a large skillet, cook tuna in oil over medium heat for 2-3 minutes on each side for medium-rare or until slightly pink in the center; remove and keep warm.
2. Combine the orange juice, onions, lemon juice, soy sauce, vinegar, brown sugar and ginger; pour into skillet. Cook for 1-2 minutes or until slightly thickened. Serve with tuna.

TUNA WITH CITRUS PONZU SAUCE

FAST FIX

STUFFED-OLIVE COD

Take advantage of the olive bar in your supermarket to put a new twist on cod. This simple high-protein, low-fat entree is a weeknight lifesaver.

—**TRIA OLSEN** QUEEN CREEK, AZ

START TO FINISH: 25 MIN.
MAKES: 4 SERVINGS

- 4 cod fillets (6 ounces each)
- 1 teaspoon dried oregano
- ¼ teaspoon salt
- 1 medium lemon, thinly sliced
- 1 shallot, thinly sliced
- ⅓ cup garlic-stuffed olives, halved
- 2 tablespoons water
- 2 tablespoons olive juice

1. Place fillets in a large nonstick skillet coated with cooking spray. Sprinkle with oregano and salt; top with lemon and shallot.
2. Scatter olives around fish; add water and olive juice. Bring to a boil. Reduce heat to low; gently cook, covered, 8-10 minutes or until fish just begins to flake easily with a fork.

SKILLET-GRILLED CATFISH

You can use this recipe with any thick fish fillet, but I suggest catfish or haddock. The bold Cajun flavor makes it out-of-this-world delicious.

—TRACI WYNNE DENVER, PA

START TO FINISH: 25 MIN.
MAKES: 4 SERVINGS

- ¼ cup all-purpose flour
- ¼ cup cornmeal
- 1 teaspoon onion powder
- 1 teaspoon dried basil
- ½ teaspoon garlic salt
- ½ teaspoon dried thyme
- ¼ to ½ teaspoon white pepper
- ¼ to ½ teaspoon cayenne pepper
- ¼ to ½ teaspoon pepper
- 4 catfish fillets (6 to 8 ounces each)
- ¼ cup butter

1. In a large resealable bag, combine the first nine ingredients. Add catfish, one fillet at a time, and shake to coat.
2. Place a large cast-iron skillet on a grill rack over medium-hot heat. Melt butter in the skillet; add catfish. Grill, covered, for 5-10 minutes on each side or until fish flakes easily with a fork.

BLACKENED HALIBUT

Serve this nicely seasoned halibut with garlic mashed potatoes, crusty bread and a fresh salad to lure in your crew. This is what my family eats when we celebrate.

—BRENDA WILLIAMS SANTA MARIA, CA

START TO FINISH: 25 MIN.
MAKES: 4 SERVINGS

- 2 tablespoons garlic powder
- 1 tablespoon salt
- 1 tablespoon onion powder
- 1 tablespoon dried oregano
- 1 tablespoon dried thyme
- 1 tablespoon cayenne pepper
- 1 tablespoon pepper
- 2½ teaspoons paprika
- 4 halibut fillets (4 ounces each)
- 2 tablespoons butter

1. In a large resealable plastic bag, combine the first eight ingredients. Add fillets, two at a time, and shake to coat.
2. In a large cast-iron skillet, cook the fillets in butter over medium heat for 3-4 minutes on each side or until fish flakes easily with a fork.

BLACKENED HALIBUT

MPLE SHRIMP
D THAI

MPLE SHRIMP PAD THAI

It's easy to make your own version of your favorite restaurant's shrimp pad Thai. No one will ever guess the secret ingredient is marinara sauce.

—**ERIN CHILCOAT** CENTRAL ISLIP, NY

RT TO FINISH: 30 MIN. • **MAKES:** 4 SERVINGS

ounces uncooked thick rice noodles
pound uncooked medium shrimp, peeled and
deveined
garlic cloves, minced
tablespoons canola oil
large eggs, beaten
cup marinara sauce
cup reduced-sodium soy sauce
tablespoons brown sugar

¼ **cup chopped dry roasted peanuts**
   Fresh cilantro leaves
1 **medium lime, cut into wedges**
   Sriracha Asian hot chili sauce or hot pepper
   sauce, optional

1. Cook noodles according to package directions.
2. Meanwhile, stir-fry shrimp and garlic in oil in a large nonstick skillet or wok until shrimp turn pink; remove and keep warm. Add eggs to skillet; cook and stir until set.
3. Add the marinara, soy sauce and brown sugar; heat through. Return shrimp to the pan. Drain noodles; toss with shrimp mixture.
4. Sprinkle with peanuts and cilantro. Serve with lime and, if desired, Sriracha.

JANE SIEMON'S TUSCAN PORTOBELLO STEW

PAGE 171

Meatless

Dishes so tasty no one will miss the meat?
It's true! Check out these lip-smacking
skillet dishes and see for yourself.

FAST FIX

TORTELLINI WITH TOMATO-CREAM SAUCE

On busy nights, take advantage of the convenience of frozen food and pantry staples to create a warm and satisfying meatless meal.

—BARBRA STANGER
WEST JORDAN, UT

START TO FINISH: 25 MIN.
MAKES: 6 SERVINGS

- 1 **package (16 ounces) frozen cheese tortellini**
- 1 **small onion, chopped**
- 2 **tablespoons olive oil**
- 3 **garlic cloves, minced**
- 1 **can (14½ ounces) diced tomatoes, undrained**
- 1 **package (10 ounces) frozen chopped spinach, thawed and squeezed dry**
- 1½ **teaspoons dried basil**
- 1 **teaspoon salt**
- ½ **teaspoon pepper**
- 1½ **cups heavy whipping cream**
- ½ **cup grated Parmesan cheese Additional grated Parmesan cheese, optional**

1. Cook tortellini according to package directions. Meanwhile, in a large skillet, saute onion in oil until tender. Add garlic; cook 1 minute longer. Add the tomatoes, spinach, basil, salt and pepper. Cook and stir over medium heat until the liquid is absorbed, about 3 minutes.

2. Stir in the cream and cheese. Bring to a boil. Reduce the heat; simmer, uncovered, for 8-10 minutes or until thickened.

3. Drain the tortellini; toss with sauce. Sprinkle with additional cheese if desired.

TORTELLINI WITH TOMATO-CREAM SAUCE

SKILLET PASTA FLORENTINE

4. Sprinkle with Parmesan cheese and remaining mozzarella cheese; cover and cook for 5 minutes longer or until the cheese is melted. Let stand for 5 minutes before serving.

SKILLET PASTA FLORENTINE

Here's a great weeknight supper that's budget-friendly, healthy—and children like it. With such a thick, cheesy topping, who'd ever guess that it's light?
—**KELLY TURNBULL** JUPITER, FL

PREP: 20 MIN. • **COOK:** 35 MIN. • **MAKES:** 6 SERVINGS

- 3 cups uncooked spiral pasta
- 1 large egg, lightly beaten
- 2 cups (16 ounces) 2% cottage cheese
- 1½ cups reduced-fat ricotta cheese
- 1 package (10 ounces) frozen chopped spinach, thawed and squeezed dry
- 1 cup (4 ounces) shredded part-skim mozzarella cheese, divided
- 1 teaspoon each dried parsley flakes, oregano and basil
- 1 jar (14 ounces) meatless spaghetti sauce
- 2 tablespoons grated Parmesan cheese

1. Cook pasta according to package directions. Meanwhile, in a large bowl, combine the egg, cottage cheese, ricotta, spinach, ½ cup of the mozzarella and herbs.
2. Drain pasta. Place half of the sauce in a large skillet; layer with pasta and remaining sauce. Top with cheese mixture.
3. Bring to a boil. Reduce heat; cover and cook for 25-30 minutes or until a thermometer reads 160°.

BLACK BEAN-SWEET POTATO SKILLET

My fiance loves sweet potatoes. By adding black beans, I came up with a nutritionally complete main dish. Its bright orange and black colors make it a natural for Halloween, but you'll want to make it all year long.
—**APRIL STREVELL** RED BANK, NJ

PREP: 15 MIN. • **COOK:** 40 MIN. • **MAKES:** 5 SERVINGS

- 1 medium onion, chopped
- 1 tablespoon olive oil
- 2 cans (15 ounces each) black beans, rinsed and drained
- 2 medium sweet potatoes, peeled and finely chopped
- 1 can (14½ ounces) vegetable broth
- 1 teaspoon minced chipotle pepper in adobo sauce
- ¼ teaspoon pepper
- ¼ teaspoon ground cinnamon
- 1¼ cups uncooked couscous

1. In a large skillet, saute onion in oil until tender. Add the beans, sweet potatoes, broth, chipotle, pepper and cinnamon.
2. Bring to a boil. Reduce heat; cover and simmer for 25 minutes. Uncover and simmer 5-10 minutes longer or until the potatoes are very tender and the mixture is thickened, stirring occasionally.
3. Meanwhile, cook the couscous according to the package directions. Serve with black bean mixture.

> **TOP TIP**
>
> Select sweet potatoes that are firm with no cracks or bruises. If stored in a cool, dark, well-ventilated place, they'll remain fresh for about 2 weeks. If the temperature is above 60°, they'll sprout sooner or become woody. Once cooked, sweet potatoes can be stored for up to 1 week in the refrigerator.

1. In a large nonstick skillet, heat 1 teaspoon of o over medium heat. Pour in eggs; cook and stir un the eggs are thickened and no liquid egg remains. Remove from pan.

2. In same skillet, heat remaining oil over mediu high heat. Add the mushrooms; cook and stir unt tender. Add coleslaw mix, garlic and ginger; cook 1-2 minutes longer or until slaw is crisp-tender. I a small bowl, mix vinegar, soy sauce and chili sauc add to pan. Stir in sprouts and eggs; heat through

3. Spread about 2 teaspoons hoisin sauce over ea tortilla to within ¼ in. of edges. Layer with ½ cu of vegetable mixture and about 1 tablespoon gree onion. Roll up tightly.

ZUCCHINI BURGERS

The patties for this omelet-like veggie burger hold together well while cooking and are hearty enough to serve bunless. In summer, I like to make them with fresh-picked zucchini.

—**KIMBERLY DANEK PINKSON** SAN ANSELMO, CA

PREP: 20 MIN. • **COOK:** 5 MIN./BATCH
MAKES: 4 SERVINGS

> 2 **cups shredded zucchini**
> 1 **medium onion, finely chopped**
> ½ **cup dry bread crumbs**
> 2 **large eggs, lightly beaten**
> ⅛ **teaspoon salt**
>   **Dash cayenne pepper**
> 3 **hard-cooked large egg whites, chopped**
> 2 **tablespoons canola oil**
> 4 **whole wheat hamburger buns, split**
> 4 **lettuce leaves**
> 4 **slices tomato**
> 4 **slices onion**

1. In a sieve or colander, drain zucchini, squeezi to remove excess liquid. Pat dry. In a small bowl, combine the zucchini, onion, bread crumbs, eggs salt and cayenne. Gently stir in cooked egg white

2. Heat 1 tablespoon oil in a large nonstick skille over medium-low heat. Drop the mixture by scan ⅔ cupfuls into the oil; press lightly to flatten. Fry in batches until patties are golden brown on both sides, using remaining oil as needed.

3. Serve on buns with lettuce, tomato and onion.

FAST FIX
MOO SHU MUSHROOM WRAPS

With so many awesome veggies out there, I'm always playing around with the ingredients in these wraps. Sometimes I add some extra protein, too—chicken, shrimp, pork, beef and tofu all work. Check for Sriracha and hoisin sauces in the Asian or international foods section of your grocery store.

—**ATHENA RUSSELL** GREENVILLE, SC

START TO FINISH: 30 MIN. • **MAKES:** 5 SERVINGS

> 4 **teaspoons sesame or canola oil, divided**
> 4 **large eggs, lightly beaten**
> ½ **pound sliced fresh mushrooms**
> 1 **package (12 ounces) broccoli coleslaw mix**
> 2 **garlic cloves, minced**
> 2 **teaspoons minced fresh gingerroot**
> 2 **tablespoons rice vinegar**
> 2 **tablespoons reduced-sodium soy sauce**
> 2 **teaspoons Sriracha Asian hot chili sauce**
> 1 **cup fresh bean sprouts**
> ½ **cup hoisin sauce**
> 10 **flour tortillas (6 inches), warmed**
> 6 **green onions, sliced**

FAST FIX

STIR-FRY RICE BOWL

My meatless version of Korean bibimbap is tasty, pretty and easy to tweak for different spice levels. Koreans typically eat this signature rice dish with beef, but I think the poached egg topping is perfect.

—DEVON DELANEY WESTPORT, CT

START TO FINISH: 30 MIN. • **MAKES:** 4 SERVINGS

- 1 **tablespoon canola oil**
- 2 **medium carrots, julienned**
- 1 **medium zucchini, julienned**
- ½ **cup sliced baby portobello mushrooms**
- 1 **cup bean sprouts**
- 1 **cup fresh baby spinach**
- 1 **tablespoon water**
- 1 **tablespoon reduced-sodium soy sauce**
- 1 **tablespoon chili garlic sauce**
- 4 **large eggs**
- 3 **cups hot cooked brown rice**
- 1 **teaspoon sesame oil**

1. In a large skillet, heat canola oil over medium-high heat. Add carrots, zucchini and mushrooms; cook and stir 3-5 minutes or until carrots are crisp-tender. Add bean sprouts, spinach, water, soy sauce and chili sauce; cook and stir just until spinach is wilted. Remove from heat; keep warm.

2. Place 2-3 in. of water in a large skillet with high sides. Bring to a boil; adjust the heat to maintain a gentle simmer. Break cold eggs, one at a time, into a small bowl; holding bowl close to the surface of the water, slip egg into water.

3. Cook, uncovered, 3-5 minutes or until whites are completely set and yolks begin to thicken but are not hard. Using a slotted spoon, lift eggs out of water.

4. Serve rice in bowls; top with the vegetables. Drizzle with sesame oil. Top each serving with a poached egg.

USCAN PORTOBELLO STEW

is heart-healthy one-skillet meal is quick and easy to
epare, yet special enough for company. I take it to my
hool's potlucks where it is devoured by teachers and
dents alike. Even the meat lovers eat it up!
ANE SIEMON VIROQUA, WI

EP: 20 MIN. • **COOK:** 20 MIN. • **MAKES:** 4 SERVINGS

2 large portobello mushrooms, coarsely chopped
1 medium onion, chopped
3 garlic cloves, minced
2 tablespoons olive oil
½ cup white wine or vegetable broth
1 can (28 ounces) diced tomatoes, undrained
2 cups chopped fresh kale
1 bay leaf
1 teaspoon dried thyme
½ teaspoon dried basil
½ teaspoon dried rosemary, crushed
¼ teaspoon salt
¼ teaspoon pepper
2 cans (15 ounces each) white kidney or
cannellini beans, rinsed and drained

In a large skillet, saute the mushrooms, onion
d garlic in oil until tender. Add the wine. Bring
a boil; cook until liquid is reduced by half. Stir in
e tomatoes, kale and seasonings. Bring to a boil.
duce heat; cover and simmer for 8-10 minutes.
Add beans; heat through. Discard the bay leaf.

USCAN PORTOBELLO STEW

**GRILLED GOAT CHEESE &
ARUGULA SANDWICHES**

FAST FIX

GRILLED GOAT CHEESE &
ARUGULA SANDWICHES

To create a more grown-up grilled cheese sandwich,
I add tangy goat cheese and peppery arugula. You can
enjoy a similar combination on pizza.
—**JESSIE APFE** BERKELEY, CA

START TO FINISH: 30 MIN. • **MAKES:** 4 SERVINGS

½ cup sun-dried tomato pesto
8 slices sourdough bread
1½ cups roasted sweet red peppers, drained and
patted dry
8 slices part-skim mozzarella cheese
½ cup crumbled goat cheese
1 cup fresh arugula
¼ cup butter, softened

1. Spread pesto over four slices of bread. Layer
with peppers, mozzarella cheese, goat cheese
and arugula; top with remaining bread. Spread
outsides of sandwiches with butter.
2. In a large skillet, toast the sandwiches over
medium heat 3-4 minutes on each side or until
golden brown and the cheese is melted.

⑤INGREDIENTS FAST FIX
POLENTA LASAGNA

Using polenta instead of pasta gives an amazing twist on lasagna. I love the easy assembly, too.

—YEVGENIYA FARRER FREMONT, CA

START TO FINISH: 25 MIN.
MAKES: 4 SERVINGS

- 1½ cups marinara sauce
- 1 teaspoon garlic powder
- 1 teaspoon herbes de Provence
- 1 tube (18 ounces) polenta, cut into 10 slices
- 1½ cups (6 ounces) shredded part-skim mozzarella cheese

1. In a small bowl, mix marinara sauce, garlic powder and herbes de Provence. Arrange half of the polenta slices in a greased 8-in. skillet. Top with half of the sauce; sprinkle with ¾ cup of cheese. Repeat layers.

2. Cook, uncovered, over medium heat for 12-14 minutes or until bubbly. Cover; cook for 2-3 minutes longer or until the cheese is melted.

NOTE Look for herbes de Provence in the spice aisle.

FAST FIX
GARBANZO-VEGETABLE GREEN CURRY

My son loves anything with coconut milk, so I keep some on hand for quick weeknight meals like this one. For a milder version, you can use red or yellow curry paste instead of green.

—MARIE PARKER MILWAUKEE, WI

START TO FINISH: 20 MIN.
MAKES: 6 SERVINGS

- 3 cups frozen cauliflower
- 2 cans (15 ounces each) garbanzo beans or chickpeas, rinsed and drained
- 1 can (13.66 ounces) coconut milk
- ¼ cup green curry paste
- ½ teaspoon salt
- 2 teaspoons cornstarch
- 1 tablespoon cold water
- 1½ cups frozen peas
- 2 packages (8.8 ounces each) ready-to-serve long grain r
- ½ cup lightly salted cashews

1. In a large skillet, combine cauliflower, beans, coconut mil curry paste and salt. Bring the mixure to a boil; cook, uncover 5-6 minutes or until cauliflowe is tender.

2. Combine the cornstarch an water until smooth; gradually stir into the skillet. Stir in peas. Bring to a boil. Cook and stir fo 2 minutes or until thickened.

3. Meanwhile, prepare the ric according to package direction Sprinkle cauliflower mixture with cashews. Serve with rice.

GARBANZO-VEGETABLE GREEN CURRY

LEMONY CHICKPEAS

These saucy chickpeas add just a little heat to our family's meatless Mondays. They're especially good over hot, fluffly brown rice.
—**APRIL STREVELL** RED BANK, NJ

START TO FINISH: 30 MIN.
MAKES: 4 SERVINGS

- 2 **cups uncooked instant brown rice**
- 1 **tablespoon olive oil**
- 1 **medium onion, chopped**
- 2 **cans (15 ounces each) chickpeas or garbanzo beans, rinsed and drained**
- 1 **can (14 ounces) diced tomatoes, undrained**
- 1 **cup vegetable broth**
- ¼ **teaspoon crushed red pepper flakes**
- ¼ **teaspoon pepper**
- ½ **teaspoon grated lemon peel**
- 3 **tablespoons lemon juice**

1. Cook rice according to the package directions. Meanwhile, in a large skillet, heat the oil over medium heat. Add onion; cook and stir 3-4 minutes or until the onion is tender.

2. Stir in chickpeas, tomatoes, broth, pepper flakes and pepper; bring to a boil. Reduce the heat; simmer, covered, 10 minutes to allow flavors to blend. Uncover; simmer 4-5 minutes or until liquid is slightly reduced, stirring occasionally. Stir in lemon peel and lemon juice. Serve with rice.

FREEZE OPTION *Freeze cooled chickpea mixture in freezer containers. To use, partially thaw in refrigerator overnight. Heat through in a saucepan, stirring occasionally and adding a little broth if necessary.*

LEMONY CHICKPEAS

FAST FIX
BEAN & PINEAPPLE SOFT TACOS

The sweet and spicy filling in these delicious soft tacos is a refreshing change from ordinary ground beef or chicken. Pair with a fresh fruit salad of melon, mango and papaya dressed with a splash of lime juice.
—**TRISHA KRUSE** EAGLE, ID

START TO FINISH: 30 MIN.
MAKES: 10 SERVINGS

- 1 can (15 ounces) black beans, rinsed and drained
- 1 large onion, chopped
- 1 medium sweet red pepper, chopped
- 1 tablespoon olive oil
- 1 can (20 ounces) unsweetened pineapple tidbits, drained
- 1 jar (16 ounces) salsa
- 1 can (4 ounces) chopped green chilies
- ¼ cup minced fresh cilantro
- 10 whole wheat tortillas (8 inches), warmed
  Sliced avocado, shredded lettuce, chopped tomatoes, shredded reduced-fat cheddar cheese, and reduced-fat sour cream, optional

1. Mash half of the beans; set aside.
2. In a large skillet, saute the onion and red pepper in oil until tender. Add the pineapple, salsa, chilies, mashed beans and remaining beans; heat through. Stir in cilantro.
3. Place ½ cup of filling on one side of each tortilla. Add toppings of your choice; fold in half. Serve immediately.

FAST FIX
ANGEL HAIR PRIMAVERA

I am sure to make pasta primavera when summer is in full swing and the vegetables are at their peak. You can toss in almost any veggie that's in season. At my house, this dish is rarely the same twice.
—**TRE BALCHOWSKY** SAUSALITO, CA

START TO FINISH: 30 MIN.
MAKES: 4 SERVINGS

- 1 tablespoon olive oil
- 2 medium zucchini, coarsely chopped
- 1 cup fresh baby carrots, halved lengthwise
- 1 cup fresh or frozen corn
- 1 small red onion, cut into thin wedges
- 1 cup cherry tomatoes, halved
- 2 garlic cloves, minced
- 1 package (4.8 ounces) Pasta Roni angel hair pasta with herbs
- ½ cup chopped walnuts, toasted
- ¼ cup shredded Parmesan cheese
  Coarsely ground pepper

1. In a large skillet, heat the oil over medium-high heat. Add the zucchini, carrots, corn and onion; cook and stir mixture for 10-12 minutes or until carrots are tender. Stir in tomatoes and garlic; cook 1 minute longer.
2. Meanwhile, prepare pasta mix according to the package directions. Add to the vegetable mixture; toss to combine. Sprinkle with walnuts, cheese and pepper.
NOTE *To toast nuts, bake in a shallow pan in a 350° oven for 5-10 minutes or cook in a skillet over low heat until lightly browned, stirring the nuts occasionally.*

ANGEL HAIR PRIMAVERA

ALSA BEAN URGERS

I created these based on a turkey burger recipe that I wanted to make even better for you. Use your orite salsa with just the heat you to make it your own.

ENNY LEIGHTY WEST SALEM, OH

EP: 15 MIN. + CHILLING
OK: 10 MIN. • **MAKES:** 4 SERVINGS

- can (15 ounces) black beans, rinsed and drained
- cup panko (Japanese) bread crumbs
- cup salsa, divided
- large egg, lightly beaten
- tablespoons minced fresh cilantro
- garlic clove, minced
- teaspoons canola oil
- whole wheat hamburger buns, split
- Sliced avocado, optional

In a large bowl, mash beans. x in bread crumbs, ½ cup of sa, egg, cilantro and garlic. pe bean mixture into four ties; refrigerate 30 minutes. In a large skillet, heat oil over dium heat. Cook the burgers minutes on each side or until ermometer reads 160°. Serve buns with remaining salsa and cado if desired.

ID YOU KNOW?

Cilantro is best when fresh. With a pungent, strong flavor, it comes from same plant as coriander seeds.

SALSA BEAN BURGERS

SALSA SPAGHETTI SQUASH

SALSA SPAGHETTI SQUASH

This satisfying dish is one of my favorite ways to use spaghetti squash. It's colorful and packed full of nutrients. You'll love how quickly it comes together.

—**CLARA COULSON MINNEY**
WASHINGTON COURT HOUSE, OH

START TO FINISH: 30 MIN. • **MAKES:** 4 SERVINGS

- 1 **medium spaghetti squash**
- 1 **medium onion, chopped**
- 2 **cups salsa**
- 1 **can (15 ounces) black beans, rinsed and drained**
- 3 **tablespoons minced fresh cilantro**
- 1 **medium ripe avocado, peeled and cubed**

1. Cut squash lengthwise in half; discard seeds. Place the squash on a microwave-safe plate, cut side down. Microwave, uncovered, on high for 15-18 minutes or until tender.

2. Meanwhile, in a nonstick skillet coated with cooking spray, cook and stir onion over medium heat until tender. Stir in salsa, beans and cilantro; heat through. Gently stir in the avocado; cook 1 minute longer.

3. When squash is cool enough to handle, use a fork to separate strands. Serve squash topped with salsa mixture.

NOTE *This recipe was tested in a 1,100-watt microwave.*

VEGETARIAN BLACK BEAN PASTA

My hearty vegetarian pasta is loaded with flavor. Use fresh rosemary when you have it on hand.

—**ASHLYNN AZAR** BEAVERTON, OR

START TO FINISH: 25 MIN. • **MAKES:** 6 SERVINGS

- 9 **ounces uncooked whole wheat fettuccine**
- 1 **tablespoon olive oil**
- 1¾ **cups sliced baby portobello mushrooms**
- 1 **garlic clove, minced**
- 1 **can (15 ounces) black beans, rinsed and drained**
- 1 **can (14½ ounces) diced tomatoes, undrained**
- 1 **teaspoon dried rosemary, crushed**
- ½ **teaspoon dried oregano**
- 2 **cups fresh baby spinach**

1. Cook fettuccine according to the package directions. Meanwhile, in a large skillet, heat oil over medium-high heat. Add mushrooms; cook and stir 4-6 minutes or until tender. Add garlic; cook 1 minute longer.

2. Stir in black beans, tomatoes, rosemary and oregano; heat through. Stir in the spinach until wilted. Drain fettuccine; add to bean mixture and toss to combine.

VEGETARIAN
BLACK BEAN PASTA

RAVIOLI WITH SNAP PEAS & MUSHROOMS

ST FIX

RAVIOLI WITH SNAP PEAS & MUSHROOMS

Here's a simple way to spruce up store-bought ravioli. The creamy, lemony sauce is a nice change from the traditional tomato-based ones.

CHARLENE CHAMBERS ORMOND BEACH, FL

START TO FINISH: 30 MIN. • **MAKES:** 8 SERVINGS

- 1 package (20 ounces) refrigerated cheese ravioli
- 1 pound fresh sugar snap peas, trimmed
- 1 tablespoon butter
- ½ pound sliced fresh mushrooms
- 3 shallots, finely chopped
- 2 garlic cloves, minced
- 2 cups fat-free evaporated milk
- 8 fresh sage leaves, thinly sliced, or 2 teaspoons rubbed sage
- 1 teaspoon grated lemon peel
- 1 teaspoon lemon-pepper seasoning
- ¼ teaspoon white pepper
- ¼ cup shredded Parmesan cheese
- ¼ cup hazelnuts, coarsely chopped and toasted

1. In a large saucepan, cook ravioli according to package directions, adding snap peas during the last 3 minutes of cooking; drain.

2. Meanwhile, in a large skillet, heat butter over medium-high heat. Add mushrooms, shallots and garlic; cook and stir until tender. Stir in milk, sage, lemon peel, lemon-pepper and white pepper; bring to a boil. Reduce the heat; simmer, uncovered, for 2 minutes or until sauce is slightly thickened.

3. Add ravioli and snap peas to sauce; heat through. Sprinkle with cheese and hazelnuts.

NOTE *To toast nuts, bake in a shallow pan in a 350° oven for 5-10 minutes or cook in a skillet over low heat until lightly browned, stirring occasionally.*

RATATOUILLE WITH POLENTA

Ratatouille is a classic vegetable stew that originated in the Provence region of France. Use the best of summer's fresh produce, and serve the stew over meaty polenta slices for a hearty main dish.

—*TASTE OF HOME* TEST KITCHEN

PREP: 20 MIN. • **COOK:** 15 MIN.
MAKES: 4 SERVINGS

- ½ **pound small fresh mushrooms, halved**
- 1 **medium sweet red pepper, chopped**
- 1 **small onion, chopped**
- 4 **teaspoons olive oil, divided**
- 4 **cups cubed peeled eggplant**
- 1 **small zucchini, chopped**
- 1 **cup cherry tomatoes**
- 2 **garlic cloves, minced**
- 1½ **teaspoons Italian seasoning**
- ½ **teaspoon salt**
- 1 **tube (1 pound) polenta, cut into ½-inch slices**
  Grated Parmesan cheese, optional

1. In a large skillet, saute the mushrooms, pepper and onion in 2 teaspoons of the oil until almost tender. Add the eggplant, zucchini, tomatoes, garlic, Italian seasoning and salt. Saute mixture for 8-10 minutes or until vegetables are tender.

2. In another skillet, cook the polenta slices in the remaining oil over medium-high heat for 3-4 minutes on each side or until lightly browned. Serve with ratatouille; sprinkle with cheese if desired.

RATATOUILLE
WITH POLENTA

PINTO BEAN TOSTADAS

Ready-to-go pinto beans and crispy corn tortillas prove how easy it is to make a healthy meal. Sometimes I add some chopped leftover meat to the tostadas, but they're equally satisfying just as they are.

—LILY JULOW LAWRENCEVILLE, GA

START TO FINISH: 30 MIN.
MAKES: 6 SERVINGS

- ¼ cup sour cream
- ¾ teaspoon grated lime peel
- ¼ teaspoon ground cumin
- ½ teaspoon salt, divided
- 2 tablespoons canola oil, divided
- 2 garlic cloves, minced
- 2 cans (15 ounces each) pinto beans, rinsed and drained
- 1 to 2 teaspoons hot pepper sauce
- 1 teaspoon chili powder
- 6 corn tortillas (6 inches)
- 2 cups shredded lettuce
- ½ cup salsa
- ¾ cup crumbled feta cheese or queso fresco
  Lime wedges

1. In a small bowl, mix sour cream, lime peel, cumin and ¼ teaspoon salt. In a large saucepan, heat 1 tablespoon oil over medium heat. Add garlic; cook and stir just until fragrant, about 45 seconds. Stir in beans, pepper sauce, chili powder and remaining salt; heat through, stirring occasionally. Keep warm.
2. Brush both sides of tortillas with remaining oil. Place a large skillet over medium-high heat. Add tortillas in two batches; cook 2-3 minutes on each side or until lightly browned and crisp.
3. To serve, arrange beans and lettuce over tostada shells; top with salsa, sour cream mixture and cheese. Serve tostadas with lime wedges.

GORGONZOLA PASTA WITH WALNUTS

Quick, easy and delicious, this is a weeknight staple at our house. Enjoy it as a side dish or double the recipe and toss in vegetarian ground meat crumbles for a heartier main dish.

—TRISHA KRUSE EAGLE, ID

START TO FINISH: 30 MIN.
MAKES: 3 SERVINGS

- 4 ounces uncooked spaghetti
- 1 large sweet onion, thinly sliced
- 2 tablespoons olive oil
- 1 garlic clove, minced
- 1 cup (4 ounces) crumbled Gorgonzola cheese
- 2 tablespoons balsamic vinegar
- ¼ teaspoon salt
- 1 tablespoon chopped walnuts, toasted

1. Cook spaghetti according to package directions. Meanwhile, in a large skillet, cook onion in the oil over medium heat for 15-20 minutes or until golden brown, stirring frequently. Add garlic; cook for 2 minutes longer. Remove from the heat.
2. Drain spaghetti; add to the skillet. Stir in the cheese, vinegar and salt. Sprinkle with walnuts.

PINTO BEAN TOSTADAS

ZIPPY ZUCCHINI PASTA

MEXICAN GRILLED CHEESE SANDWICHES

A little salsa goes a long way in these quick, no-fuss sandwiches. Perked up with sweet peppers, they're flavorful, fun and ideal on busy weeknights.

—*TASTE OF HOME* TEST KITCHEN

START TO FINISH: 25 MIN. • **MAKES:** 4 SERVINGS

- 1 medium sweet yellow pepper, chopped
- 1 medium green pepper, chopped
- 2 teaspoons olive oil
- 8 slices rye bread
- 2 tablespoons mayonnaise
- 1 cup fresh salsa, well drained
- ¾ cup shredded Mexican cheese blend
- 2 tablespoons butter, softened

1. In a small skillet, saute the peppers in oil until tender. Spread four bread slices with mayonnaise. Layer with peppers, salsa and cheese. Top with remaining bread. Butter outsides of sandwiches.

2. In a small skillet over medium heat, toast the sandwiches for 2-4 minutes on each side or until cheese is melted.

ZIPPY ZUCCHINI PASTA

Here's the perfect meal for two, with leftovers for one the next day. A colorful combination of zucchini and canned tomatoes is delicious over quick-cooking angel hair pasta. We like the extra zip from crushed red pepper flakes.

—**KATHLEEN TIMBERLAKE** DEARBORN HEIGHTS, MI

START TO FINISH: 15 MIN. • **MAKES:** 3 SERVINGS

- 1 package (7 ounces) angel hair pasta or thin spaghetti
- 2 small zucchini, cut into ¼-inch pieces
- 2 garlic cloves, minced
- 3 tablespoons olive oil
- 1 can (14½ ounces) Mexican diced tomatoes, undrained
- ¼ cup minced fresh parsley
- 1 teaspoon dried oregano
- ⅛ to ½ teaspoon crushed red pepper flakes

1. Cook pasta according to package directions. Meanwhile, in a large skillet, saute zucchini and garlic in oil until zucchini is crisp-tender.

2. Add the tomatoes, parsley, oregano and pepper flakes; heat through. Drain the pasta; serve with zucchini mixture.

MEXICAN GRILLED CHEESE SANDWICHES

EMON-GARLIC REAM FETTUCCINE

been making this for my family for years. It's both
ple and indulgent enough to make it a go-to recipe.
NNE MILLER GLENFIELD, NY

EP: 25 MIN. • **COOK:** 15 MIN. • **MAKES:** 4 SERVINGS

- teaspoons grated lemon peel
- teaspoons minced fresh parsley
- garlic cloves, minced
- ounces uncooked fettuccine

UCE

- cup butter
- small onion, chopped
- garlic cloves, minced
- teaspoon grated lemon peel
- cup heavy whipping cream
- teaspoon salt
- teaspoon pepper

4 ounces cream cheese, cubed
2 tablespoons lemon juice
2 plum tomatoes, chopped
2 teaspoons minced fresh parsley
  Grated Parmesan cheese, optional

1. In a small bowl, mix lemon peel, parsley and garlic. Cook fettuccine according to the package directions; drain.

2. For sauce, in a large skillet, heat butter over medium-high heat. Add the onion; cook and stir 2-3 minutes or until tender. Add garlic and lemon peel; cook 1 minute longer. Stir in the cream, salt and pepper. Whisk in the cream cheese until melted. Remove from the heat; cool slightly. Stir in the lemon juice.

3. Add pasta, tomatoes and parsley to skillet; toss to combine. Serve immediately with the lemon peel mixture and, if desired, Parmesan cheese.

FAST FIX

SQUASH FAJITAS WITH GOAT CHEESE

I like to pair unusual ingredients to create new and exciting twists on traditional foods. These fajitas are one of my specialties.

—**DEBRA KEIL** OWASSO, OK

START TO FINISH: 30 MIN.
MAKES: 4 SERVINGS

- 2 **pounds yellow summer squash, sliced**
- 1 **large sweet onion, chopped**
- 2 **tablespoons olive oil**
- 4 **garlic cloves, minced**
- 1 **teaspoon pepper**
- ½ **teaspoon salt**
- 8 **flour tortillas (8 inches)**
- 1 **log (4 ounces) fresh goat cheese, crumbled**
- 2 **tablespoons minced fresh parsley**

1. In a large skillet, saute squash and onion in the oil until tender. Add the garlic, pepper and salt; cook 1 minute longer.
2. Spoon onto tortillas. Top with cheese and sprinkle with parsley. Fold in sides.

FAST FIX

CREAMY EGGPLANT & MUSHROOM MONTE CRISTO

I know how important veggies are, so I sneak them into food in creative ways. I'm proud to say the eggplant sandwich is a hit with my son.

—**MACEY ALLEN** GREEN FOREST, AR

START TO FINISH: 30 MIN.
MAKES: 4 SERVINGS

- 5 **tablespoons olive oil, divided**
- 6 **slices eggplant (½ inch thick), halved**

CREAMY EGGPLANT & MUSHROOM MONTE CRISTO

- 2½ **cups sliced fresh shiitake or baby portobello mushrooms (about 6 ounces)**
- 1 **large garlic clove, minced**
- ½ **teaspoon salt**
- ¼ **teaspoon pepper**
- 2 **large eggs**
- 2 **tablespoons 2% milk**
- ½ **cup garlic-herb spreadable cheese (about 3 ounces)**
- 8 **slices wide-loaf white bread**

1. In a large nonstick skillet, heat 1 tablespoon of oil over medium heat. Add eggplant; cook 2-3 minutes on each side or until tender and lightly browned. Remove from pan.
2. In the same pan, heat 2 tablespoons oil over medium heat. Add mushrooms; cook and stir 2-3 minutes or until tende[r] Add garlic, salt and pepper; co[o] 1 minute longer. Remove from pan; wipe skillet clean.
3. In a shallow bowl, whisk th[e] eggs and milk until blended. Spread 1 tablespoon herb chee[se] over each slice of bread. Layer four slices with the eggplant a[nd] mushrooms; top vegetables wi[th] the remaining bread.
4. In same pan, heat 1 tablesp[oon] oil over medium heat. Careful[ly] dip both sides of sandwiches i[n] egg mixture, allowing each side to soak for 5 seconds. Place tw[o] sandwiches in the skillet; toast for 2-3 minutes on each side o[r] until golden brown. Repeat wi[th] remaining oil and sandwiches.

ORTOBELLO & BASIL CHEESE TORTELLINI

rtobello mushrooms and satisfying cheese tortellini ke this earthy, elegant dish perfect for either a quick, ual dinner or a more formal meal. I often use fresh il from my garden.

MARY SHIVERS ADA, OK

EP: 15 MIN. • **COOK:** 20 MIN. • **MAKES:** 4 SERVINGS

- package (19 ounces) frozen cheese tortellini
- pound sliced baby portobello mushrooms
- small onion, chopped
- cup butter, cubed
- garlic cloves, minced
- cup reduced-sodium chicken broth
- cup heavy whipping cream
- teaspoon salt
- teaspoon pepper
- cup grated Parmesan cheese
- tablespoons minced fresh basil or 2 teaspoons dried basil

Cook tortellini according to package directions. Meanwhile, in a large skillet, saute mushrooms d onion in butter until tender. Add garlic; cook 1 minute longer. Stir in the broth. Bring to a boil. duce heat; simmer, uncovered, for 12-15 minutes until liquid is reduced by half.

Add cream, salt and pepper. Cook 4-5 minutes ger or until slightly thickened. Drain tortellini; d to skillet. Stir in cheese and basil.

PORTOBELLO & BASIL CHEESE TORTELLINI

FAST FIX
COCONUT-GINGER CHICKPEAS & TOMATOES

This is my go-to quick dish. When you add tomatoes, you can also toss in some chopped green peppers to make it even more colorful.

—MALA UDAYAMURTHY SAN JOSE, CA

START TO FINISH: 30 MIN. • **MAKES:** 6 SERVINGS

- 2 tablespoons canola oil
- 2 medium onions, chopped (about 1⅓ cups)
- 3 large tomatoes, seeded and chopped (about 2 cups)
- 1 jalapeno pepper, seeded and chopped
- 1 tablespoon minced fresh gingerroot
- 2 cans (15 ounces each) chickpeas or garbanzo beans, rinsed and drained
- ¼ cup water
- 1 teaspoon salt
- 1 cup light coconut milk
- 3 tablespoons minced fresh cilantro
- 4½ cups hot cooked brown rice
   Additional minced fresh cilantro, optional

1. In a large skillet, heat oil over medium-high heat. Add the onions; cook and stir until crisp-tender. Add the tomatoes, jalapeno and ginger; cook and stir 2-3 minutes longer or until tender.
2. Stir in chickpeas, water and salt; bring to a boil. Reduce heat; simmer, uncovered, 4-5 minutes or until liquid is almost evaporated. Remove from heat; stir in coconut milk and cilantro.
3. Serve with the rice; sprinkle with additional cilantro if desired.
NOTE *Wear disposable gloves when cutting hot peppers; the oils can burn skin. Avoid touching your face.*

DID YOU KNOW?

Fresh gingerroot is available in your grocer's produce section. It should have a smooth skin. If wrinkled and cracked, the root is dry and past its prime. When stored in a heavy-duty resealable plastic bag, unpeeled gingerroot can be frozen for up to 1 year. When needed, simply peel and grate.

VEGGIE BEAN TACOS

I can't wait for the fresh corn and just-picked tomatoes to be in season so I can enjoy authentic Mexican dishes like these tasty tacos.
—**TONYA BURKHARD** DAVIS, IL

PREP: 20 MIN. • **COOK:** 20 MIN.
MAKES: 6 SERVINGS

- 2 **cups fresh corn**
- 2 **tablespoons canola oil, divided**
- 4 **medium tomatoes, seeded and chopped**
- 3 **small zucchini, chopped**
- 1 **large red onion, chopped**
- 3 **garlic cloves, minced**
- 1 **cup black beans, rinsed and drained**
- 1 **teaspoon minced fresh oregano or ¼ teaspoon dried oregano**
- ½ **teaspoon salt**
- ¼ **teaspoon pepper**
- 12 **corn tortillas (6 inches), warmed**
- ¾ **cup shredded Monterey Jack cheese**
- ¼ **cup salsa verde**
- 1 **medium ripe avocado, peeled and thinly sliced**
  Reduced-fat sour cream, optional

1. In a large skillet, saute corn in 1 tablespoon oil until lightly browned. Remove and keep warm. In the same skillet, saute tomatoes, zucchini and onion in remaining oil until tender. Add garlic; cook 1 minute longer. Stir in the beans, oregano, salt, pepper and corn; heat through.

2. Divide filling among tortillas. Top with cheese, salsa, avocado and, if desired, sour cream.

VEGGIE BEAN TACOS

ENNE WITH
OMATOES
WHITE BEANS

I learned how to make this dish from friends in Genoa, Italy, where they're known for eating tasty combinations of gies, pasta and beans. You also substitute feta cheese ive this a Greek twist.

RISHA KRUSE EAGLE, ID

RT TO FINISH: 30 MIN.
KES: 4 SERVINGS

ounces uncooked penne
pasta
tablespoons olive oil
garlic clove, minced
cans (14½ ounces each)
Italian diced tomatoes,
undrained

1 can (15 ounces) white kidney
or cannellini beans, rinsed
and drained
1 package (10 ounces) fresh
spinach, trimmed
¼ cup sliced ripe olives
½ teaspoon salt
¼ teaspoon pepper
½ cup grated Parmesan cheese

1. Cook the pasta according to package directions. Meanwhile, in a large skillet, heat oil over medium-high heat. Add garlic; cook and stir for 1 minute. Add tomatoes and beans. Bring to a boil. Reduce the heat; simmer, uncovered, 5-7 minutes to allow flavors to blend.

2. Add the spinach, olives, salt and pepper; cook and stir over medium heat until the spinach is wilted. Drain pasta; top with tomato mixture and cheese.

PENNE WITH TOMATOES
& WHITE BEANS

VEGETABLE PASTA WITH SUN-DRIED TOMATO SAUCE

Sun-dried tomato spread is a blend of sun-dried tomatoes, tomato paste and olive oil. Use it as a spread on toast or instead of tomato paste in recipes. It's delicious!
—*TASTE OF HOME* TEST KITCHEN

PREP: 20 MIN. • **COOK:** 15 MIN.
MAKES: 6 SERVINGS

2 cups uncooked bow tie pasta
1¼ cups half-and-half cream
⅓ cup sun-dried tomato spread
1 large sweet red pepper,
julienned
1 large sweet yellow pepper,
julienned
1 cup sliced fresh mushrooms
1 small onion, sliced
5 teaspoons olive oil
1 package (10 ounces) frozen
peas, thawed
½ teaspoon salt
¼ teaspoon pepper
Minced fresh parsley and
grated Parmesan cheese,
optional

Cook pasta according to package directions. Meanwhile, in a small bowl, combine the cream and sun-dried tomato spread until blended. In a large skillet, saute peppers, mushrooms and onion in oil until crisp-tender. Reduce heat. Add cream mixture; bring to a gentle boil. Cook and stir for 2 minutes. Stir in the peas, salt and pepper. Drain the pasta; add to the sauce mixture. Cook for 5 minutes or until mixture is heated through. Garnish with parsley and cheese if desired.

CURRIED TOFU WITH RICE

Get your protein from tofu in a bold-tasting dish. It's packed with curry and cilantro, and with all that flavor going on, you won't even miss the meat!

—**CRYSTAL JO BRUNS** ILIFF, CO

PREP: 15 MIN. • **COOK:** 20 MIN. • **MAKES:** 4 SERVINGS

- 1 **package (12.3 ounces) extra-firm tofu, drained and cubed**
- 1 **teaspoon seasoned salt**
- 1 **tablespoon canola oil**
- 1 **small onion, chopped**
- 3 **garlic cloves, minced**
- ½ **cup light coconut milk**
- ¼ **cup minced fresh cilantro**
- 1 **teaspoon curry powder**
- ¼ **teaspoon salt**
- ¼ **teaspoon pepper**
- 2 **cups cooked brown rice**

1. Sprinkle tofu with the seasoned salt. In a large nonstick skillet coated with cooking spray, saute the tofu in oil until lightly browned. Remove and keep warm.

2. In the same skillet, saute the onion and garlic for 1-2 minutes or until crisp-tender. Stir in the coconut milk, cilantro, curry, salt and pepper. Bring to a boil. Reduce heat; simmer, uncovered, 4-5 minutes or until sauce is slightly thickened. Stir in tofu; heat through. Serve with rice.

FAST FIX ▶

LINGUINE WITH BROCCOLI RABE & PEPPERS

Broccoli rabe is one of my favorite vegetables. This dish preps in a flash because you cook the broccoli right along with the pasta. And before you know it, a colorful and nutritious dinner is ready.

—**GILDA LESTER** MILLSBORO, DE

START TO FINISH: 25 MIN. • **MAKES:** 6 SERVINGS

- 1 **pound broccoli rabe**
- 1 **package (16 ounces) linguine**
- 3 **tablespoons olive oil**
- 2 **anchovy fillets, finely chopped, optional**
- 3 **garlic cloves, minced**
- ½ **cup sliced roasted sweet red peppers**
- ½ **cup pitted Greek olives, halved**
- ½ **teaspoon crushed red pepper flakes**
- ¼ **teaspoon pepper**
- ⅛ **teaspoon salt**
- ½ **cup grated Romano cheese**

1. Cut ½ in. off ends of broccoli rabe; trim woo[d] stems. Cut stems and leaves into 2-in. pieces. Co[ok] linguine according to package directions, adding broccoli rabe during the last 5 minutes of cooki[ng] Drain, reserving ½ cup of the pasta water.

2. Meanwhile, in a large skillet, heat the oil over medium-high heat. Add anchovies and garlic; c[ook] and stir 1 minute. Stir in red peppers, olives, pep[per] flakes, salt and pepper.

3. Add linguine and broccoli rabe to skillet; toss to combine, adding reserved pasta water as desi[red] to moisten. Serve with cheese.

LINGUINE WITH BROCCOLI RABE & PEPPERS

INDIAN SPICED CHICKPEA WRAPS

Raita, an Indian condiment made with yogurt, elevates this vegetarian dish into a satisfying gourmet wrap. I sometimes substitute diced mango or cucumber for the pineapple and add fresh herbs like cilantro or mint.

JENNIFER BECKMAN FALLS CHURCH, VA

START TO FINISH: 30 MIN.
MAKES: 4 SERVINGS (1⅓ CUPS SAUCE)

RAITA
- 1 cup (8 ounces) reduced-fat plain yogurt
- ½ cup drained unsweetened pineapple tidbits
- ¼ teaspoon salt
- ¼ teaspoon ground cumin

WRAPS
- 2 teaspoons canola oil
- 1 small onion, chopped
- 1 tablespoon minced fresh gingerroot
- 2 garlic cloves, minced
- ½ teaspoon curry powder
- ¼ teaspoon each salt, ground cumin and ground coriander
- ¼ teaspoon cayenne pepper, optional
- 1 can (15 ounces) chickpeas or garbanzo beans, rinsed and drained
- 1 cup canned crushed tomatoes
- 4 whole wheat tortillas (8 inches), warmed
- 3 cups fresh baby spinach

1. In a small bowl, mix raita ingredients; set aside.
2. For wraps, in a nonstick skillet coated with cooking spray, heat oil over medium-high heat. Add onion; cook and stir until tender. Add ginger, garlic and seasonings; cook and stir 1 minute longer.
3. Stir in chickpeas and tomatoes. Bring to a boil. Reduce heat; simmer, uncovered, for 5-8 minutes or until slightly thickened, stirring occasionally.
4. Near the center of each tortilla, arrange spinach and chickpea mixture; top with the raita. Roll up tightly; serve immediately.

**DEBI MITCHELL'S
JALAPENO BUTTERMILK CORN
BREAD** *PAGE 193*

Sizzling Side Dishes & More

Cast-iron-baked breads, garden-fresh favorites, pasta classics...it's a snap to round out menus with these easy additions.

FAST FIX

HOT AND ZESTY QUINOA

What a fun way to spice up dinner! Featuring a bit of a kick, this skillet side offers more protein and makes an easy, interesting change from potatoes or rice.

—**SANDRA LETIZIA** PROVIDENCE, RI

START TO FINISH: 25 MIN.
MAKES: 4 SERVINGS

- 1 **cup water**
- ½ **cup quinoa, rinsed**
- 1 **small onion, finely chopped**
- 1 **teaspoon olive oil**
- 2 **garlic cloves, minced**
- 1 **can (10 ounces) diced tomatoes and green chilies**
- 2 **tablespoons chopped marinated quartered artichoke hearts**
- 2 **tablespoons grated Parmesan cheese**

1. In a small saucepan, bring water to a boil. Add the quinoa. Reduce heat; cover and simmer for 12-15 minutes or until liquid is absorbed. Remove from the heat; fluff with a fork.
2. In a large skillet, saute onion in the oil until tender. Add garlic; cook for 1 minute longer. Add the tomatoes and green chilies. Bring to a boil over medium heat. Reduce heat; simmer, uncovered, for 10 minutes. Stir in quinoa and artichoke; heat through. Sprinkle with cheese.
NOTE *Look for quinoa in the cereal, rice or organic food aisle.*

(5) INGREDIENTS FAST FIX

BROCCOLI WITH ASIAGO

Here's one of the best and simplest ways I've found to serve broccoli. It's also good with Parmesan if you don't have Asiago cheese.

—**CJINTEXAS,** *TASTE OF HOME*
ONLINE COMMUNITY

START TO FINISH: 20 MIN.
MAKES: 4 SERVINGS

- 1 **bunch broccoli, cut into spears**
- 4 **teaspoons minced garlic**
- 2 **tablespoons olive oil**
- ¼ **teaspoon salt**
  Dash pepper
- 1 **cup (4 ounces) shaved Asiago cheese**

1. Place the broccoli in a large skillet; cover with water. Bring a boil. Reduce heat; cover and simmer for 5-7 minutes or unt broccoli is tender. Drain well. Remove and keep warm.
2. In the same skillet, saute th garlic in oil for 1 minute. Stir in the broccoli, salt and pepper. Top with cheese.

BROCCOLI WITH ASIAGO

MUSHROOM & PEAS RICE PILAF

Anything goes in a rice pilaf, so add peas and baby portobello mushrooms for a spring-like burst of color and a variety of textures.
—**STACY MULLENS** GRESHAM, OR

START TO FINISH: 25 MIN.
MAKES: 6 SERVINGS

- 1 **package (6.6 ounces) rice pilaf mix with toasted almonds**
- 1 **tablespoon butter**
- 1½ **cups fresh or frozen peas**
- 1 **cup sliced baby portobello mushrooms**

1. Prepare pilaf according to package directions.
2. In a large skillet, heat butter over medium heat. Add the peas and mushrooms; cook and stir 6-8 minutes or until tender. Stir in rice.

TOP TIP

As long as you're whipping up Mushroom & Peas Rice Pilaf, why not double or triple the recipe for busy nights? Divide the extra pilaf into 1 cup portions and transfer each to a resealable freezer storage bag. Squeeze out the air, flatten the bag and seal. Simply take out portions as needed and reheat in the microwave.

MUSHROOM & PEAS
RICE PILAF

BRANDY-GLAZED CARRO

RANDY-GLAZED CARROTS

ınd this recipe about 10 years ago in an old
kbook from a thrift store and changed the sugar
ılled for to honey. Once these carrots are glazed,
y are not just delicious, but they look pretty, too.
ʌMMY LANDRY SAUCIER, MS

RT TO FINISH: 30 MIN.
KES: 12 SERVINGS (¾ CUP EACH)

pounds fresh baby carrots
cup butter, cubed
cup honey
cup brandy
cup minced fresh parsley
teaspoon salt
teaspoon pepper

ı large skillet, bring ½ in. of water to a boil. Add
rots. Cover and cook for 5-9 minutes or until
ıp-tender. Drain and set aside. In the same
ılet, cook butter and honey over medium heat
ıil butter is melted. Remove from heat; stir in
ındy. Bring to a boil; cook until liquid is reduced
ıbout ½ cup. Add the carrots, parsley, salt and
ıper; heat through.

LAPENO BUTTERMILK
ƆRN BREAD

ıu're from the South, you have to have a good
ın bread recipe. Here's a healthier version of my
ım's traditional corn bread.
ıEBI MITCHELL FLOWER MOUND, TX

ɛP: 15 MIN. • **BAKE:** 20 MIN. • **MAKES:** 8 SERVINGS

cup self-rising flour
cup yellow cornmeal
cup buttermilk
cup egg substitute
tablespoon canola oil, divided
tablespoons honey
tablespoon reduced-fat mayonnaise
cup fresh or frozen corn, thawed
tablespoons shredded reduced-fat cheddar
cheese
tablespoons finely chopped sweet red pepper
to 1 jalapeno pepper, seeded and finely chopped

1. Preheat oven to 425°. In a large bowl, whisk flour
and cornmeal. In another bowl, whisk buttermilk,
egg substitute, 2 tablespoons oil, honey and the
mayonnaise. Pour remaining oil into a cast-iron
or 8-in. ovenproof skillet; place skillet in oven for
4 minutes.

2. Meanwhile, add buttermilk mixture to flour
mixture; stir just until moistened. Fold in corn,
cheese and peppers.

3. Carefully tilt and rotate skillet to coat bottom
with oil; add batter. Bake 20-25 minutes or until
a toothpick inserted in center comes out clean.
Serve warm.

NOTE *As a substitute for 1 cup of self-rising flour,
place 1½ teaspoons baking powder and ½ teaspoon
salt in a measuring cup. Add all-purpose flour to
measure 1 cup. Also, wear disposable gloves when
cutting hot peppers; the oils can burn skin. Avoid
touching your face.*

DID YOU KNOW?

Corn bread can be made light! If you're looking
for a corn bread that pares back calories and fat,
look no further than Jalapeno Buttermilk Corn
Bread. It uses honey as a sweetener without adding
processed sugar, and reduced-fat products keep
things lighter than traditional recipes. No one will
realize they're eating fewer calories!

FAST FIX
HERBED NOODLES WITH EDAMAME

Give meals a pop of color with my stovetop recipe. All the fresh herbs make it feel extra-special even though it's oh-so easy!

—**MARIE RIZZIO** INTERLOCHEN, MI

START TO FINISH: 30 MIN.
MAKES: 4 SERVINGS

- 3½ cups uncooked egg noodles
- 2 tablespoons butter
- 1 green onion, sliced
- 1 tablespoon finely chopped sweet red pepper
- ½ cup frozen shelled edamame, thawed
- ¼ cup reduced-sodium chicken broth
- 1 tablespoon minced fresh parsley
- 1½ teaspoons minced fresh marjoram
- 1½ teaspoons minced fresh chives
- 1 tablespoon olive oil
- ¼ cup grated Romano cheese

1. Cook noodles according to package directions. Meanwhile, in a large skillet, heat butter over medium-high heat. Add onion and red pepper; cook and stir until tender. Stir in edamame and broth; heat through. Add the herbs.

2. Drain the noodles and add to skillet; toss to combine. Transfer to a serving plate. Drizzle with oil and sprinkle with cheese.

FAST FIX
CURRIED FRIED RICE WITH PINEAPPLE

This special fried rice, often known as Khao Pad, is popular in Thai restaurants. It has a bit of heat, a little sweetness and some crunch.

—**JOANNA YUEN** SAN JOSE, CA

START TO FINISH: 30 MIN.
MAKES: 8 SERVINGS

- 4 tablespoons canola oil, divided
- 2 large eggs, beaten
- 1 small onion, finely chopped
- 2 shallots, finely chopped
- 3 garlic cloves, minced
- 4 cups cold cooked rice
- 1 can (8 ounces) unsweetened pineapple chunks, drained
- ½ cup lightly salted cashews
- ½ cup frozen peas
- ⅓ cup minced fresh cilantro
- ¼ cup raisins
- 3 tablespoons chicken broth
- 2 tablespoons fish sauce
- 1½ teaspoons curry powder
- 1 teaspoon sugar
- ¼ teaspoon crushed red pepper flakes

1. In a large skillet or wok, heat 1 tablespoon oil over medium-high heat; add eggs. As eggs set, lift the edges, letting uncooked portion flow underneath. When the eggs are completely cooked, remove to a plate and keep warm.

2. In the same pan, stir-fry onion and shallots in the remaining until tender. Add the garlic; cook 1 minute longer. Stir in the rice, pineapple, cashews, peas, cilantro, raisins, broth, fish sauce, curry, sugar and pepper flakes; heat through. Chop the egg into small pieces; add to the rice mixture.

CURRIED FRIED RICE WITH PINEAPPLE

LOADED CHEDDAR-
CORN POTATO
PATTIES

Golden, crunchy and delicious mashed potato patties are seasoned with cheese, corn and green onions. These crispy little loaded potato patties are a perfect side, and if you make them smaller, they're a great hand-held appetizer.

—DARLENE BRENDEN SALEM, OR

START TO FINISH: 30 MIN.
MAKES: 1 DOZEN (1 CUP SAUCE)

- **1 cup (8 ounces) sour cream**
- **2 tablespoons plus ⅓ cup thinly sliced green onions**
- **2 cups mashed potato flakes**
- **⅓ cup cornmeal**
- **1¾ teaspoons garlic salt**
- **½ teaspoon smoked paprika**
- **2 cups 2% milk**
- **1 package (10 ounces) frozen corn, thawed**
- **1 cup (4 ounces) shredded extra-sharp cheddar cheese**

In a small bowl, mix the sour cream and 2 tablespoons green onion; refrigerate until serving.

In a large bowl, mix the potato flakes, cornmeal, garlic salt and paprika. Add the milk, corn, cheese and the remaining green onions; mix until blended. Using ⅓ cupfuls, shape mixture into twelve 3½-in. patties.

Heat a large nonstick skillet coated with cooking spray over medium heat. Cook the patties in batches for 2-3 minutes on each side or until golden brown. Serve with sauce.

O'LARRY'S SKILLET POTATOES

O'LARRY'S SKILLET POTATOES

My husband, Larry, uses all fresh ingredients when he prepares his famous O'Larry's Skillet Potatoes. These zippy potatoes have colorful bits of red pepper.

—KERRY AMUNDSON OCEAN PARK, WA

START TO FINISH: 30 MIN. • **MAKES:** 10 SERVINGS

- 2 **pounds potatoes, cut into ½-inch cubes**
- 1 **medium onion, finely chopped**
- 1 **medium sweet red pepper, chopped**
- 1 **teaspoon Caribbean jerk seasoning**
- 1 **teaspoon salt**
- ¼ **cup olive oil**
- 2 **garlic cloves, minced**

1. Place potatoes in a large saucepan and cover with water. Bring to a boil. Reduce heat; cover and simmer for 5-10 minutes or until almost tender. Drain.

2. In a large skillet, saute the potatoes, onion, red pepper, jerk seasoning and salt in oil until potatoes are golden brown and vegetables are tender. Add garlic; cook 1 minute longer.

BROCCOLI CAULIFLOWER COMBO

Shallots, basil and broth rev up the earthy flavors of this nutritious vegetable medley. And the bright green color dresses up any plate!

—CLARA COULSON MINNEY WASHINGTON COURT HOUSE, OH

START TO FINISH: 25 MIN. • **MAKES:** 6 SERVINGS

- 4 **cups fresh broccoli florets**
- 2 **cups fresh cauliflowerets**
- 3 **shallots, chopped**
- ½ **cup reduced-sodium chicken broth or vegetable broth**
- 1 **teaspoon dried basil**
- ½ **teaspoon seasoned salt**
- ⅛ **teaspoon pepper**

In a large skillet, combine all ingredients. Cover and cook over medium heat for 6-8 minutes or until the vegetables are crisp-tender, stirring mixture occasionally.

GOLDEN SWEET ONION CORN BREAD

your cast-iron skillet to use with this hearty corn
bread. Make extra Cranberry Butter. It's also great on
morning bagels and livens up cooked poultry entrees.
—TASTE OF HOME TEST KITCHEN

PREP: 35 MIN. • **BAKE:** 20 MIN. + STANDING
MAKES: 8 SERVINGS

- tablespoons butter
- large sweet onion, halved and thinly sliced
- teaspoons chopped seeded jalapeno pepper
- teaspoon chili powder, divided
- tablespoons brown sugar, divided
- ½ cups all-purpose flour
- cup yellow cornmeal
- tablespoons sugar
- teaspoons baking powder
- teaspoon kosher salt
- teaspoon baking soda
- ¼ cups buttermilk
- large eggs, lightly beaten
- cup butter, melted
- cup shredded cheddar cheese
- can (4 ounces) chopped green chilies

CRANBERRY BUTTER
- cup whole-berry cranberry sauce
- teaspoon grated lime peel
- cup butter, softened

In a 10-in. cast-iron skillet, melt 2 tablespoons
butter; tilt to coat bottom and sides. Add the onion,
jalapeno and ¼ teaspoon chili powder; cook over
medium-low heat until onion is lightly browned
and tender. Stir in 1 tablespoon of the brown sugar
until dissolved; set aside.

In a large bowl, combine the flour, cornmeal,
sugar, baking powder, salt, baking soda, and the
remaining chili powder and brown sugar. In a
small bowl, whisk the buttermilk, eggs and
melted butter. Stir into the dry ingredients just
until moistened. Fold in the cheese and chilies.
Pour over onion mixture in skillet. Bake at
375° for 20-25 minutes or until golden brown.
Meanwhile, in a small saucepan, cook cranberry
sauce and lime peel over low heat until heated
through. Cool completely.

4. Let corn bread stand for 10 minutes. Invert
corn bread onto a serving platter; cut into wedges.
Pour cranberry mixture over softened butter;
serve with corn bread.

NOTE *Wear disposable gloves when cutting hot
peppers; the oils can burn skin. Avoid touching
your face.*

FAST FIX
HERBED PEAS
Fresh herbs create peas that please! Here's a great
side that I love serving along with meaty entrees.
—**MARY ANN DELL** PHOENIXVILLE, PA

START TO FINISH: 25 MIN. • **MAKES:** 8 SERVINGS

- ⅓ cup butter
- 6 cups fresh or frozen peas
- ¾ cup thinly sliced green onions
- 3 tablespoons minced fresh parsley
- 3 tablespoons minced fresh basil
- 1 teaspoon sugar
- ¾ teaspoon salt
- ½ teaspoon pepper

In a large skillet, heat butter over medium-high
heat. Add peas and green onions; cook and stir
until tender. Stir in the remaining ingredients.

HERBED PEAS

PEPPER SQUASH SAUTE

I double the ingredients when I'm making this recipe because it's just as good reheated later in the week.

—JANICE MCCLOSKEY HOWARD, PA

START TO FINISH: 25 MIN.
MAKES: 4 SERVINGS

- 1 **small onion, chopped**
- ⅓ **cup each chopped green, sweet red and yellow pepper**
- 1 **tablespoon butter**
- 1 **medium zucchini, chopped**
- 1 **medium yellow summer squash, chopped**
- 1 **medium carrot, shredded**
- 2 **garlic cloves, minced**
- ½ **teaspoon salt**
- ¼ **teaspoon pepper**

In a large nonstick skillet, saute onion and peppers in butter for 3-4 minutes. Stir in the zucchini, summer squash and carrot; saute 3-4 minutes or until vegetables are tender. Add garlic; cook 1 minute longer or until tender. Sprinkle with salt and pepper.

HOW TO

MINCE AND CHOP

❶ To mince or chop, hold the handle of a chef's knife with one hand, and rest the fingers of your other hand on the top of the blade near the tip.
❷ Using the handle as a guide, move knife in an arc across the food in a rocking motion until pieces are the desired size.

PEPPER SQUASH SAUTE

AUTEED ORANGE-
LAZED BABY
ARROTS

e's a wonderful accompaniment
ust about any main dish at any
e of year. The carrots are sauteed
sweet orange butter sauce with
ique blend of spices.
—NGELA BARTOW CATO, WI

RT TO FINISH: 30 MIN.
KES: 4 SERVINGS

pound fresh baby carrots
tablespoons butter

3 **tablespoons thawed orange**
juice concentrate
¼ **teaspoon dried thyme**
¼ **teaspoon paprika**
¼ **teaspoon ground cumin**
⅛ **teaspoon salt**
⅛ **teaspoon pepper**

In a large skillet, saute carrots
in butter for 8 minutes. Stir in
the remaining ingredients; cook
for 2 minutes longer. Reduce the
heat; cover skillet and simmer
for 8-10 minutes or until carrots
are tender.

**SAUTEED ORANGE-GLAZED
BABY CARROTS**

SCALLOPED
POTATOES AU
GRATIN

I found I could
cut down the
time in preparing
scalloped
potatoes by first
simmering them
on top of the stove in an ovenproof
skillet and then slipping it into the
oven to finish them nicely with
a brown crust.
—LILY JULOW LAWRENCEVILLE, GA

PREP: 35 MIN. **BAKE:** 15 MIN.
MAKES: 2 SERVINGS

2 **cups thinly sliced peeled**
potatoes (about 2 large)
2 **teaspoons all-purpose flour**
Dash each salt, pepper and
ground nutmeg
2 **teaspoons butter**
⅔ **to 1 cup half-and-half cream**
⅓ **cup shredded Gouda cheese**

1. Place half of the potatoes in
a greased small cast-iron or
ovenproof skillet; sprinkle with
1 teaspoon flour. Repeat layers.
Sprinkle with salt, pepper and
nutmeg. Dot with butter.
2. Add enough cream to fill
skillet about three-fourths full.
Bring to a boil over medium-high
heat. Reduce the heat; simmer,
uncovered, for 15-20 minutes
or until most of the liquid in the
skillet is absorbed.
3. Carefully place skillet in oven.
Bake, uncovered, at 350° for
10-15 minutes or until bubbly
and potatoes are tender. Sprinkle
with the cheese; bake 5 minutes
longer or until cheese is melted.

RIGATONI CHARD TOSS

I wanted to get my firefighter husband to eat more fruits and veggies to help lower his cholesterol and triglycerides. Fresh chard and tomatoes add fiber and vitamins, but we actually love it for the flavor. While he would never admit to eating healthy food to his buddies at the firehouse, this dish is one of many that made his trips to the doctor much more pleasant!

—**CAROLYN KUMPE** EL DORADO, CA

PREP: 25 MIN. • **COOK:** 20 MIN. • **MAKES:** 10 SERVINGS

- 8 **ounces uncooked rigatoni or large tube pasta**
- 2 **tablespoons olive oil**
- 1 **bunch Swiss chard, coarsely chopped**
- 1 **small onion, thinly sliced**
- 2 **garlic cloves, minced**
- 3 **medium tomatoes, chopped**
- 1 **can (15 ounces) white kidney or cannellini beans, rinsed and drained**
- ½ **teaspoon salt**
- ⅛ **teaspoon crushed red pepper flakes**
- ⅛ **teaspoon fennel seed, crushed**
- ⅛ **teaspoon pepper**
- ¼ **cup minced fresh basil**
- ½ **cup grated Parmesan cheese**

1. Cook rigatoni according to package directions.
2. Meanwhile, in a large skillet, heat the oil over medium-high heat. Add Swiss chard and onion; cook and stir 4 minutes. Add garlic; cook 2 minutes longer. Stir in tomatoes, beans, salt, pepper flakes, fennel and pepper. Cook for 3-4 minutes longer or until chard is tender.
3. Drain rigatoni, reserving ¼ cup pasta water. Add rigatoni, pasta water and basil to skillet; toss to combine. Serve with cheese.

RIGATONI CHARD TOSS

LEMONY GREEN BEANS

You can throw together a tasty side in just minutes using ingredients you probably already have on hand.

—JENNIFER TARANTINO
RUTHERFORD, NJ

START TO FINISH: 20 MIN.
MAKES: 6 SERVINGS

- ¼ cup chicken broth
- 2 tablespoons olive oil
- 1½ pounds fresh green beans, trimmed
- ¾ teaspoon lemon-pepper seasoning
  Lemon wedges

In a large skillet, heat the chicken broth and oil over medium-high heat. Add green beans; cook and stir until crisp-tender. Sprinkle with lemon-pepper. Serve with lemon wedges.

SAUTEED CORN WITH CHEDDAR

My husband likes only this kind of corn, so I make it about once a week. Plus, it's so easy that anyone could make it in a jiffy!

SARAH COPE DUNDEE, NY

START TO FINISH: 10 MIN.
MAKES: 2 SERVINGS

- 1½ cups frozen corn, thawed
- ⅛ teaspoon salt
- ⅛ teaspoon pepper
- 1 tablespoon butter
- ¾ cup shredded cheddar cheese

In a small skillet, saute the corn, salt and pepper in butter until tender. Stir in cheese.

LEMONY GREEN BEANS

ITALIAN DRESSED BROCCOLI

Here's a tangy treatment for broccoli that the whole family will enjoy. It tastes terrific with Italian-themed meals, but would work equally well alongside almost any main dish.

—TASTE OF HOME TEST KITCHEN

START TO FINISH: 20 MIN.
MAKES: 5 SERVINGS

- 4 cups fresh broccoli florets
- 1 medium onion, halved and sliced
- ⅔ cup water
- ⅓ cup Italian salad dressing
- 1 tablespoon butter
- ½ teaspoon dried oregano
- ¼ teaspoon garlic powder
- ¼ teaspoon dried parsley flakes
- ¼ teaspoon salt

Place the broccoli, onion and water in a large skillet. Bring to a boil. Reduce heat; cover and simmer for 3 minutes. Add the remaining ingredients. Cook and stir over medium heat for 2-4 minutes or until vegetables are tender and liquid is reduced.

KASHA VARNISHKES

One of the great Jewish comfort foods, kasha is easy to put together, and leftovers make a surprisingly delicious breakfast. Find buckwheat groats with other grains or in the kosher foods section.

—JOANNE WEINTRAUB
MILWAUKEE, WI

PREP: 10 MIN. • **COOK:** 25 MIN.
MAKES: 8 SERVINGS

- 4 **cups uncooked bow tie pasta**
- 2 **large onions, chopped**
- 1 **cup sliced fresh mushrooms**
- 2 **tablespoons canola oil**
- 1 **cup roasted whole grain buckwheat groats (kasha)**
- 1 **large egg, lightly beaten**
- 2 **cups chicken broth, heated**
- ½ **teaspoon salt**
  Dash pepper
  Minced fresh parsley

1. Cook the pasta according to package directions. Meanwhile, saute onions and mushrooms in oil in a large skillet until lightly browned, about 9 minutes. Remove from pan and set aside.
2. Combine buckwheat groats and egg in a small bowl; add to the same skillet. Cook and stir over high heat for 2-4 minutes or until buckwheat is browned, separating grains with the back of a spoon. Add the hot broth, salt and pepper.
3. Bring to a boil; add the onion mixture. Reduce heat; cover and simmer for 10-12 minutes or until liquid is absorbed. Drain pasta; add to the pan and heat through. Sprinkle with parsley.

FAST FIX
SPEEDY SPANISH RICE

Mexican food is big with our family; in fact, one of my nephews loves this dish so much that he always requests it for his special birthday dinner, and I'm happy to comply!

—ANGIE RORICK FORT WAYNE, IN

START TO FINISH: 25 MIN.
MAKES: 4 SERVINGS

- 1½ **cups uncooked instant brown rice**
- 1 **medium onion, chopped**
- 1 **small green pepper, chopped**
- 1 **tablespoon butter**
- 1 **garlic clove, minced**
- 1½ **cups water**
- 1 **tablespoon minced fresh cilantro**
- 2 **teaspoons ground cumin**
- 1½ **teaspoons chicken bouillon granules**
- ¼ **teaspoon pepper**
- 1 **cup picante sauce**

1. In a large nonstick skillet, saute the rice, onion and green pepper in butter until the rice is lightly browned and vegetables are crisp-tender. Add garlic; cook 1 minute longer. Stir in the water, cilantro, cumin, bouillon and pepper; bring to a boil. Reduce the heat; cover and simmer for 5 minutes.
2. Remove from the heat; let stand for 5 minutes. Fluff with a fork. Stir in picante sauce.

SPEEDY SPANISH RICE

SHREDDED GINGERED
BRUSSELS SPROUTS

SHREDDED GINGERED BRUSSELS SPROUTS

Even people who normally don't care for Brussels sprouts will ask for a second helping of these.

—JAMES SCHEND
PLEASANT PRAIRIE, WI

START TO FINISH: 25 MIN.
MAKES: 6 SERVINGS

- 1 **pound fresh Brussels sprouts (about 5½ cups)**
- 1 **tablespoon olive oil**
- 1 **small onion, finely chopped**
- 1 **tablespoon minced fresh gingerroot**
- 1 **garlic clove, minced**
- ½ **teaspoon salt**
- 2 **tablespoons water**
- ¼ **teaspoon pepper**

1. Trim Brussels sprouts. Cut the sprouts lengthwise in half; cut crosswise into thin slices.

2. Place a large skillet over medium-high heat. Add the Brussels sprouts; cook and stir 2-3 minutes or until sprouts begin to brown lightly. Add oil and toss to coat. Stir in onion, ginger, garlic and salt. Add water; reduce heat to medium and cook, covered, 1-2 minutes or until vegetables are tender. Stir in the pepper.

FAST FIX

CREAMY SWEET CORN WITH OKRA

A bit of cream and a few crumbles of bacon lightly coat these delightful veggies the whole family will love.
—*TASTE OF HOME* TEST KITCHEN

START TO FINISH: 20 MIN. • **MAKES:** 4 SERVINGS

- 1 small onion, chopped
- 2 tablespoons butter
- 1 garlic clove, minced
- 3 cups frozen corn, thawed
- 1 cup frozen sliced okra, thawed
- ¼ cup half-and-half cream
- 2 slices ready-to-serve fully cooked bacon, chopped
- 1 tablespoon sugar
- ½ teaspoon salt
- ¼ teaspoon pepper

In a large skillet, saute the onion in butter until tender. Add the garlic; cook 1 minute longer. Stir in the remaining ingredients; heat through.

CREAMY SWEET CORN WITH OKRA

MUSHROOM FRIED RICE

After moving, I couldn't find a Chinese restaurant that met my tastes. So I decided to create my own Asian-inspired dishes. This is one of my favorites, and it can be served as a side dish or vegetarian entree.
—JACOB KITZMAN SEATTLE, WA

PREP: 25 MIN. • **COOK:** 10 MIN. • **MAKES:** 8 SERVINGS

- 1 teaspoon plus 2 tablespoons sesame oil, divided
- 3 large eggs, beaten
- 2 tablespoons canola oil
- 2 small onions, finely chopped
- 6 medium fresh mushrooms, thinly sliced
- 2 teaspoons minced garlic
- 1 teaspoon minced fresh gingerroot
- 4 cups cold cooked rice
- 1 cup frozen peas, thawed
- ¼ cup reduced-sodium soy sauce
- ¼ teaspoon salt
- ¼ teaspoon pepper
- 3 green onions, thinly sliced
  Optional ingredients: Chinese-style mustard, duck sauce and additional soy sauce

1. In a large skillet, heat 1 teaspoon sesame oil over medium-high heat. Add eggs to skillet. Cook and stir until set. Remove to a plate; set aside.
2. In the same skillet, heat the canola oil and the remaining sesame oil. Saute the onions and mushrooms for 2-3 minutes or until mushrooms are tender. Add garlic and ginger; saute mixture 1-2 minutes longer.
3. Stir in the rice, peas, soy sauce, salt and pepper. Chop egg into small pieces; stir into skillet and heat through. Stir in green onions. Serve with mustard, duck sauce and additional soy sauce if desired.

TOP TIP

Need to use up leftover fried rice? Simply combine it with cooked chicken, beef or shrimp for a no-fuss meal-in-one dinner. You can also use the rice as a filling for stuffed peppers, mix it into ground beef for a change-of-pace meat loaf or add it to a kettle of simmering chicken stock for a hearty soup with a tasty flair.

HERB & OLIVE OIL CORN BREAD

Add to the cornmeal mixture; stir just until moistened. Stir in ½ cup cheese.

3. Carefully remove hot skillet from oven. Add remaining oil to skillet; tilt pan to coat the bottom and sides. Add batter, spreading evenly. Sprinkle with remaining cheese.

4. Bake 12-15 minutes or until golden brown and a toothpick inserted in the center comes out clean. Cut into wedges; serve warm.

COUNTRY-STYLE TOMATOES

You've heard of fried green tomatoes, but have you tried fried ripe tomatoes? Sandwich slices together with cream cheese filling when tomatoes are in season.
—**CATHERINE DWYER** FREEDOM, NH

PREP: 25 MIN. • **COOK:** 10 MIN./BATCH
MAKES: 8 SERVINGS

- 4 **large tomatoes**
- 1 **package (8 ounces) cream cheese, softened**
- ¼ **cup minced fresh parsley**
- 1½ **teaspoons minced fresh basil or ½ teaspoon dried basil**
- 1 **garlic clove, minced**
- ¼ **teaspoon salt**
- ¼ **cup all-purpose flour**
- 1 **cup panko (Japanese) bread crumbs**
- 1 **large egg**
- 1 **tablespoon 2% milk**
- 3 **tablespoons butter**
- 3 **tablespoons olive oil**

1. Cut each tomato into four thick slices; place on paper towels to drain. Meanwhile, in a small bowl, beat the cream cheese, parsley, basil, garlic and salt until blended. Spread cream cheese mixture over eight tomato slices; top with the remaining tomato slices.

2. Place the flour and bread crumbs in separate shallow bowls. In another bowl, whisk egg and milk. Coat the top and bottom of each sandwich with flour, dip into egg mixture, then coat with the crumbs.

3. In a large skillet, heat the butter and oil over medium heat. Fry tomato sandwiches in batches for 3-4 minutes on each side or until golden brown. Drain on paper towels.

ERB & OLIVE OIL CORN BREAD

I rely on my cast-iron skillet to bake a moist corn bread. I love the way the rosemary and thyme come through, and the Italian cheese blend makes it all the more special.
—**MARY LISA SPEER** PALM BEACH, FL

P: 25 MIN. • **BAKE:** 15 MIN. • **MAKES:** 8 SERVINGS

- cup cornmeal
- cup all-purpose flour
- tablespoon sugar
- tablespoon grated Parmesan cheese
- ½ teaspoons baking powder
- teaspoon minced fresh rosemary or ¼ teaspoon dried rosemary, crushed
- teaspoon minced fresh thyme or ¼ teaspoon dried thyme
- teaspoon salt
- large egg
- cup buttermilk
- tablespoons olive oil, divided
- cup plus 2 tablespoons shredded Italian cheese blend, divided

Preheat oven to 425°. Place an 8-in. cast-iron llet in oven; heat skillet 10 minutes. Meanwhile, in a large bowl, whisk the first ht ingredients. In another bowl, whisk egg, termilk and 2 tablespoons oil until blended.

FAST FIX

HEALTHY ZUCCHINI PANCAKES

Fun and flavorful, rustic veggie pancakes make a wonderfully versatile side dish. They're also a great solution for what to do with a harvest of garden-fresh zucchini!

—**DIANA JOHNSON** AUBURN, WA

START TO FINISH: 25 MIN.
MAKES: 8 PANCAKES

- 1 cup shredded zucchini
- ¼ cup panko (Japanese) bread crumbs
- 2 green onions, chopped
- 1 large egg
- 3 tablespoons minced fresh parsley
- 1 tablespoon snipped fresh dill
- 1 garlic clove, minced
- ¼ cup crumbled feta cheese
- 3 teaspoons olive oil, divided

1. In a sieve or colander, drain zucchini, squeezing to remove the excess liquid. Pat dry. In a small bowl, combine zucchini, bread crumbs, onions, egg, parsley, dill, garlic and cheese.
2. Heat 1½ teaspoons oil in a large nonstick skillet over medium-low heat. Drop batter by heaping tablespoonfuls into oil; press lightly to flatten. Fry in batches until golden brown on both sides, using remaining oil as needed.

⑤ INGREDIENTS FAST FIX

DILL POTATO WEDGES

These are my absolute favorites; I've been making them for years!

—**JEANNIE KLUGH** LANCASTER, PA

START TO FINISH: 15 MIN.
MAKES: 4 SERVINGS

- 1 tablespoon olive oil
- 1 package (20 ounces) refrigerated red potato wedges
- ½ teaspoon salt
- ½ teaspoon pepper
- 2 tablespoons grated Parmesan cheese
- 1 teaspoon snipped fresh dill or ¼ teaspoon dill weed

In a large skillet, heat oil over medium heat. Add the potato wedges; sprinkle with salt and pepper. Cook for 10-12 minutes or until tender and golden brown, stirring occasionally. Remove from the heat; sprinkle with cheese and dill.

DILL POTATO WEDGES

CHAPATI BREADS

My daughter and I used to make Indian flatbread frequently. It's so fun and goes well with any spiced dish. We use the extras to make sandwich wraps.

—JOYCE MCCARTHY SUSSEX, WI

PREP: 20 MIN. • **COOK:** 5 MIN./BATCH
MAKES: 10 SERVINGS

CHAPATI BREADS

- 1½ cups all-purpose flour
- ½ cup whole wheat flour
- 1 teaspoon salt
- ¼ teaspoon garlic powder
- ¾ cup hot water
- 2 tablespoons olive oil

In a large bowl, combine the flours, salt and garlic powder. Stir in the water and oil. Turn onto a floured surface; knead 10-12 times. Divide dough into 10 portions. On a lightly floured surface, roll each portion into 6-in. circle.

In a large nonstick skillet, cook breads over medium heat for 1 minute on each side or until lightly browned. Keep warm.

DID YOU KNOW?

Chapati is an Indian bread that usually calls for only a handful of ingredients and a trusty skillet. Some recipes replace the water with milk for a softer product or use different oils to change the flavor. Regardless, these easy breads are a fun change-of-pace even on busy weeknights.

SAUTEED SPRING VEGETABLES

SAUTEED SPRING VEGETABLES

Summer squash, asparagus and sweet red onion help usher in the flavors of the warmer months. For an Asian flavor twist, substitute soy sauce for the balsamic vinegar (reduce the salt because soy sauce is full of sodium). Use red pepper flakes for a little added heat.

—BILLY HENSLEY MOUNT CARMEL, TN

PREP: 20 MIN. + MARINATING • **COOK:** 10 MIN.
MAKES: 9 SERVINGS

- 2 medium yellow summer squash, sliced
- 1 pound fresh asparagus, trimmed and cut into 1½-inch pieces
- 1 medium zucchini, sliced
- 1 small red onion, cut into thin wedges
- 1 cup green pepper strips
- ½ cup sweet red pepper strips

MARINADE

- ¼ cup olive oil
- 2 tablespoons balsamic vinegar
- 1 tablespoon lemon juice
- 2 garlic cloves, minced
- ½ teaspoon salt
- ½ teaspoon pepper
- ⅛ to ½ teaspoon crushed red pepper flakes

1. Place the vegetables in a large bowl. In a small bowl, whisk the marinade ingredients. Pour over the vegetables; toss to coat. Cover and refrigerate for up to 1 hour.

2. In a large skillet, saute vegetable mixture in batches for 3-6 minutes or until crisp-tender.

TOP TIP

To prepare asparagus, rinse stalks well in cold water. Snap off the stalk ends as far down as they will easily break when gently bent, or cut off the tough white portion. If stalks are large, use a vegetable peeler to gently peel the tough area of the stalk from the end to just below the tip. If tips are large, scrape off scales with a knife.

RB GARDEN VEGETABLES

ve a garden and wanted to highlight all the
etables and herbs that I grow. This medley
the perfect way to do just that.
LIE STELLA CHAMPLIN, MN

RT TO FINISH: 30 MIN. • **MAKES:** 2 SERVINGS

- **pound fresh green beans, trimmed**
- **cup fresh sugar snap peas**
- **tablespoon olive oil**
- **cup julienned zucchini**
- **cup julienned yellow summer squash**
- **teaspoon each minced fresh rosemary, sage, basil and thyme**
- **teaspoon crushed red pepper flakes**
- **tablespoons crumbled blue cheese**

small skillet over medium heat, cook beans
peas in oil for 3 minutes. Add the zucchini,
ash, herbs and pepper flakes; cook and stir
minutes longer or until the vegetables are
p-tender. Sprinkle vegetables with cheese
before serving.

NT OF LEMON
QUASH SAUTE

vely touch of lemon adds refreshing tang to this
er-simple veggie blend.
STE OF HOME TEST KITCHEN

RT TO FINISH: 20 MIN. • **MAKES:** 4 SERVINGS

- **medium yellow summer squash, sliced**
- **medium carrots, sliced**
- **small onion, sliced**
- **tablespoons olive oil**
- **garlic clove, minced**
- **teaspoon grated lemon peel**
- **teaspoon dried rosemary, crushed**
- **teaspoon pepper**
- **teaspoon salt**

large skillet, saute the squash, carrots and
on in oil for 5-7 minutes or until tender. Add
remaining ingredients; cook 1 minute longer.

---

⑤INGREDIENTS FAST FIX

CRANBERRY-WALNUT
BRUSSELS SPROUTS

Brussels sprouts are a food that picky eaters often
refuse to eat. This recipe might change their minds. You
can add garlic and other dried fruits for extra flavor.
—**JENNIFER ARMELLINO** LAKE OSWEGO, OR

START TO FINISH: 20 MIN. • **MAKES:** 4 SERVINGS

- ¼ **cup olive oil**
- 1 **pound fresh Brussels sprouts, trimmed and halved lengthwise**
- ½ **cup dried cranberries**
- 2 **tablespoons water**
- ⅓ **cup chopped walnuts**
- 2 **tablespoons balsamic vinegar**

1. In a large skillet, heat the oil over medium heat.
Place Brussels sprouts in pan, cut side down; cook
4-5 minutes or until bottoms are browned.
2. Add the cranberries and water; cook, covered,
for 1-2 minutes or until the Brussels sprouts are
crisp-tender. Stir in walnuts; cook and stir until
water is evaporated. Stir in vinegar.

**CRANBERRY-WALNUT
BRUSSELS SPROUTS**

FAST FIX

AU GRATIN POTATO PANCAKES

Family and friends say these flavorful pancakes are among the best they've ever tasted. They go especially well with barbecued ribs or chicken, but can substitute for almost any potato dish.

—CATHY HALL LYNDHURST, VA

START TO FINISH: 25 MIN. • **MAKES:** 8 POTATO PANCAKES

- 2 **cups mashed potatoes (without added milk and butter)**
- 1 **large egg, lightly beaten**
- 1 **tablespoon minced chives**
- 1 **teaspoon minced fresh parsley**
- ¾ **teaspoon salt**
- ⅛ **teaspoon dried minced garlic**
- ⅛ **teaspoon pepper**
  Dash dried rosemary, crushed
- ½ **cup shredded sharp cheddar cheese**
- 4 **tablespoons canola oil, divided**

1. In a large bowl, combine the first eight ingredients. Stir in cheese.

2. Heat 2 tablespoons oil in a large nonstick skillet over medium heat. Drop batter by ¼ cupfuls into oil; press lightly to flatten. Cook in batches for 2-3 minutes on each side or until golden brown, using remaining oil as needed. Drain on paper towels.

AU GRAT
POTATO PANCAK▶

BUTTERNUT SQUASH ROLLS

With their cheery yellow color and delicious aroma, these appealing rolls will brighten any buffet. I've found them a great way to use up leftover squash.

—BERNICE MORRIS MARSHFIELD, MO

PREP: 30 MIN. + RISING
BAKE: 20 MIN. • **MAKES:** 2 DOZEN

- 1 **package (¼ ounce) active dry yeast**
- 1 **cup warm milk (110° to 115°)**
- ¼ **cup warm water (110° to 115°)**
- 3 **tablespoons butter, softened**
- 2 **teaspoons salt**
- ½ **cup sugar**
- 1 **cup mashed cooked butternut squash**
- 5 **to 5½ cups all-purpose flour, divided**

In a large bowl, dissolve yeast in milk and water. Add the butter, salt, sugar, squash and 3 cups of flour; beat until smooth. Add enough of the remaining flour to form a soft dough.

Turn onto a floured surface; knead until smooth and elastic, about 6-8 minutes. Place in a greased bowl, turning once to grease top. Cover and let rise in a warm place until doubled, about 1 hour.

Punch dough down. Form into rolls; place in two greased 10-in. cast-iron skillets or 9-in. round baking pans. Cover and let the dough rise until doubled, about 30 minutes.

Bake at 375° for 20-25 minutes or until golden brown.

BOK CHOY AND RADISHES

BOK CHOY AND RADISHES

This simple, good-for-you recipe captures the flavors of spring.

—ANN BAKER TEXARKANA, TX

START TO FINISH: 25 MIN.
MAKES: 8 SERVINGS

- 1 **head bok choy**
- 2 **tablespoons butter**
- 1 **tablespoon olive oil**
- 12 **radishes, thinly sliced**
- 1 **shallot, sliced**
- 1 **teaspoon lemon-pepper seasoning**
- ¾ **teaspoon salt**

1. Cut off and discard root end of bok choy, leaving stalks with leaves. Cut the green leaves from stalks. Cut leaves into 1-in. slices; set aside. Cut the white stalks into 1-in. pieces.

2. In a large skillet, cook the bok choy stalks in the butter and oil for 3-5 minutes or until crisp-tender. Add the radishes, shallot, lemon-pepper, salt and reserved leaves; cook and stir vegetables for 3 minutes or until mixture is heated through.

FAST FIX ▸
CALICO CORN CAKES

Served with salsa on the side, fluffy corn cakes make a fantastic side for nearly any main dish, and especially those with Southwestern flair. You can also try them with sour cream for a cool burst.

—TASTE OF HOME TEST KITCHEN

START TO FINISH: 25 MIN.
MAKES: 3 SERVINGS

- ¼ **cup chopped onion**
- ¼ **cup chopped green pepper**
- 1 **teaspoon canola oil**
- ¼ **cup all-purpose flour**
- 2 **tablespoons yellow cornmeal**
- ½ **teaspoon sugar**
- ¼ **teaspoon salt**
- ¼ **teaspoon dried oregano**
- ⅛ **teaspoon baking powder**
- ⅛ **teaspoon ground cumin**
- 1 **large eggs, lightly beaten**
- ¼ **cup 2% milk**
- 1 **cup frozen corn, thawed**
- 1 **tablespoon diced pimientos**
- ½ **cup salsa**

1. In a small skillet, saute onion and green pepper in the oil until tender; set aside. In a large bowl, whisk the flour, cornmeal, sugar, salt, oregano, baking powder, cumin, egg and milk just until combined. Fold in the corn, pimientos and onion mixture.

2. Heat a large skillet coated with cooking spray; drop batter by ¼ cupfuls into skillet. Cook cakes for 3 minutes on each side or until golden brown. Serve with salsa.

CALICO CORN CAKES

ACON AND GARLIC REEN BEANS

ing white wine, lemon juice garlic gives a little kick to green ns. It was enough to turn our traditional holiday side into ar-round favorite.

—HANNON REYNOSO
ERSFIELD, CA

RT TO FINISH: 30 MIN.
KES: 8 SERVINGS

thick-sliced bacon strips, chopped
small onion, thinly sliced
tablespoons butter
tablespoon olive oil
garlic cloves, minced
cup white wine or chicken broth

9 cups frozen french-style green beans, thawed
½ teaspoon salt
½ teaspoon garlic powder
¼ teaspoon pepper
2 to 3 tablespoons lemon juice

1. In a large skillet, cook bacon over medium heat until crisp. Remove to paper towels with a slotted spoon; drain. In the same skillet, saute onion in butter and oil until tender. Add garlic; cook 1 minute longer. Stir in the wine; bring to a boil. Simmer mixture, uncovered, for 5-8 minutes or until liquid is reduced by half.
2. Add the green beans, salt, garlic powder and pepper; heat through. Stir in the lemon juice and bacon.

BACON AND GARLIC GREEN BEANS

VEGGIE-TOPPED POLENTA SLICES

We didn't have many items in the kitchen one night, so this side came from a stroke of genius, I guess.

—JENN TIDWELL FAIR OAKS, CA

PREP: 20 MIN. • **COOK:** 20 MIN.
MAKES: 4 SERVINGS

1 tube (1 pound) polenta, cut into 12 slices
2 tablespoons olive oil, divided
1 medium zucchini, chopped
2 shallots, minced
2 garlic cloves, minced
3 tablespoons reduced-sodium chicken broth
½ teaspoon pepper
⅛ teaspoon salt
4 plum tomatoes, seeded and chopped
2 tablespoons minced fresh basil or 2 teaspoons dried basil
1 tablespoon minced fresh parsley
½ cup shredded part-skim mozzarella cheese

1. In a large nonstick skillet, cook the polenta in 1 tablespoon oil over medium heat for 9-11 minutes on each side or until golden brown.
2. Meanwhile, in another large skillet, saute zucchini in remaining oil until tender. Add shallots and garlic; cook 1 minute longer. Add the broth, pepper and salt. Bring to a boil; cook until liquid is almost evaporated.
3. Stir in the tomatoes, basil and parsley; heat through. Serve with polenta; sprinkle with cheese.

**JO ANN SHEEHAN'S
CRAN-APPLE COBBLER**
PAGE 220

Sweets, Snacks & Party Starters

Get the most out of your skillet with these finger-licking appetizers, no-fuss bites and comforting desserts.

⑤ INGREDIENTS FAST FIX ▸

BEEF NACHOS SUPREME

Your clan will love these beefed up nachos. They come together in a flash even when you customize your taco seasonings and toppings.

—ROSE LAURITSEN LINDALE, GA

START TO FINISH: 25 MIN.
MAKES: 2 SERVINGS

- ½ **pound lean ground beef (90% lean)**
- ¾ **cup water**
- ⅔ **cup condensed tomato soup, undiluted**
- 2 **tablespoons taco seasoning**
- ¾ **cup uncooked instant rice**
  Optional toppings: shredded lettuce, shredded cheddar cheese, salsa and/or sour cream
  Tortilla chips

1. In a large skillet, cook beef over medium heat until no longer pink; drain. Stir in the water, soup and taco seasoning. Bring to a boil. Stir in rice. Cover and remove from the heat. Let stand for 5 minutes or until rice is tender.

2. Spoon onto two serving plates. Top with lettuce, cheese, salsa and sour cream if desired. Serve with chips.

TOP TIP

When browning ground beef or other ground meat, use a pastry blender to break up larger pieces shortly before the meat is completely cooked. This makes the texture much more suitable for chili, stews, soups and casseroles.

BEEF NACHOS SUPREME

SKILLET BLUEBERRY SLUMP

I've been eating slump for nearly decades! My mother-in-law started the tradition with a recipe ...ng for wild blueberries. She ...ved hers warm with a pitcher ...resh farm cream. It doesn't get ...re down-home than that!

—LEANORE EBELING BREWSTER, MN

PREP: 25 MIN. • **BAKE:** 20 MIN.
MAKES: 6 SERVINGS

- cups fresh or frozen blueberries
- cup sugar
- cup water
- teaspoon grated lemon peel
- tablespoon lemon juice
- cup all-purpose flour
- tablespoons sugar
- teaspoons baking powder
- teaspoon salt
- tablespoon butter
- ½ cup 2% milk
  Vanilla ice cream

1. Preheat oven to 400°. In a 10-in. cast-iron or ovenproof skillet, combine the first five ingredients; bring to a boil. Reduce heat; simmer, uncovered, for 9-11 minutes or until the fruit is slightly thickened, stirring occasionally.

2. Meanwhile, in a small bowl, whisk the flour, sugar, baking powder and salt. Cut in butter until mixture resembles coarse crumbs. Add the milk; stir just until moistened.

3. Drop batter in six portions on top of the simmering blueberry mixture. Transfer to oven. Bake, uncovered, for 17-20 minutes or until the dumplings are golden brown. Serve slump warm with ice cream.

SKILLET BLUEBERRY SLUMP

SALISBURY MEATBALLS

Saucy and so simple, these jazzed-up meatballs will help you turn out dinner in no time on any busy night.

—MARIA REGAKIS SAUGUS, MA

START TO FINISH: 20 MIN.
MAKES: 4 SERVINGS

- 1 large sweet onion, halved and thinly sliced
- 1 tablespoon brown sugar
- 3 tablespoons butter
- 2 jars (12 ounces each) beef gravy
- 1 package (12 ounces) frozen fully cooked homestyle meatballs, thawed
  Hot cooked egg noodles

In a large skillet, saute onion and brown sugar in butter until onion is tender. Add the gravy and meatballs. Bring to a boil. Reduce heat; simmer, uncovered, for 4-6 minutes or until meatballs are heated through, stirring occasionally. Serve with noodles.

PHILLY CHEESESTEAK BITES

Here's a deliciously downsized version of the famous Philly cheesesteak. For perfect bite-size snacks or party appetizers, layer the sandwich ingredients on waffle-cut fries instead of buns.

—*TASTE OF HOME* TEST KITCHEN

PREP: 30 MIN. • **COOK:** 5 MIN. • **MAKES:** 1½ DOZEN

- 1 package (22 ounces) frozen waffle-cut fries
- 1 medium onion, halved and sliced
- ½ small green pepper, halved and sliced
- ½ small sweet red pepper, halved and sliced
- 3 tablespoons canola oil, divided
- ½ teaspoon salt, divided
- ¾ pound beef ribeye steak, cut into thin strips
- ¼ teaspoon pepper
- 3 tablespoons ketchup
- 6 tablespoons process cheese sauce

1. Bake 18 large waffle fries according to package directions (save remaining fries for another use). Meanwhile, in a large skillet, saute onion and peppers in 1 tablespoon oil until tender. Sprinkle with ⅛ teaspoon salt. Remove and keep warm.

2. In the same pan, saute steak in the remaining oil in batches for 45-60 seconds or until desired doneness. Sprinkle with pepper and remaining sa On each waffle fry, layer the beef, onion mixture, ketchup and cheese sauce. Serve warm.

ED VELVET CREPE CAKES

well worth the time to make this beautiful and
cious cake. Each thin layer is separated by a rich and
amy filling. Treat your family on special occasions
n this sweet sensation.

RYSTAL HEATON ALTON, UT

EP: 1¼ HOURS • **COOK:** 25 MIN.
KES: 2 CREPE CAKES (8 SERVINGS EACH)

- package red velvet cake mix (regular size)
- ¼ cups whole milk
- cup all-purpose flour
- large eggs
- large egg yolks
- cup butter, melted
- teaspoons vanilla extract

OSTING

- packages (8 ounces each) cream cheese,
  softened
- ¼ cups butter, softened
- teaspoon salt
- 2 cups confectioners' sugar
- teaspoons vanilla extract
  Fresh blueberries

In a large bowl, combine the cake mix, milk,
ur, eggs, egg yolks, butter and vanilla; beat
ow speed for 30 seconds. Beat on medium
2 minutes.

Heat a lightly greased 8-in. nonstick skillet
er medium heat; pour ¼ cup batter into center
skillet. Lift and tilt pan to coat bottom evenly.
ok until the top appears dry; turn and cook
20 seconds longer. Remove to a wire rack.
peat with remaining batter, greasing skillet
eeded. When cool, stack crepes with waxed
per or paper towels in between.

For frosting, in a large bowl, beat the cream
ese, butter and salt until fluffy. Add the
fectioners' sugar and vanilla; beat until the
sting is smooth.

To assemble two crepe cakes, place one crepe
each of two cake plates. Spread each with one
nded tablespoon frosting to within ½ in. of
es. Repeat layers until all the crepes are used.
ead the remaining frosting over tops and sides
repe cakes. Garnish with blueberries.

SKILLET CHERRY COBBLER

Once a week, my husband and I enjoy a candlelight
dinner after our children are fed and in bed. This
dessert is the perfect size for two, and we look forward
to it on those special date nights. If you like apple or
blueberry pie filling better, try it with one of those.
—**KARI DAMON** RUSHFORD, NY

START TO FINISH: 30 MIN. • **MAKES:** 2 SERVINGS

- ½ cup biscuit/baking mix
- 1½ teaspoons sugar
- ½ to 1 teaspoon grated orange peel
- 2 tablespoons 2% milk
- 1 cup cherry pie filling
- ¼ cup orange juice

1. In a small bowl, combine the biscuit mix, sugar
and orange peel. Stir in milk just until moistened;
set aside.

2. In a small nonstick skillet, combine pie filling
and the orange juice; bring to a boil, stirring
occasionally. Drop biscuit mixture in two mounds
onto boiling cherry mixture. Reduce heat; cover
and simmer for 10 minutes. Uncover; simmer for
5-7 minutes longer or until a toothpick inserted
into a dumpling comes out clean.

SKILLET CHERRY COBBLER

CRAN-APPLE COBBLER

My cranberry-packed cobbler is the crowning glory o many of our late fall and winter meals. My family isn't big on pies, so we make this favorite dessert for all ou Thanksgiving and Christmas celebrations. The aroma of cinnamon and fruit is irresistible.

—**JO ANN SHEEHAN** RUTHER GLEN, VA

PREP: 20 MIN. • **BAKE:** 30 MIN. • **MAKES:** 6-8 SERVINGS

- 2½ cups sliced peeled apples
- 2½ cups sliced peeled firm pears
- 1 to 1¼ cups sugar
- 1 cup fresh or frozen cranberries, thawed
- ½ cup water
- 3 tablespoons quick-cooking tapioca
- 3 tablespoons Red Hots
- ½ teaspoon ground cinnamon
- 2 tablespoons butter

TOPPING
- ¾ cup all-purpose flour
- 2 tablespoons sugar
- 1 teaspoon baking powder
- ¼ teaspoon salt
- ¼ cup cold butter, cubed
- 3 tablespoons milk
   Vanilla ice cream

1. In a large, oven-safe skillet, combine the first eight ingredients; let stand for 5 minutes. Cook a stir over medium heat until mixture comes to a f rolling boil, about 18 minutes. Dot with butter.
2. In a small bowl, combine the flour, sugar, baki powder and salt in a bowl. Cut in the butter until mixture resembles coarse crumbs. Stir in milk u a soft dough forms.
3. Drop topping by heaping tablespoons onto ho fruit. Bake at 375° for 30-35 minutes or until gol brown. Serve warm with ice cream.

FAST FIX

BANANA RUM SUNDAES

You can serve a mouthwatering dessert on busy weeknights when it takes just minutes to make. The warm, sweet fruit; crunchy nuts; and cold, smooth ice cream are a winning combination.

—**DENISE ALBERS** FREEBURG, IL

START TO FINISH: 20 MIN. • **MAKES:** 6 SERVINGS

- 3 tablespoons butter
- ¾ cup packed brown sugar
   Dash ground nutmeg
- 4 medium firm bananas, halved and sliced
- ¼ cup golden raisins
- ¼ cup rum
- 2 tablespoons sliced almonds, toasted
- 1 quart vanilla ice cream

1. In a large nonstick skillet, melt the butter over medium-low heat. Stir in brown sugar and nutmeg until blended.
2. Remove from the heat; add the bananas, raisins, rum and almonds. Cook over medium heat, stirring gently, for 3-4 minutes or until bananas are glazed and slightly softened. Serve with ice cream.

CRAN-APPLE COBBLER

VANILLA & CINNAMON-KISSED APPLE LATKES

Instead of using traditional potatoes, take latkes to the dessert realm with shredded apples and a sweet mix of orange juice, cinnamon and vanilla.

—CANDY MCMENAMIN
LEXINGTON, SC

PREP: 20 MIN. • **COOK:** 5 MIN./BATCH
MAKES: 3 DOZEN

- 2 **tablespoons confectioners' sugar**
- 2 **tablespoons ground cinnamon**
- 4 **cups all-purpose flour**
- ⅔ **cup sugar**
- 2 **teaspoons baking powder**
- ½ **teaspoon salt**
- 2 **cups orange juice**
- 1 **cup 2% milk**
- 4 **large eggs, lightly beaten**
- 1 **teaspoon vanilla extract**
- 2¾ **pounds apples (about 6 large apples), peeled and shredded**
- ¾ **cup canola oil**

1. In a small bowl, combine the confectioners' sugar and the cinnamon; set aside.

2. In a large bowl, combine the flour, sugar, baking powder and salt. Stir in the orange juice, milk, eggs and vanilla until blended; fold in apples.

3. Heat 2 tablespoons oil in a large nonstick skillet over medium heat. Drop batter by ¼ cupfuls into oil; press lightly to flatten. Fry in batches until golden brown on both sides, using remaining oil as needed. Drain on paper towels. Sprinkle with cinnamon-sugar.

**VANILLA & CINNAMON-KISSE
APPLE LATKE**

CINNAMON-SUGAR APPLE PIE

Apple pie baked in a cast-iron skillet is a real stunner. This beauty, with its buttery, flaky crust and tender fruit filling, is a guaranteed winner.

RENEE SCHETTLER ROSSI
NEW YORK, NY

PREP: 1 HOUR + CHILLING
BAKE: 65 MIN. + COOLING
MAKES: 10 SERVINGS

- 2 cups all-purpose flour
- 1 teaspoon salt
- ¾ cups cold lard
- 6 to 8 tablespoons cold 2% milk

FILLING

- 2 cups sugar
- 1 teaspoon ground cinnamon
- 1 teaspoon ground ginger
- 8 cups thinly sliced peeled tart apples (about 9 medium)
- 1 tablespoon bourbon, optional
- 2 tablespoons all-purpose flour
- Dash salt
- 2 tablespoons cold butter, cubed

TOPPING

- 1 tablespoon 2% milk
- 2 teaspoons coarse sugar

1. In a large bowl, mix flour and salt; cut in lard until crumbly. Gradually add milk, tossing with a fork until dough holds together when pressed. Divide dough in half. Shape each into a disk; wrap in plastic wrap. Refrigerate for 1 hour or overnight.

2. For filling, in a large bowl, mix sugar, cinnamon and ginger. Add apples and toss to coat. Cover; let stand 1 hour to allow the apples to release their juice, stirring the mixture occasionally.

3. Drain apples, reserving syrup. Place the syrup and, if desired, bourbon in a small saucepan; bring to a boil. Reduce heat; simmer liquid, uncovered, for 20-25 minutes or until mixture thickens slightly and turns a medium amber color. Remove from heat; cool completely.

4. Preheat oven to 400°. Toss drained apples with flour and salt. On a lightly floured surface, roll one half of the dough to a circle ⅛-in. thick; transfer to a 10-in. cast-iron or other deep ovenproof skillet. Trim pastry even with rim. Add the apple mixture. Pour cooled syrup over top; dot with butter.

5. Roll remaining dough to a circle ⅛-in. thick. Place over filling. Trim, seal and flute edge. Cut slits in top. Brush milk over the pastry; sprinkle with coarse sugar. Place on a foil-lined baking sheet. Bake 20 minutes.

6. Reduce oven setting to 350°. Bake 45-55 minutes longer or until crust is golden brown and the filling is bubbly. Cool pie on a wire rack.

CINNAMON-SUGAR
APPLE PIE

COWBOY BEEF DIP

In a foods class, a group of us developed this recipe for the North Dakota State Beef Bash Competition. We won the contest, and now my family requests this dip for all our special gatherings!

—**JESSICA KLYM** DUNN CENTER, ND

PREP: 20 MIN. • **COOK:** 25 MIN. • **MAKES:** 3 CUPS

- 1 **pound ground beef**
- 4 **tablespoons chopped onion, divided**
- 3 **tablespoons chopped sweet red pepper, divided**
- 2 **tablespoons chopped green pepper, divided**
- 1 **can (10¾ ounces) condensed nacho cheese soup, undiluted**
- ½ **cup salsa**
- 4 **tablespoons sliced ripe olives, divided**
- 4 **tablespoons sliced pimiento-stuffed olives, divided**
- 2 **tablespoons chopped green chilies**
- 1 **teaspoon chopped seeded jalapeno pepper**
- ¼ **teaspoon dried oregano**
- ¼ **teaspoon pepper**
- ¼ **cup shredded cheddar cheese**
- 2 **tablespoons sour cream**
- 2 **to 3 teaspoons minced fresh parsley**
  Tortilla chips

1. In a large skillet, cook the beef, 3 tablespoons onion, 2 tablespoons red pepper and 1 tablespoon green pepper over medium heat until the meat is no longer pink; drain. Stir in the soup, salsa, 3 tablespoons of the ripe olives, 3 tablespoons of the pimiento-stuffed olives, chilies, jalapeno, oregano and pepper. Bring to a boil. Reduce heat; simmer, uncovered, for 5 minutes.

2. Transfer to a serving dish. Top with cheese, sour cream and parsley; sprinkle with the remaining onion, peppers and olives. Serve the dip with tortilla chips.

NOTE *Wear disposable gloves when cutting hot peppers; the oils can burn skin. Avoid touching your face.*

---

⑤ INGREDIENTS   FAST FIX

CARAMEL-PECAN APPLE SLICES

Here's a warm, decadent side dish. Ready to eat in only 15 minutes, the apples are also good alongside a pork entree or spooned over vanilla ice cream.

—**CAROL GILLESPIE** CHAMBERSBURG, PA

START TO FINISH: 15 MIN. • **MAKES:** 6 SERVINGS

- ⅓ **cup packed brown sugar**
- 2 **tablespoons butter**
- 2 **large apples, cut into ½-inch slices**
- ¼ **cup chopped pecans, toasted**

In a large skillet, cook and stir brown sugar and butter over medium heat until sugar is dissolved. Add apples; cook, uncovered, over medium heat 5-7 minutes or until tender, stirring occasionally. Stir in pecans. Serve warm.

NOTE *To toast nuts, cook in a skillet over low heat until lightly browned, stirring occasionally, or bake in a shallow pan in a 350° oven for 5-10 minutes.*

ZUCCHINI PATTIES WITH DILL DIP

These crisp-tender zucchini patties are a nice vegetarian alternative to crab cakes and have the same great taste, thanks to the seafood seasoning. They always get gobbled up in a flash.

—**KELLY MAXWELL** PLAINFIELD, IL

PREP: 25 MIN. • **COOK:** 10 MIN.
MAKES: 2 DOZEN (¾ CUP DIP)

- cup sour cream
- tablespoons minced fresh dill
- teaspoon lemon juice
- teaspoon salt
- teaspoon pepper
- cups shredded zucchini
- cup seasoned bread crumbs
- teaspoon seafood seasoning
- teaspoon garlic powder

- 1 large egg, lightly beaten
- 2 tablespoons butter, melted
- 1 large carrot, chopped
- ¼ cup finely chopped onion
- ¼ cup all-purpose flour
- ½ cup canola oil

1. For dip, in a small bowl, combine the first five ingredients. Cover and refrigerate until serving.

2. Place zucchini in a colander to drain; squeeze to remove excess liquid. Pat dry; set aside.

3. In a large bowl, combine the bread crumbs, seafood seasoning and garlic powder. Stir in the egg and butter until blended. Add the carrot, onion and zucchini.

4. Place flour in a shallow bowl. Shape zucchini mixture into 24 small patties; coat with flour.

5. Heat oil in a large skillet; fry patties, a few at a time, for 3-4 minutes on each side or until lightly browned. Drain on paper towels. Serve with dip.

ZUCCHINI PATTIES WITH DILL DIP

FAST FIX

SAUCY SPICED PEARS

We serve these tangy, saucy pears over angel food cake, pound cake or with a little yogurt or vanilla ice cream. Sprinkle with mint or your favorite dessert toppings.

—JOY ZACHARIA CLEARWATER, FL

START TO FINISH: 20 MIN.
MAKES: 4 SERVINGS

- ½ cup orange juice
- 2 tablespoons butter
- 2 tablespoons sugar
- 2 teaspoons lemon juice
- 1 teaspoon vanilla extract
- 1 teaspoon ground ginger
- ¼ teaspoon ground cinnamon
- ⅛ teaspoon salt
- ⅛ teaspoon ground allspice
- ⅛ teaspoon cayenne pepper, optional
- 3 large Bosc pears (about 1¾ pounds), cored, peeled and sliced
  Thinly sliced fresh mint leaves, optional

1. In a large skillet, combine the first nine ingredients and, if desired, cayenne. Cook over medium-high heat 1-2 minutes or until the butter is melted, stirring occasionally.

2. Add pears; bring to a boil. Reduce heat to medium; cook, uncovered, 3-4 minutes or until sauce is slightly thickened and pears are crisp-tender, stirring occasionally. Cool slightly. If desired, top with mint.

SAUCY SPICED PEARS

FIGGY APPLE BRIE TART

holiday gatherings often included baked brie. I transformed to a dessert that's both savory sweet. It makes a wonderful etizer, too.

RISTIE SCHLEY SEVERNA PARK, MD

EP: 25 MIN. • **BAKE:** 15 MIN.
KES: 8 SERVINGS

- tablespoons butter, softened
- cup sugar
- large apples
- cup dried figs, halved
- pound Brie cheese, rind removed, sliced
- sheet refrigerated pie pastry

1. Preheat oven to 425°. Spread butter over the bottom of a 10-in. cast-iron or ovenproof skillet; sprinkle evenly with sugar.

2. Peel, quarter and core apples; arrange in a circular pattern over sugar, rounded side down. Place figs around apples. Place the skillet over medium heat; cook for 10-12 minutes or until sugar is caramelized and apples have softened slightly. Remove from heat; top with cheese.

3. Unroll the pastry sheet; place over apples, tucking under edges. Place skillet in oven on an upper rack; bake 15-18 minutes or until crust is golden brown. Cool in pan 5 minutes. Carefully invert onto a serving plate; serve warm.

FIGGY APPLE BRIE TART

PLUM UPSIDE-DOWN CAKE

The delicate flavor of plums is a pleasing change of pace from pineapple in this upside-down cake.

—**BOBBIE TALBOTT** VENETA, OR

PREP: 15 MIN. • **BAKE:** 40 MIN.
MAKES: 8-10 SERVINGS

- ⅓ cup butter
- ½ cup packed brown sugar
- 2 pounds fresh plums, pitted and halved
- 2 large eggs
- ⅔ cup sugar
- 1 cup all-purpose flour
- 1 teaspoon baking powder
- ¼ teaspoon salt
- ⅓ cup hot water
- ½ teaspoon lemon extract
  Whipped cream, optional

1. Melt the butter in a 10-in. cast-iron or ovenproof skillet. Sprinkle brown sugar over the butter. Arrange plum halves, cut side down, in a single layer over sugar; set aside.

2. In a large bowl, beat the eggs until thick and lemon-colored; gradually beat in sugar. Combine the flour, baking powder and salt; add to egg mixture and mix well. Blend water and lemon extract; beat into batter. Pour over plums.

3. Bake at 350° for 40-45 minutes or until a toothpick inserted near the center comes out clean. Immediately invert onto a serving plate. Serve warm with whipped cream if desired.

⟨5⟩ INGREDIENTS FAST FIX ▸

CHOCOLATE CHIP QUESADILLA

Dessert is simple with this sweet finale. It's quick, chocolaty, out of the ordinary and calls for just a handful of easy ingredients.

—IRENE RUNDELL HASKELL, OK

START TO FINISH: 15 MIN.
MAKES: 2 SERVINGS

- 2 tablespoons honey
- 2 flour tortillas (6 inches)
- ½ teaspoon ground cinnamon
- 2 tablespoons semisweet chocolate chips
- 1 teaspoon canola oil

1. Drizzle the honey over one tortilla; sprinkle with cinnamon and chocolate chips. Top with remaining tortilla.
2. In a small skillet, cook the quesadilla in oil over medium heat for 1-2 minutes on each side or until lightly browned. Cut into four wedges. Serve immediately.

CORNMEAL TOWERS WITH STRAWBERRIES & CREAM

My kids love to help make these towers. They measure, mix, whisk and build the stacks. It's become a family tradition and a perfect summer dessert.

—JOSIE SHAPIRO SAN FRANCISCO, CA

PREP: 40 MIN. • **COOK:** 5 MIN./BATCH
MAKES: 12 SERVINGS

- 3 large egg whites
- 1 cup heavy whipping cream
- 1 cup cornmeal
- 1 cup all-purpose flour
- 1½ teaspoons baking powder
- ½ teaspoon ground cardamom
- ¼ teaspoon salt
- 1¼ cups 2% milk
- 1 cup whole-milk ricotta cheese
- ¼ cup orange juice
- 2 tablespoons honey
- 1 teaspoon almond extract
- 1 to 2 tablespoons butter
- 1 pound fresh strawberries, sliced
- 2 tablespoons sugar

1. Place the egg whites in a small bowl; let stand at room temperature 30 minutes. Meanwhile, in a small bowl, beat the cream until soft peaks form; refrigerate, covered, until serving.
2. In a large bowl, whisk the cornmeal, flour, baking powder, cardamom and salt. In another bowl, mix milk, ricotta cheese, orange juice, honey and extra until blended. Add ricotta chee mixture to cornmeal mixture; stir just until moistened. With clean beaters, beat egg whites on high speed until stiff but no dry; fold into batter.
3. Heat a griddle or a large nonstick skillet over medium heat; grease with butter. Fillin a ¼-cup measure halfway wit batter, pour batter onto griddl or skillet. Cook until edges beg to dry and bottoms are golden brown. Turn; cook until secon side is golden brown. Cool the pancakes slightly.
4. In a bowl, toss strawberries with sugar. For each serving, stack three pancakes, layering each pancake with strawberri and whipped cream.

CORNMEAL TOWERS WITH STRAWBERRIES & CREAM

QUESO FUNDIDO

Dig in to this hot one-skillet dip and enjoy the gooey cheese and extra spicy kick from chorizo.

—JULIE MERRIMAN SEATTLE, WA

PREP: 20 MIN. • **BAKE:** 15 MIN.
MAKES: 6 CUPS

- 1 pound uncooked chorizo
- 2 cups fresh or frozen corn, thawed
- 1 large red onion, chopped
- 1 poblano pepper, chopped
- 8 ounces fresh goat cheese, crumbled
- 2 cups cubed Monterey Jack cheese
- 1 cup cubed pepper jack cheese
- 1 large tomato, seeded and chopped
- 3 green onions, thinly sliced
  Blue corn tortilla chips

Preheat the oven to 350°. Crumble the chorizo into a 10-in. cast-iron or ovenproof skillet; add corn, red onion and pepper. Cook over medium heat for 6-8 minutes or until meat is fully cooked; drain. Stir in the cheeses.

Bake 14-16 minutes or until bubbly. Sprinkle with tomato and green onions. Serve with chips.

DID YOU KNOW

Chorizo is a coarsely ground fresh or smoked pork sausage with Mexican, Spanish and Portuguese origins. It gets its reddish color from traditional flavorings such as paprika or chili powder. It's used in a wide variety of egg, soup, casserole and Mexican dishes.

QUESO FUNDIDO

1. In a large bowl, combine first five ingredients. Cover and chill until serving. For crab cakes, in a large bowl, combine the egg, cheese, bread crumbs, mayonnaise, onion, parsley, mustard, seafood seasoning and pepper. Fold in the crab. Refrigerate for at least 30 minutes.

2. With floured hands, shape the mixture by 2 tablespoonfuls into ½-in.-thick patties. In a large skillet over medium heat, cook crab cakes in oil in batches for 3-4 minutes on each side or until golden brown. Serve with sauce.

FAST FIX▸

CHICKEN CHILI NACHOS

Spicy nachos with plenty of chicken and two kinds of beans make a fun and filling snack.

—KAREN HORNING ROCKFORD, IL

START TO FINISH: 25 MIN. • **MAKES:** 8 SERVINGS

- 1 **pound boneless skinless chicken breasts, cub**
- 1 **can (10 ounces) diced tomatoes and green chilies, undrained**
- 1 **can (16 ounces) kidney beans, rinsed and drained**
- 1 **can (16 ounces) chili beans, undrained**
- 1 **teaspoon paprika**
- 1 **teaspoon ground cumin**
- ½ **teaspoon cayenne pepper**
- 1 **package (13½ ounces) tortilla chips**
- 1½ **cups (6 ounces) shredded Mexican cheese blend**

1. In a large skillet coated with cooking spray, saute the chicken until no longer pink. Add the tomatoes; cook over medium-high heat for 3 minutes or until tomato juice is reduced. Stir in the beans, paprika, cumin and cayenne; cook for 5 minutes or until heated through.

2. Arrange the tortilla chips on two large microwave-safe plates; sprinkle each with ¼ cup of cheese. Top with the chicken mixture and the remaining cheese. Microwave, uncovered, on high for 25-30 seconds or until cheese is melted.

CRAB CAKES WITH CHESAPEAKE BAY MAYO

I placed my personal stamp on my Aunt Ellie's crab cake recipe by changing up some of her ingredients. They're served with a tart and tangy creamy sauce. You can use them in an appetizer spread or as a terrific first-course for a more formal dinner.

—MICHELLE CRITCHELL MOON, VA

PREP: 20 MIN. + CHILLING • **COOK:** 10 MIN./BATCH
MAKES: 16 APPETIZERS

- ½ **cup sour cream**
- ½ **cup mayonnaise**
- 2 **tablespoons sweet pickle relish**
- 1 **tablespoon spicy brown mustard**
- ¼ **teaspoon seafood seasoning**

CRAB CAKES
- 1 **large egg, beaten**
- ¼ **cup grated Parmesan cheese**
- ¼ **cup seasoned bread crumbs**
- ¼ **cup mayonnaise**
- 2 **tablespoons finely chopped onion**
- 1 **tablespoon minced fresh parsley**
- 1 **tablespoon spicy brown mustard**
- ½ **teaspoon seafood seasoning**
- ⅛ **teaspoon pepper**
- 3 **cans (6 ounces each) lump crabmeat, drained**
- ¼ **cup canola oil**

SAME-BEEF
OT STICKERS

oy these pot stickers as a late-
t snack. They also work well as
ick appetizer for family parties.

AROLYN TURNER RENO, NV

P: 20 MIN. • **COOK:** 10 MIN./BATCH
KES: 2 DOZEN

- **pound lean ground beef (90% lean)**
- **tablespoons reduced-sodium soy sauce**
- **tablespoon sesame oil**
- **teaspoons chili garlic sauce**
- **teaspoons onion powder**
- **teaspoon garlic salt**
- **teaspoon dried parsley flakes**
- **pot sticker or gyoza wrappers**
- **large egg, lightly beaten**
- **teaspoons sesame or olive oil, divided**
- **cup water, divided**

1. In a large bowl, combine the first seven ingredients. Place 1 tablespoon of the beef mixture in the center of each pot sticker wrapper. (Cover wrappers with a damp towel until ready to use.)

2. Moisten wrapper edges with egg. Fold wrapper over filling; seal edges, pleating the front side several times to form a pleated pouch. Stand pot stickers on a work surface to flatten bottoms; curve slightly to form crescent shapes, if desired.

3. In a large skillet, heat 1½ teaspoons sesame oil over medium-high heat. Arrange half of the pot stickers in concentric circles in pan, flat side down; cook 1-2 minutes or until bottoms are lightly browned. Carefully add ¼ cup water (water may spatter); reduce heat to medium. Cook, covered, 3-5 minutes or until water is almost absorbed and filling is cooked through.

4. Cook, uncovered, 1-2 minutes or until bottoms are crisp and water is completely evaporated. Repeat with remaining pot stickers.

NOTE *Wonton wrappers may be substituted for pot sticker and gyoza wrappers. Stack two or three wonton wrappers on a work surface; cut into circles with a 3½-in. biscuit or round cookie cutter. Fill and cook as directed.*

CURRY SPICED CASHEWS

Spiced cashews contrast with the sweet, dried cranberries in this quick combo. Feel free to swap walnuts, almonds or pecans for the cashews.

—**LOUISE GILBERT** QUESNEL, BC

PREP: 20 MIN. + COOLING
MAKES: 2½ CUPS

- 2 **cups salted cashews**
- 1 **tablespoon olive oil**
- 2 **teaspoons curry powder**
- 1 **garlic clove, minced**
- 1 **teaspoon Worcestershire sauce**
- ¾ **teaspoon ground cumin**
- ¼ **teaspoon cayenne pepper**
- ½ **cup dried cranberries**

In a large nonstick skillet, cook cashews over medium heat until toasted, about 4 minutes. Add the oil, curry powder, garlic, Worcestershire sauce, cumin and cayenne. Cook and stir for 2-4 minutes or until cashews are well coated. Spread on foil to cool completely. Stir in cranberries; store in an airtight container.

SESAME-BEEF
POT STICKERS

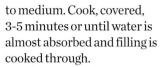

FAST FIX

CHILI CON QUESO EL DORADO

Used as a dip or on burgers, chicken or pork, this creamy queso sauce is spiced with chilies, chipotle peppers and hot pepper sauce. I like my dip with kick!

—**CAROLYN KUMPE** EL DORADO, CA

START TO FINISH: 25 MIN.
MAKES: 4 CUPS

- 1 cup chopped green onions
- 1 tablespoon olive oil
- 1 garlic clove, minced
- 4 cans (4 ounces each) chopped green chilies
- 2 chipotle peppers in adobo sauce, finely chopped
- 2 cans (5 ounces each) evaporated milk
- 2 cups (8 ounces) shredded Monterey Jack cheese
- ¼ cup minced fresh cilantro
- ⅛ teaspoon salt
- 2 to 4 drops hot pepper sauce
  Tortilla chips

1. In a large saucepan, saute the onions in oil until tender. Add garlic; cook 1 minute longer. Add the chilies and chipotle peppers; cook 2 minutes longer. Gradually stir in milk; heat through.

2. Remove from the heat; stir in cheese until melted. Stir in the cilantro, salt and pepper sauce. Serve warm with tortilla chips.

FAST FIX

GREEK SANDWICH BITES

Here's an appetizer that tastes a lot like traditional spanakopita bu is much less work to make.

—**LYNN SCULLY** RANCHO SANTA FE

START TO FINISH: 25 MIN.
MAKES: 16 APPETIZERS

- 1 medium onion, finely chopped
- 1 tablespoon olive oil
- 2 garlic cloves, minced
- 1 pound fresh baby spinach
- 1 cup (4 ounces) crumbled feta cheese
- ¼ cup pine nuts, toasted
- ¼ teaspoon salt
- ¼ teaspoon pepper
- ⅛ teaspoon ground nutmeg
- 8 slices Italian bread (½ inc thick)
- 4 teaspoons butter, softene

1. In a large nonstick skillet, saute onion in oil until tender Add garlic; cook 1 minute long Stir in the spinach; cook and s until wilted. Drain. Stir in the feta, pine nuts, salt, pepper an nutmeg.

2. Spread over four bread slic top with the remaining bread Spread outsides of sandwiche with butter. Grill sandwiches, uncovered, over medium hea for 3-4 minutes or until bread browned and cheese is melter turning once. Cut each sandw into quarters.

CHILI CON QUESO
EL DORADO

CRAB ASPARAGUS QUESADILLAS

RAB ASPARAGUS UESADILLAS

s deliciously different recipe gives fresh asparagus d crabmeat a little Mexican flare. The quesadillas are hearty enough to be served as a main course.

URTIS GUNNARSON SYCAMORE, IL

ART TO FINISH: 20 MIN. **• MAKES:** 6 SERVINGS

- flour tortillas (8 inches)
- cups (8 ounces) shredded reduced-fat Mexican cheese blend
- cup chopped fresh asparagus, cooked
- cup chopped imitation crabmeat
- tablespoons plus ¾ cup picante sauce, divided
- teaspoons canola oil
- tablespoons fat-free sour cream
- 2 large ripe olives, sliced

1. On two tortillas, layer each with ½ cup cheese, ½ cup asparagus, ¼ cup crab, 1 tablespoon picante sauce and remaining cheese. Top with remaining tortillas; press down lightly.

2. In a small skillet coated with cooking spray, cook one quesadilla at a time in oil for 2 minutes on each side or until cheese is melted. Cut each quesadilla into six wedges. Serve with sour cream, olives and remaining picante sauce.

DID YOU KNOW

Imitation crabmeat, also called surimi, is fish that is shaped, flavored and colored to resemble crab. Typically made from Alaskan pollock (a lean, firm fish with a delicate flavor), it has both natural and artificial flavors as well as artificial coloring.

FAST FIX

FRUITY DESSERT CREPE

Filled with a tropical-tasting pudding mixture and topped with fresh fruit, this dessert crepe is sure to be an impressive conclusion to a special brunch or dinner for two.

—VIRGINIA DECKER MOJAVE, CA

START TO FINISH: 15 MIN.
MAKES: 2 SERVINGS

- ¼ cup 2% milk
- 2 tablespoons beaten egg
- 3 tablespoons biscuit/baking mix
- 1 snack-size cup (3½ ounces) vanilla pudding
- ½ small banana, sliced
- 2 tablespoons flaked coconut
- ¼ teaspoon almond extract
- 3 fresh strawberries, sliced
- ½ medium kiwifruit, peeled and sliced

1. In a small bowl, combine the milk and egg. Add biscuit mix and mix well. Heat a 10-in. nonstick skillet coated with cooking spray; pour batter into center of skillet. Lift and tilt pan to evenly coat bottom. Cook until top appears dry; turn and cook 15-20 seconds longer. Remove to a wire rack.

2. Transfer pudding to a small bowl; fold in the banana, coconut and extract. Spoon down center of crepe; fold sides over filling. Top with strawberries and kiwi.

FRUITY DESSERT CREPE

ANDIED PUMPKIN
ICE PECANS

ll be tempted to eat an entire
l of these sweet and spicy nuts,
rab a handful before you put
n out. They'll be gone in a flash!

LIE PUDERBAUGH BERWICK, PA

P: 15 MIN. + COOLING
KES: 2 CUPS

- **tablespoons butter**
- **cup sugar**
- **teaspoon pumpkin pie spice**
- **teaspoon vanilla extract**
- **cups pecan halves**

1. In a large heavy non-stick skillet, melt butter over medium heat. Stir in the sugar. Cook until mixture turns an amber color, about 3-4 minutes, stirring occasionally (the mixture will separate while it cooks).

2. Stir in pie spice and vanilla; add pecans. Reduce heat; cook and stir 3-4 minutes longer or until pecans are toasted. Spread onto foil to cool. Store nuts in an airtight container.

NDIED PUMPKIN
CE PECANS

(5) INGREDIENTS FAST FIX

CHOCOLATE CINNAMON TOAST

Looking for a fun dessert or snack? Cinnamon bread is toasted to perfection in a skillet, then topped with chocolate and fresh fruit.

—**JEANNE AMBROSE** MILWAUKEE, WI

START TO FINISH: 10 MIN.
MAKES: 1 SERVING

- 1 **slice cinnamon bread**
- 1 **teaspoon butter, softened**
- 2 **tablespoons 60% cacao bittersweet chocolate baking chips**
  Sliced banana and strawberries, optional

Spread both sides of bread with butter. In a small skillet, toast bread over medium-high heat for 2-3 minutes on each side, topping with chocolate chips after turning. Remove from heat; spread melted chocolate evenly over toast. If desired, top with bananas and strawberries.

RAINBOW PEPPER APPETIZERS

Company will quickly polish off this colorful pepper medley. The crisp-tender veggies are topped with chopped olives and cheese.

—MARION KARLIN WATERLOO, IA

START TO FINISH: 20 MIN.
MAKES: 3 DOZEN

- ½ **each medium green, sweet red, yellow and orange peppers**
- 1 **cup (4 ounces) shredded Monterey Jack cheese**
- 2 **tablespoons chopped ripe olives**
- ¼ **teaspoon crushed red pepper flakes, optional**

1. Cut each pepper half into nine pieces. Place skin side down in an ungreased ovenproof skillet; sprinkle with cheese, olives and pepper flakes if desired.

2. Broil 3-4 in. from the heat for 5-7 minutes or until peppers are crisp-tender and cheese is melted.

FOCACCIA BARESE

This recipe has been in my mom's family for several generations and is one of the most-requested dishes whenever I'm invited to a party. I'm not allowed to attend unless I bring my focaccia!

—DORA TRAVAGLIO
MOUNT PROSPECT, IL

PREP: 30 MIN. + RISING
BAKE: 30 MIN. • **MAKES:** 8 SERVINGS

- 1⅛ **teaspoons active dry yeast**
- ¾ **cup warm water (110° to 115°), divided**
- ½ **teaspoon sugar**
- ⅓ **cup mashed potato flakes**
- 1½ **teaspoons plus 2 tablespoons olive oil, divided**
- ¼ **teaspoon salt**
- 1¾ **cups bread flour**

TOPPING
- 2 **medium tomatoes, thinly sliced**
- ¼ **cup pitted Greek olives, halved**
- 1½ **teaspoons minced fresh or dried oregano**
- ½ **teaspoon coarse salt**

1. In a large bowl, dissolve yeast in ½ cup warm water. Add sugar; let stand for 5 minutes. Add the potato flakes, 1½ teaspoons oil, salt, 1 cup flour and remaining water. Beat until smooth. Stir in enough of the remaining flour to form a soft dough.

2. Turn onto a floured surface; knead until smooth and elasti about 6-8 minutes. Place in a greased bowl, turning once to grease the top. Cover and let ri in a warm place until doubled, about 1 hour. Punch dough do Cover and let rest for 10 minut

3. Place 1 tablespoon olive oil a 10-in. cast-iron or ovenproo skillet; tilt pan to evenly coat. Add dough; shape dough to fit pan. Cover and let dough rise until doubled, about 30 minut

4. With fingertips, make seve dimples over top of dough. Bru with remaining tablespoon of Blot the tomato slices with pa towels. Arrange the tomato sli and olives over dough; sprinkl with oregano and salt.

5. Bake at 375° for 30-35 minutes or until golden brown

FOCACCIA BARESE

CHOCOLATE-HAZELNUT BANANA CREPES

[CH]OCOLATE-HAZELNUT
[B]ANANA CREPES

[Wa]rm bananas and Nutella make the perfect pair when [roll]ed into these light and luscious homemade crepes. [Enjo]y them for breakfast, dessert or a snack.

[K]ATHY HALL LYNDHURST, VA

[PRE]P: 15 MIN. + CHILLING • **COOK:** 15 MIN.
[MAK]ES: 10 SERVINGS

[2] **large eggs**
[2] **large egg whites**
[1¼] **cup water**
[¾] **cup 2% milk**
[1] **tablespoon canola oil**
[1½] **cup all-purpose flour**
[1] **tablespoon sugar**
[¼] **teaspoon salt**
[3] **tablespoons butter**
[3] **tablespoons brown sugar**
[4] **medium bananas, peeled and sliced**
[¾] **cup Nutella**

1. In a large bowl, whisk the eggs, egg whites, water, milk and oil. Combine the flour, sugar and salt; add to egg mixture and mix well. Refrigerate for 1 hour.

2. Heat a lightly greased 8-in. nonstick skillet over medium heat; pour ¼ cup batter into the center of the skillet. Lift and tilt pan to coat bottom evenly. Cook until the top appears dry; turn and cook for 15-20 seconds longer. Remove crepe to a wire rack. Repeat with remaining batter, greasing skillet as needed. When cool, stack crepes with waxed paper or paper towels in between.

3. In a large skillet, melt butter over medium-low heat. Stir in the brown sugar until blended. Add bananas; cook for 2-3 minutes or until the bananas are glazed and slightly softened, stirring gently. Remove from the heat.

4. Spread Nutella over each crepe; top with the bananas. Roll up and serve.

**MARTHA HASEMAN'S
COOKOUT CARAMEL S'MORES**
PAGE 242

Campfire Classics

Campers agree: food simply tastes better cooked over an open flame! Get ready for some good eats with the hearty ideas found here.

WALKING TACOS

This chili is perfect for al fresco dining, whether it's an overnight adventure trip, a picnic at the park or a backyard barbecue around a crackling bonfire. All the ingredients go right into the chips bag, so there are no dishes to wash. And while the chili simmers, you can get in a round of Texas hold'em.

—BEVERLY MATTHEWS PASCO, WA

PREP: 10 MIN. • **COOK:** 30 MIN.
MAKES: 5 SERVINGS

- 1 **pound ground beef**
- 1 **envelope reduced-sodium chili seasoning mix**
- ¼ **teaspoon pepper**
- 1 **can (10 ounces) diced tomatoes and green chilies**
- 1 **can (15 ounces) Ranch Style beans (pinto beans in seasoned tomato sauce)**
- 5 **packages (1 ounce each) corn chips**
  Toppings: shredded cheddar cheese, sour cream and sliced green onions

1. In a large skillet, cook beef over medium heat 6-8 minutes or until no longer pink, breaking into crumbles; drain. Stir in chili seasoning mix, pepper, tomatoes and beans; bring to a boil. Reduce the heat; simmer, uncovered, for 20-25 minutes or until chili is thickened, stirring occasionally.
2. Just before serving, cut open corn chip bags. Add the beef mixture and toppings as desired.

WALKING TACOS

CAMPFIRE FRIED FISH

Here's a classic recipe that will have you cooking up a shore lunch in no time. Fry up whatever type of fish you've caught that day.

—TASTE OF HOME TEST KITCHEN

PREP: 15 MIN. • **COOK:** 10 MIN./BATCH
MAKES: 6 SERVINGS

- 2 **large eggs**
- ¾ **cup all-purpose flour**
- ½ **cup cornmeal**
- 1 **teaspoon salt**
- 1 **teaspoon paprika**
- 3 **pounds walleye, bluegill or perch fillets**
  Canola oil

In a shallow bowl, whisk eggs. In a large resealable plastic bag, combine the flour, cornmeal, salt and paprika. Dip the fillets in eggs, then roll in flour mixture.

Add ¼ in. of oil to a large cast-iron skillet; place skillet on grill rack over medium-hot heat. Fry fillets in oil in batches for 3-4 minutes on each side or until fish flakes easily with a fork.

CAKE & BERRY CAMPFIRE COBBLER

Warm cobbler is one of our favorite ways to end a busy day of fishing, hiking, swimming or rafting. Many times, Mom tops each serving with a scoop of ice cream.

—JANE DRESS BOISE, ID

PREP: 10 MIN. • **GRILL:** 30 MIN.
MAKES: 12 SERVINGS

- 2 **cans (21 ounces each) raspberry pie filling**
- 1 **package yellow cake mix (regular size)**
- 1¼ **cups water**
- ½ **cup canola oil**
  Vanilla ice cream, optional

1. Prepare grill or campfire for low heat, using 16-20 charcoal briquettes or large wood chips.
2. Line a Dutch oven with heavy-duty aluminum foil; add the pie filling. In a large bowl, combine the cake mix, water and oil. Spread over pie filling.
3. Cover Dutch oven. When briquettes or wood chips are covered with white ash, place Dutch oven directly on top of 8-10 of them. Using long-handled tongs, place remaining briquettes on pan cover.
4. Cook for 30-40 minutes or until the filling is bubbly and a toothpick inserted in the topping comes out clean. To check the cobbler for doneness, use the tongs to carefully lift the cover. Serve with ice cream if desired.
EDITOR'S NOTE *This recipe does not use eggs.*

CAKE & BERRY CAMPFIRE COBBLER

FAST FIX

SESAME DILL FISH

Crispy fillets are a snap to make. A grocery store special on fish motivated me to adapt a pork recipe for fish in this quick-cooking dish.
—LINDA HESS CHILLIWACK, BC

START TO FINISH: 15 MIN.
MAKES: 4 SERVINGS

- ½ cup dry bread crumbs
- ¼ cup sesame seeds
- ½ teaspoon dill weed
- ¼ teaspoon salt
- ¾ cup plain yogurt
- 1 pound catfish or other whitefish fillets
- ¼ cup canola oil
  Lemon wedges, optional

1. In a shallow bowl, combine the bread crumbs, sesame seeds, dill and salt. Place the yogurt in another bowl. Dip fish fillets in yogurt; shake off excess, then dip in crumb mixture.
2. Heat oil in a large nonstick skillet. Fry fillets over medium-high heat for 2-3 minutes on each side or until the fish flakes easily with a fork. Serve with lemon if desired.

COOKOUT CARAMEL S'MORES

Nothing beats creating sweet campfire memories as we toast the marshmallows for this special treat. Your family will love the ooey-gooey twist, with caramel and chocolate syrup to make it extra yummy.
—MARTHA HASEMAN HINCKLEY, IL

START TO FINISH: 10 MIN.
MAKES: 4 SERVINGS

- 8 large marshmallows
- 4 whole graham crackers, halved
- 2 teaspoons chocolate syrup
- 2 teaspoons caramel ice cream topping

Using a long-handled fork, toast the marshmallows 6 in. from medium heat or campfire until marshmallows are golden brown, turning occasionally. Place two marshmallows on each of four graham cracker halves. Drizzle with the chocolate syrup and caramel topping. Top with the remaining crackers.

COOKOUT CARAMEL S'MORES

CAMPFIRE BUNDLES

I created this recipe on a family camping trip. I'd brought along a hodgepodge of ingredients, so I just threw them all together in a foil packet. Everyone said that the bundles were delicious. Now I grill them at home, and the results are just as pleasing.

—**LAURI KRAUSE** JACKSON, NE

PREP: 15 MIN. • **GRILL:** 1 HOUR
MAKES: 6 SERVINGS

- 1 large sweet onion, sliced
- 1 each large green, sweet red and yellow pepper
- 4 medium potatoes, cut into ¼-inch slices
- 6 medium carrots, cut into ¼-inch slices
- 1 small head cabbage, sliced
- 2 medium tomatoes, chopped
- 1 to 1½ pounds smoked Polish sausage, cut into ½-inch slices
- ½ cup butter, cubed
- 1 teaspoon salt
- ½ teaspoon pepper

1. Place the vegetables on three pieces of double-layered heavy-duty foil (about 18 in. square). Top with the sausage; dot with butter. Sprinkle with salt and pepper. Fold foil around mixture and seal tightly.

2. Grill, covered, over medium heat for 30 minutes. Turn and grill 30 minutes longer or until the vegetables are tender. Open foil carefully to allow the steam to escape.

CAMPFIRE BUNDLES

INDIVIDUAL CAMPFIRE STEW

INDIVIDUAL CAMPFIRE STEW

These packets are perfect for grilling or whipping up over a campfire. I can get several outdoor chores done while they're cooking.

MARGARET HANSON-MADDOX MONTPELIER, IN

PREP: 15 MIN. • **GRILL:** 25 MIN.
MAKES: 4 SERVINGS

- 1 **large egg, lightly beaten**
- ¾ **cup dry bread crumbs**
- ¼ **cup ketchup**
- 1 **tablespoon Worcestershire sauce**
- 1 **teaspoon seasoned salt**
- 1 **pound lean ground beef (90% lean)**
- 2 **cups frozen shredded hash brown potatoes, thawed**
- 1 **cup diced carrots**
- 1 **cup condensed cream of chicken soup, undiluted**
- ¼ **cup milk**

1. Prepare grill for indirect heat. In a large bowl, combine the first five ingredients. Crumble beef over mixture and mix well. Shape into four patties. Place each patty on a greased double thickness o heavy-duty foil (about 12 in. square); sprinkle ea with potatoes and carrots.

2. Combine soup and milk; spoon over meat and vegetables. Fold foil around the mixture and sea tightly. Grill, covered, over indirect medium hea for 25-30 minutes or until meat is no longer pink and potatoes are tender. Open the foil carefully t allow steam to escape.

AMPFIRE CHEESE ASH BROWN CKETS

ng by the campfire? This easy nbo of potatoes, bacon and ese makes a terrific hash. We to serve it with eggs and fresh de gallo.

INA NISTICO MILWAUKEE, WI

RT TO FINISH: 30 MIN.
KES: 4 SERVINGS

- **package (28 ounces) frozen O'Brien potatoes, thawed**
- **cups (5 ounces) shredded cheddar cheese, divided**
- **bacon strips, cooked and chopped**
- **teaspoon salt**
- **teaspoon pepper**
- **Hard-cooked eggs and pico de gallo, optional**

1. Prepare campfire or grill for medium-high heat. Toss potatoes with ¾ cup cheese, bacon, salt and pepper.
2. Divide mixture among four 18x12-in. pieces of heavy-duty nonstick foil, placing food on dull side of foil. Fold foil around potato mixture, sealing tightly.
3. Place packets over campfire or grill; cook 6-9 minutes on each side or until potatoes are tender. Open packets carefully to allow steam to escape; sprinkle with remaining cheese. If desired, serve with eggs and pico de gallo.

CAMPFIRE HASH

In our area we are able to camp almost all year-round. My family invented this skillet recipe using ingredients we all love so we could enjoy them on the campfire. The hearty meal tastes so good after a full day of outdoor activities.
—**JANET DANILOW** WINKLEMAN, AZ

PREP: 15 MIN. • **COOK:** 40 MIN.
MAKES: 6 SERVINGS

- 1 **large onion, chopped**
- 2 **tablespoons canola oil**
- 2 **garlic cloves, minced**
- 4 **large potatoes, peeled and cubed (about 2 pounds)**
- 1 **pound smoked kielbasa or Polish sausage, halved and sliced**
- 1 **can (4 ounces) chopped green chilies**
- 1 **can (15¼ ounces) whole kernel corn, drained**

1. In a large ovenproof skillet over medium heat, cook and stir onion in oil under tender. Add garlic; cook 1 minute longer. Add potatoes. Cook, uncovered, for 20 minutes, stirring occasionally.
2. Add kielbasa; cook and stir until the meat and potatoes are tender and browned, about 10-15 minutes. Stir in the chilies and corn; heat through.

CAMPFIRE CHEESE
HASH BROWN PACKETS

General Index

This handy index lists recipes by food category and major ingredient so you can find recipes that suit your needs.

GENERAL INDEX **249**

Alphabetical Index